Anna Bowman Dodd, E. Eldon Deane

Cathedral Days

A Tour in Southern England

Anna Bowman Dodd, E. Eldon Deane

Cathedral Days
A Tour in Southern England

ISBN/EAN: 9783337005139

Printed in Europe, USA, Canada, Australia, Japan

Cover: Foto ©Andreas Hilbeck / pixelio.de

More available books at **www.hansebooks.com**

CATHEDRAL DAYS

A TOUR IN SOUTHERN ENGLAND

BY

ANNA BOWMAN DODD

AUTHOR OF "THREE NORMANDY INNS," "ON THE BROADS,"
"GLORINDA," "STRUTHERS," ETC.

Illustrated from Sketches and Photographs

BY

E. ELDON DEANE

NEW EDITION

BOSTON
LITTLE, BROWN, AND COMPANY
1899

Dedication.

To Silvie, of Sosiego,

THE FRIEND FOR HOLIDAYS, AND ALL OTHER DAYS.

NEW YORK, 1899.

NOTE.

The names of the various Inns mentioned in the text are mainly fanciful, and for obvious reasons. The frequent changes of both management and name of hotels or hostelries would make any attempt to guide a traveller inevitably misleading.

A. B. D.

CONTENTS.

CHAPTER		PAGE
I.	THE PROJECT	7
II.	ARUNDEL	13
III.	SLINDON AND BOGNOR	47
IV.	CHICHESTER	68
V.	GOODWOOD	94
VI.	FAREHAM.—WALTHAM.—THE VALLEY OF THE ITCHEN	110
VII.	WINCHESTER	135
VIII.	A COLLEGE AND AN ALMSHOUSE	161
IX.	HURSLEY AND ROMSEY ABBEY	190
X.	SALISBURY	214
XI.	STONEHENGE.—WARMINSTER.—LONGLEAT.—FROME	247
XII.	BATH	274
XIII.	THE DRIVE TO WELLS.—AN ENCHANTED NIGHT	298
XIV.	WELLS, AN ENCHANTED CITY	314
XV.	TO GLASTONBURY	314
XVI.	TO EXETER	366
XVII.	FAREWELL TO BALLAD	386

ILLUSTRATIONS.

EXETER GUILDHALL	*Frontispiece*
ARUNDEL CASTLE	14
OLD PAROCHIAL CHURCH, ARUNDEL	34
CHICHESTER CROSS	74
CHICHESTER CATHEDRAL	82
OLD SCULPTURES, CHICHESTER	90
OLD HOUSES IN CLOSE, WINCHESTER	142
WINCHESTER CATHEDRAL	144
CHANTRIES, WINCHESTER	156
ST. CROSS HOSPITAL	180
ROMSEY ABBEY, TRANSEPT AND NAVE	206
NUN'S DOOR, ROMSEY ABBEY	210
SALISBURY	214
SALISBURY CATHEDRAL, FROM THE CLOISTER	232
GATEWAY TO CATHEDRAL CLOSE, SALISBURY	244
STONEHENGE	254
LONGLEAT HOUSE	262
OLD ROMAN BATHS, BATH	292
BISHOP'S PALACE, WELLS CATHEDRAL	332
WELLS CATHEDRAL, FROM MOAT	338
WELLS CATHEDRAL, FROM THE WELLS	342
ARCH, GLASTONBURY	357
TITHE BARN, GLASTONBURY	364
THE NAVE, EXETER CATHEDRAL	382

CATHEDRAL DAYS.

CHAPTER I.

THE PROJECT.

ONE night in London, in the crowded latter end of June, a small number of us were sitting under the quiet stars, in a certain friend's charming garden, after a long evening of pleasure. There had been music and talk and laughter, into the small hours, in the great studio, from whose open windows a few of us had stepped forth, at the bidding of our host, into the coolness and fragrance of the night. We sat under the trees near a trickling fountain, whose liquid voice at first was the only one which filled the sweet night air; but soon, through puffs of smoke, others joined in its babble. The talk drifted into that closer, more intimate form of conversation which midnight and summer in conjunction so often induce. It was an hour for confidences. Caught in this embrace of night, with London hushed and still, and only nature stirring in mysterious whispers, each of us in turn had been involuntarily betrayed into an avowal of his personal plans or desires. The talk, in a word, had come to have something of the charm and something also of the intimacy of the confessional. One had proclaimed his approaching nuptials; another her forthcoming book,— almost as great a venture; a third had expressed his secret desire to run away from life and hide himself behind the Rockies or under the shadow of the Pyramids; and still a fourth confessed to his having only recently signed a Mephistophelian bond to do that very thing, to go forth into the Great Desert and to bring back something of its desolation and its grandeur in verse.

Boston and I, having some years ago settled our mutual destiny, having no book in view and no tragic sense of unrest, could only add the comparatively tame and commonplace avowal of our modest purpose to run away from the world, but only so far as English lanes and by-paths. This announcement was the signal for a simultaneous attack, for an explosion of advice. If there is any one thing a friend thinks he can interfere with righteously, it is another man's plans, — after they have all been settled and made.

"Of course you'll coach it," briskly said the nearest man, in a tone as if to settle the matter. "Go alone? Just two of you! Absurd! You'll die of ennui. Make up a party."

"Only, whoever you ask, don't make it a party of more than six, and don't take more than two ladies," — this from a deeper tone amid the shadows of the foliage.

"You are entirely right," cried a third, under one of the farther palms. "I never knew more than six to get through a trip without trouble. One can get along with two women, but more — "

Then a laugh went round, which died into the trickle of the splashing fountain. Suddenly some one else puffed out a great volley of smoke, and began again.

"And don't take luggage. Send it on by train. It's a wretched nuisance, always slipping about, and it fags the horses."

"Why go in for England?" broke in a new voice; "it's beastly tame. The Tyrol's the best driving, and you get at least a bit of drama in your scenery, —

peasants in costume, and all that. England has n't any scenery."

"It has cathedrals," I ventured to suggest.

"Oh! cathedrals — well, so has France. Now, there's Normandy and Brittany. No one's done that yet on four wheels, and it's crammed full of architecture."

"Horrible waste of time, — England!"

Whereupon Boston assured the company, that, not being an Englishman, he found it impossible to agree with them; that at least before condemning the country, he proposed to know something of its beauties and defects, and further courageously avowed our intention of "doing it" in a much humbler fashion than from the throne-like elevation of a coach. And would it be best to hire or buy our modest little trap?

Whereupon there was a chorus of disapproving comments.

"Oh, you'll have to buy, out and out."

"Horse'll go lame, sure to, if you have only one."

"If you don't take a servant, who is to look out for you, — for your horse and your luggage? Oh no, the thing is n't feasible. Coaching's the only safe or comfortable way. Now, I know a man—" And the voice went on, with admirable zeal and kindliness, to dilate on the advantages to be derived from an acquaintance with this latter individual.

But better even than this kindly meant zeal was an invitation from one of the older gentlemen to run down to his country-house in Kent on the coming Sunday, and talk the thing over quietly.

The subject was canvassed to such purpose that we ended by putting ourselves completely in our wise friend's hands. He decided that we were to depend on local traps, taking a horse and carriage from one town to another. The inns all along our proposed route, which was to include the southern cathedral towns, were admirable, and the roads were perfect. As for scenery, while lacking perhaps the wider horizons and the romantic character of the Northlands, Southern England was delightfully diversified along the coast by sea and land views, and the towns were charmingly picturesque. Altogether, our friend having travelled over his own country, knew it and loved it. He bade us God-speed with a smile prophetic of our coming enjoyment. We were to go by train from London to Arundel; and thence, from that most beautiful of the Sussex towns, we were to start forth on our six weeks' driving-tour.

Inside of twenty-four hours we were on our way to the Sussex Downs.

CHAPTER II.

ARUNDEL.

ARUNDEL might be, and doubtless was, the most beautiful of the Sussex towns; but as we had confided to each other before we left London, we should only stop there long enough to hire a horse and trap. It would be a capital place from which to start.

But Arundel itself had decided quite differently. It was a charming little town,—a fact of which it appeared to be almost humanly cognizant. Like all beauties, conscious of its attractions it resented being used for purposes of mere utility. Was Arundel, forsooth, with its grassy banks and its lovely river, its fascinating old Elizabethan streets, its splendid castle, and its bran-new cathedral, to be thus snubbed by two impertinent transatlantic travellers? Was it to be debased to the level of a livery-stable? Arundel, fortunately, was a thousand years older than these young American upstarts. She knew a trick or two. She had not gone on fascinating all England for centuries past, without having learned every art that belongs to a consummate coquette. As for these young Americans, she would make short work of them.

And she did. First, she presented us at the railway-station with a huge bouquet. We could even have our choice of three. There were the masses of poppies, dyeing the meadows with their scarlet flames; there were the fragrant trim hedgerows, as odorous as a bride's garland; and there were also the low, sweet-flowering river-banks. These floral offerings were accompanied by a smile. She leaned over the hill, and shot it down at us over the thick-clustering roofs and chimneys, from the very citadel of the huge and noble castle itself.

Alighting at the neat, bright Arundel station was, in a word, like being dropped into the midst of a blooming garden. What with the odors and honeysuckle perfume, the dashing sparkling river, the town running up the steep hill to the castle's turreted walls, the rustic setting of the outlying farms, the velvety hills covered with

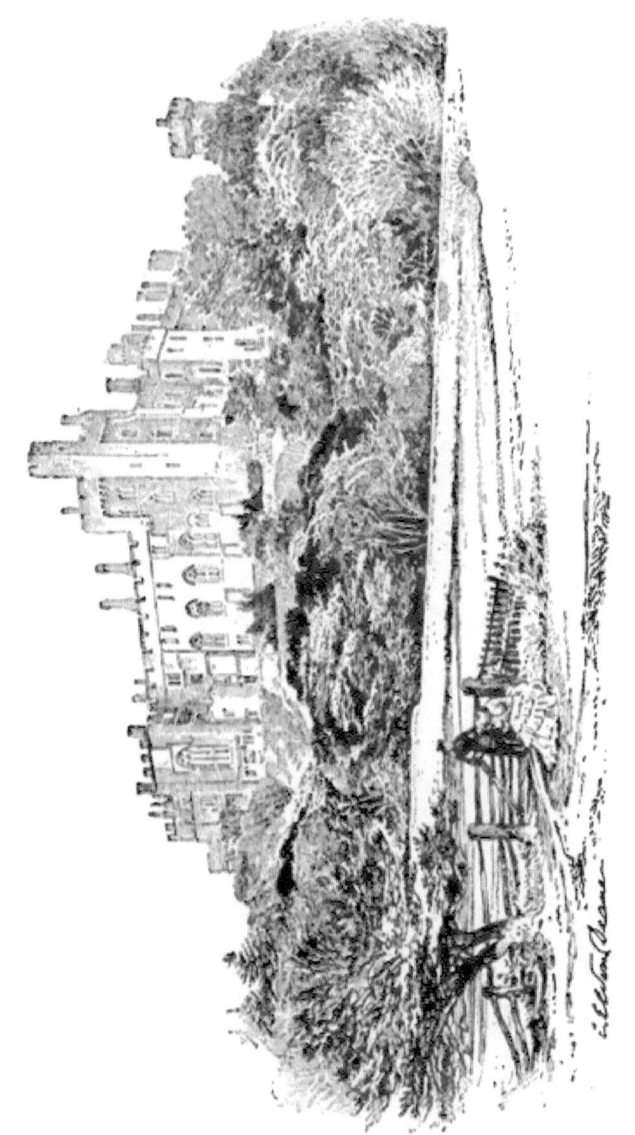

ARUNDEL CASTLE. *Page 14.*

browsing sheep and brilliant-skinned cattle,— an enchanting vision of summer and of picturesque beauty appeared to have stepped forth to greet us.

"I think, perhaps, Boston, we might stop over *one* day," I remarked, as we drove through the streets of the town to our inn.

"Yes; it would be a pity to miss seeing the place, now we are here. There seems to be a good deal in it, after all," Boston replied, quite as if we had arranged it with our imaginations to find it interesting from the outset.

The glimpses which we caught of the town on our drive up the steep High Street were of the fragmentary, incomplete order peculiar to such approaches. We had a confused sense of meadows, of houses closely packed together, of distant vistas of a vast park with the downs beyond as a background, and of the great castle's turrets, these latter making admirable bits in perspective along the crest of the hillside.

Our experiences with the true life of the town began with the entrance into our inn.

Quite as a matter of course, we had our choice of two. To have only one inn in a town, and that one good, would make the path of the traveller too smooth. A rival establishment is always started, apparently, on the principle that one's enjoyment in this world must be made as difficult and as complex as possible. Equally, of course, there being two inns, whichever one we chose it would follow that we would regret our choice and repentingly wish we had gone to the other. The Bridges Inn — which we had decided against, moved by the higher-sounding Norfolk Arms' title — presented, we found as we passed it, an alluring combination of charms. It stood in an attitude of bewitching grace on the river-bank, looking out upon the meadows, the castle, and the downs, through windows embowered in blooming vines.

But once inside of the Norfolk Arms, we knew that happily our first choice had been the right one. The chiefest among the excellences of the Arms was that it stood in the very centre of the little town, on High Street. The neighborhood was of the most distinguished, as only a Frenchman knows how to say it. We discovered at once that the Norfolk Arms was nothing if not an aristocrat. In assuming the name of the famous family whose castle walls almost adjoined those of its ambitious namesake, the Arms had evidently made up its mind to maintain the family reputation for dignity and virtue. It announced, at the very outset, a high-bred indifference to ornament which was too obvious to be unintentional. Its external austere simplicity was the protest of the aristocrat against the plebeian aids of picturesque accessories. A single large golden cluster of grapes hung, it is true, from the sign-board; but this was the only concession to the popular but vulgar demand for symbolic parade. The interior of this most self-respecting inn was in keeping with its outward meagreness of decorative embellishment. The rooms were large and spacious, but not luxuriously furnished. There was a conscious air of respectability about the tall beds, the stiff upright buffets, and the erect dining-room chairs, as if to assure the inmates of these dignified apartments that they were in the very best society.

We discovered that the epitome of the conscious air of aristocratic rectitude which pervaded this admirable inn was embodied in our waiter. He was more than a person, — he was a personage. He appeared to be an individual of high-rank antecedents. From the first he gave us to understand, by a number of disdainful little ways, that his being a provincial at all was purely a matter of accident. This transition had evidently not been effected without disastrous results on his character : it had made him a pessimist. He took the darkest possible views of life in general, and of the travelling public in particular. He appeared, from the start, to have taken a melancholy view of us and of our luggage. The compactness and limited number of our boxes seemed to afflict him with dim forebodings both of the transiency of our stay and of the limitations of our purse. At the end of the second day, however, we noticed that he had become more cheerful.

"It must have been the dinner we ordered last evening," said Boston. "If a little thing like that can raise his spirits, why, we will keep it up. But he is a gloomy specimen, is n't he?"

The gloom settled down upon him later the same evening. It was occasioned by a little obtuseness on Boston's part. Under the impulse of the knowledge that there were a number of interesting places about and in Arundel which must be visited in the next few days, and not having as yet either guide-book or map at hand, Boston sought to extract a little useful information from Walters. Boston was too true an American not to see in every other man a being born for the express purpose of answering questions.

"Walters, when is the castle open?"

"The castle, sir, is never open to visitors. Only the dairy and the keep, sir, are open. The tickets can be 'ad 'ere, sir." This was delivered with a commendable alacrity of utterance. The succeeding questions were, however, answered with less and less readiness. Later there came a perceptible deepening of the gloom under which Walters appeared habitually to endure existence. Then came a pause all at once in both questions and answers. During the pause Walters gave Boston's pocket a pregnant glance.

"Oh!" said Boston in an undertone, his fingers obeying mechanically the meaning conveyed in this portentous look. He took out a silver coin. After its contact with Walters' palm the cloud of his melancholy appeared to lift for a few seconds.

"What nonsense, Boston, to have tipped him!" I protested as he left the room. "Can't one ask a question in England without having to pay for it?"

"It appears not. You saw that I only did what was expected of me."

"That's because we are Americans. An Englishman would n't have given him a penny."

"It is Englishmen who taught him the habit, not Americans. Tipping is a national product. Every one is tipped in England, from the lord to the beggar. Only, when it gets into the upper circles it goes by another name."

I noticed, however, that in spite of Boston's philosophic acceptance of this national custom, conversation with Walters, even of the most Socratian order of dialogue, having been found to be expensive, became more and more feeble.

On the following morning we saw such a spectacle in the courtyard as made us still more sensible that certain customs in England are tenaciously rooted. The cook and two assistants were busily handling a number of huge joints, which were suspended on hooks from the inner archway. This archway was the only mode of egress or ingress from the inn-door to the street without. The meats were hanging in full view under the brick arch, as if it had been a butcher's stall instead of the neat approach to an inn. I cannot say that there was any dripping of gore, but there was an unpleasant suggestion of recent bleeding under the knife.

"The courtyard apparently is the inn's open-air ice-chest," I remarked to Boston, after our first start of amazement.

"No; it is an original and altogether inexpensive method of announcing the day's *menu*," Boston replied to my suggestion. Subsequent experiences resulted in our forming even less favorable opinions of the innkeeper's designs upon his guests. The next morning we noticed that the huge quarter of lamb had disappeared.

"We had best order the beef to-day, or to-morrow we shall wish that we had."

"It is altogether the most ingenious method of enforcing speedy consumption of viands that was ever invented. Talk of Yankee ingenuity, indeed!" answered Boston, in a semi-burst of indignation.

There was, in truth, no escape from the fate which would befall us in case of a too prolonged indifference to these mute but terrible appeals to our sense of economy. There came upon us, at the last, the grewsome habit of fascinated calculation, as we eyed the meats day after day. We could not help conjecturing how the dampness of one day or the heat of another would affect their complexions, and then critically surveying them to see whether their pink and white had suffered.

This was not the only proof we encountered that the sensibility of English stomachs is of a different order from that of American organs. No one else but ourselves appeared even so much as to glance at the pendent carnivorous array.

Our large sitting-room window opened directly on the town's main thoroughfare. One little street, at right angles with the larger, broader High Street, seemed to have stepped into our windows, so close did its houses appear. Our sitting-room windows, we declared, were thus as good as a stage-box. All the life and the picturesqueness of the town could be enjoyed without stirring from the depths of our easy-chairs. The stage, we discovered on the second day of our arrival, was charmingly set. The brooding quiet had given place to lively activity. The streets were full of noise and bustle, of a true holiday clatter and buzz. It was Saturday, — market-day; and from early morning carts and wagons had been standing about in the open square.

Wagoners and teamsters were soon out shopping. The tiny shops in a half-hour were so full that they were spilling over, country-people swarming out into the open streets and over the narrow sidewalks. The charming old Elizabethan houses, with the rich shadows beneath their deep projecting eaves, the quaint signs, the diamond-shaped panes, needed just this mass of rustic life moving beneath the window-ledges to give to this picturesque frontage this last touch of completeness. The street itself could hardly have happened twice, I think, even in England. It began its existence, as we discovered later, with the bridge which crosses the Arun. Its progress up the hillside had the wandering, straying irregularity peculiar to old streets which have grown up independent of municipal intention. It ended, at the summit of the hill, with some towers and turrets whose crenellated tops were green and mossy among the trees, — these towers and turrets being only a portion of the vast corona which adorned the castle's fortified walls.

We were about to start forth on a visit to the castle when the sound came up to us from the street, through the open sitting-room window, of the scraping of a fiddle. A moment later, snatches of song broke forth from a low window directly opposite. We stopped to listen. There was a moment of hesitation before the song came full and clear; for voices, like soldiers, must be thoroughly drilled to fall directly into rhythmic accord. Then the song burst out, firm and swelling with the might of the strong male voices. It was a lovely bit of part-singing, with sweet minor changes and full deep bass harmonies in it. Then, after a little, there were pausings and haltings. The singers apparently were at something else besides their singing. We could see, as we leaned out, a group of men in the house opposite, sitting about a long table. They were playing cards, and there was a huge tankard of beer at each man's elbow. I devoutly prayed that the depth of the tankard might prolong the length of the song; but in a few minutes the song was done. The men came out, twenty or more in number, — strong, lusty-looking fellows, with the sun's red seal burnt upon their faces. They climbed into one of the big wagons, gave a deep-throated cheer to their hostess, and were off. The landlady stood looking after them, with both hands in her pockets, smiling a broad farewell. Then the little door swallowed her up.

"What was that singing over the way?" I asked the chambermaid as we passed her on the stairs. The previous answers of this neat and most respectful of her sex to my questions had not impressed me with the belief that she also was infected with the British habit of turning a passing dialogue into a financial speculation. She had never failed to enliven her civility with a smile.

"It's a bean feast, mum."

"A bean feast? And what is that?"

"It's the workingmen's outings, mum,— a kind of harvest feast, mum."

So rural England still played and sang a little! There was a time, I know, when she sang better than any one else,— when she could beat the world in her own line. In the old madrigal days England was a nest of singing-birds. But I had supposed that the cruel fate which overtakes all great singers had come to her: I understood that she had lost her voice. It was pleasant to know that her method had been so good it had survived till now among its grain and bean fields, if abandoned by the great.

What was not so pleasant was the braying of a horrible assemblage of instruments called a band.

This latter was attached to a trick and monkey show which had taken its place, early on this holiday Saturday, at the bottom of High Street. Its hideous blare of sound had kept the village astir and abroad for five long hours. Where the crowds came from that kept the dogs performing and the monkeys playing their monotonous tricks, and how an otherwise sane and sensible English village could endure having its peace and quiet disturbed by such a roar and din as issued from the cracked trumpet and the squeaky fiddle, surpassed comprehension. The band and its torturing music had the pervasiveness of all vulgarity; it filled the village like an intolerable presence. We shut the windows; but the discords, like jubilant furies, screamed at us through the key-hole. We sought refuge in the graveyard at the top of the street, — this at ten at night, when fatigue and desperation had turned us loose upon the world, seeking where we might hide our tortured ears; but through the darkness of the night came the blare of that terrible trumpet, like a yell of some devil cheated out of his prey. At eleven, finally, the last villager had seen the last trick, and silence fell, like a great peace, on the still air. The next morning the great hideous cart had disappeared. It had doubtless moved on to another suffering village.

"Do you suppose it has gone to Chichester?" I asked, in despair, of Boston.

"I presume it has. It's probably doing the towns,— it is taking its summer tour, as we are," was Boston's comforting answer.

"Then I stay where I am."

I take pleasure in warning any unwary traveller against a similar fate. The name of that trick and monkey show was Whitcomb's. Whenever he meets Mr. Whitcomb I advise him to take the next train — if it be for Hades.

It was owing to these and other adventures with the more homely features of Arundel's town-life, that we found ourselves too late that afternoon for a visit to the castle. But the hour was perfect for an inspection of its battlemented walls. To escape them, in whatever direction one turned in the town, would have been difficult. Such a vast architectural mass as Arundel Castle, implanted in Saxon, Roman, and feudal military necessities, strikes its roots deep and wide. The town appeared, by comparison, to be but an accidental projection on the hillside. The walls grew out of the town as the trunks of a great tree shoot forth from the ground, — of a different growth, but an integral part of it.

Topographically, Arundel had only a few features, yet they were fine enough to form a rich ensemble. There was the castle, huge, splendid, impressive, set like a great gray pearl on the crown of the hill. On one side spread the town; on the other, the tall trees of the castle park begirt its towers and battlements. At the foot of the hill ran the river, — a beautiful sinuous stream, which curved its course between the Down hillsides, out through the plains, to the sea. Whatever may have been the fate of the town in former times, held perhaps at a distance far below in the valley, — during troublous times when the castle must be free for the more serious work of assault or defence, — it no longer lies at the foot of its great protector. In friendly confidence it seems to sit, if not within its arms, at least beside its knee. But in spite of these changed relations, all the good old prejudices, I fancy, are not done away with. In spite of certain excited statements from our socialistic brotherhood, the castle and the village are hardly as yet on visiting terms. Nothing appears easier than the fulfilment of these and other specious prophecies, away from the proofs. But somehow, when one looks up at such a vast and splendid castle as this, impregnable as its walls, and contrasts the simple plebeian little town beside it, one's belief in the glorious principle of the equality of men dwindles into pitiful conjecture. One wonders whether, after all, the castle will not survive these and other agitations and agitators, as its very existence is proof of its power to resist far more formidable sieges.

There is no escaping the conclusion that a duke, when one is confronted with his castle, does seem a personage whose state is secure.

The noise and the clatter of the main thoroughfare, and even the long stretch of the castle walls, we had soon passed, in our walk that afternoon, reaching the quiet of its upper streets. The principal dwelling-streets of the pretty town run laterally across the hillside, as if for once even a village house-builder could prove he knew best how to stand when he wished to look out upon a picture. Beneath us, swimming in light, stretched the great canvas of the open country. Through doorways and open windows there were enchanting views framed in old casements and Tudor pilasters. The eye swept past open doorways into broad halls, with their quaint old-time furniture of high-shouldered chairs and carved settle, straight out to the lovely Sussex valley, which stretched itself towards the horizon like an endless carpet, with its inwrought pattern of waving grain, oaks, and hayricks. With such pictures to gain, even our best manners were not proof against the temptation presented by the tiny diamond-shaped open lattices. The houses seemed in conspiracy with our impertinence, some of them standing boldly out on the sidewalk, as if bent on looking up and down the street. Others more modest, whose deprecating air of shyness we respected, retreated behind with demurely drawn shutters, — timid creatures holding fans before their pretty faces. There were ancient and modern styles apparent, in the architectural fashions we passed in review, the gable-roofed Elizabethan and the broad low Georgian being the most noticeable. There were also modern reproductions of both, — very precise and perfect reproductions, which imposed on no one.

What pleased us even better than the houses was the human life that they sheltered, and which looked out at us through the old windows. There were some fresh, fair faces, that only needed ruffs and stomachers to be in admirable keeping with the ancient architectural setting. Fine last-century figures, strong-featured, with gentle eyes, ceased their knitting to glance up, over silver-rimmed spectacles, at the sound of our voices.

One face we met, which seemed strangely out of keeping with such surroundings. It was a curiously un-English face. It belonged to a man who was hurrying past us, with a book in his hand, on the cover of which there was a large gilt cross. The face was long and dark, clean-shaven, with deep-set wary eyes, and a sly curve on the full lips. It needed neither the abbé's long fluttering coat nor its purple lining to tell us it was the face of a priest. As he neared the great castle gateway, I saw it open, the keeper within bowing as the abbé passed beyond.

I remembered then that the castle was a great Catholic stronghold, the Dukes of Norfolk being among the few great families which have remained faithful, since the Conquest, to the See of Rome. The present Duke of Norfolk, by reason of the fervor of his piety, his untiring zeal and magnificent generosity, is recognized as the head of the Catholic party in England. To learn that he was at present on a pilgrimage to Lourdes, and that such was his yearly custom, seemed to shorten distance for us. It made the old — its beliefs, its superstitions, its unquestioning ardor of faith — strangely new. It invested the castle, which appealed to our consciousness as something remote and alien, with the reality of its relation to mediæval life and manners.

The little cathedral which crowns the hill — the most prominent object for miles about, after the castle — is the gift of the present Duke. It is a pretty structure, pointed Gothic in style, conscientiously reproduced with all the aids of flying buttresses, niches, pinnacles, and arches. It was doubtless a splendid gift. Perhaps in the twenty-first century, when the weather has done its architectural work on the exterior, and when the interior has been finely dimmed with burnt incense, when stained glass and sculptured effigies of saints have been donated by future dukes, it will be a very imposing edifice indeed.

But all the beauty of ecclesiastical picturesqueness lies across the way. Hidden behind the lovely beech-arched gateway rests the old parochial church. In spite of restoration the age of six centuries is written unmistakably on the massive square belltower, the thirteenth-century traceries, and the rich old glass. It is guarded by a high wall from the adjoining castle-walls, as if the castle still feared there were something dangerously infectious in the mere propinquity of such heresies.

It has had its turn at the sieges that have beset the castle. From the old tower there came a rattling hail when Waller's artillery flashed forth its fire upon the Royalist garrison in the castle. The old bells that peal out the Sunday chimes seem to retain something of the jubilant spirit of that martial time. There was a brisk military vigor in their clanging, suggestive of command rather than of entreaty, as if they were more at home when summoning fighters than worshippers.

All is peace now. The old church sits in the midst of its graves, like an old patriarch surrounded by the dead whom he has survived.

We were curious to see which church would have the greater number of worshippers, — how many of his townsfolk the Duke had managed to hold faithful to the Pope. The Ducal influence had, we found, prevailed over her Majesty's less ancient established church. At the little cathedral there was, we found on the first Sunday morning of our stay, a marked Catholic majority. In spite of the more splendid ceremonial at St. Philip de Neri, in spite of the pomp of scarlet-robed priests and the glory of a double choir, in spite of the subtle intoxication of the incense and the pictorial attractions of burning tapers and flower-decked altars, it was the simpler, the more earnest worship in the old church beneath the cypresses that touched our hearts and made us one with the worshippers. There was a ring in the responses, and a fervor in the way the hymns burst forth from the fresh, strong English throats, drowning the less-meaning music of the birds twittering at the open door, that made one know and feel, with full strength of inherent conviction, just why it is that an Englishman is by instinct a Protestant. His religion must appeal to his understanding; it must stir his soul. He is not satisfied with being moved superficially. He is not poet enough to possess vast perspectives, or so delicately organized that he can vibrate to purely sensuous imageries. There is precision even in the English imagination, as there are limitations to English sensibilities.

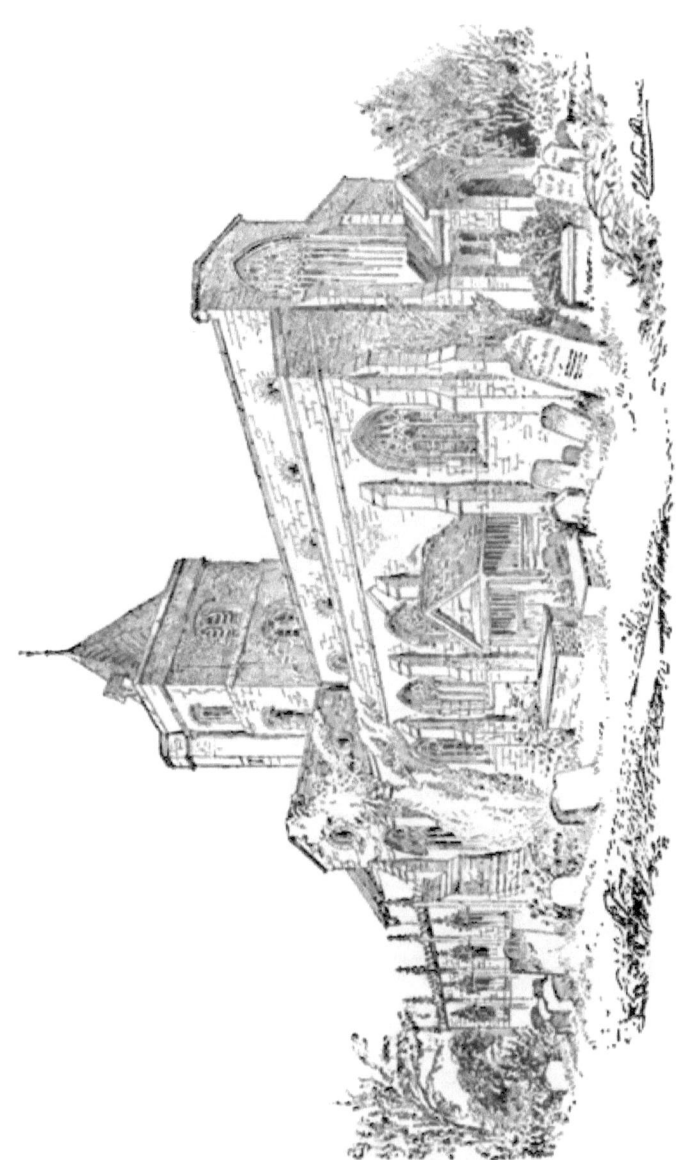

Old Parochial Church, Arundel.

It is good to see, however, that some of the virtues which the Englishman as a Protestant has prayed for, have come to him. Fresh from London and the site of Smithfield, it was edifying to see Catholics and Protestants worshipping, in gentle amity, within sight of one another. Is it by reason of the efficacy of their prayers that this grace of toleration has been borne in upon them, or is it due to the lesson which the inefficacy of their mutual roasting has taught them?

Doubtless both. The prayers made the martyrs, whose stuff of glorious stubbornness made sizzling under a slow fire appeal to the economies of the nation. It must have seemed, at the last, a waste in kindling-wood. The attempt to roast their religion out of the martyrs was in the end, doubtless, discovered to be only a more expensive method of thoroughly baking in their beliefs.

That all the good townsfolk of Arundel had not been to church on this lovely July morning might have been inferred from the look of the sky and the quality of the air, to breathe which was like sipping perfumed dew.

We ourselves had proof of this backsliding. On Arundel Bridge there was assembled a congregation of open-air worshippers which would have filled a fairly capacious church.

Arundel Bridge possessed an order of attraction, we discovered, quite apart from any other feature of the town. It appeared to be the open-air clubroom, the fashionable promenade, the lounging-place of the entire population. At whatever hour of the day one chanced to pass it, there was always to be found a knot of idlers gathered about its parapet, leaning on strong elbows, looking out upon the river life. Even the passers-by stopped, took a turn at lounging, and chatted for a brief moment ere they went their way. We also had fallen into this pleasant habit; as who would not, with a silver river rippling beneath one, banks odorous and green above, the town breaking into charming perspectives, the great castle hanging overhead, and the Down hillsides rushing tumultuously into the plains? Besides, close at hand, was the Bridges Inn. And we liked to be near it, and watch its prettiness and activity, and talk over our regret at not being there, much as a disappointed lover nurses his hurt and coquets with his despair.

Perhaps there is more in lounging than the never-idle dream of. It may be that the idlers form the ideal leisure class, — a class too aristocratic to work for knowledge, yet to whom it comes by sheer force of the long measure of time at their command. Certain it is, that unless we had joined these loungers on the bridge we should never have known so much of the real life and history of the little town. We should never, for instance, have discovered, unless our eyes had proved it to us, that Arundel was a port. Yet such it is. The river banks are prolific with signs of unmistakable maritime activity. Ships we saw, riding in from the sea, looking indeed as if projected into this inland landscape for purely operatic purposes of stage grouping. They anchored along the reedy banks, their cargoes as gravely unloading as if there were nothing incongruous in a full-rigged ship lying at anchor amid the grasses and poppies of an inland meadow.

It is the river that plays stage-manager. It is in league with the sea. Old Ocean's strong pulse throbs its buoyant life through this slender artery. At noon the river rests, barely breathing in its swoon of sleep. At morn and evening it rises, swelling with tidal fury, rushing past its banks with the zest of an athlete.

Wherever there is a ship, there are always any number of men with their hands in their pockets, and with no visible occupation in life except that of watching her. Why is it that a man never wearies of looking at a ship, — as he does, for instance, of contemplating his wife or his house or his horse? Is it because a ship possesses the ideal feminine charm, — is never quite to be counted upon, — is fugitive, illusive, a creature of the winds and the tides, ever ready to open her white wings and to sail away from him? In the eyes of the men who are given to watching ships and ship-life, one can detect a peculiar look of intentness, an air of alertness, as if they were perpetually on the lookout for the ship which will surely come in. It is the sea which brings with it this element of expectancy. It is everywhere the breeder of expectation and the renewer of hope, as it is the great mother of energy and ambition.

On this particular morning of our half-hour's lounging, a little incident occurred to enliven the quiet and the stillness. A boat was coming up river with tremendous swiftness. The tide was flowing inward with the rush of a torrent. The boat with its four oarsmen was borne along on the wings of the wind as if it had been a feather. There was no rowing, the men letting the tide do their work for them. Opposite the Bridges Inn some skilful steering was done, the boat being brought up in workmanlike style. For two of the men to clamber up the iron ladder into an open window of the hotel, while the other two shot the boat out, shoving it into the weeds along the banks, from which it was lifted as if it had been a thing of paper, and carried up the bank, was but the work of a few seconds.

"They 're come to breakfast," was the knowing remark of my next neighbor, a stout villager of florid aspect, addressing no one in particular.

From the fringe of on-lookers there was no response, except that the smoking went on a little more vigorously. After a pause another voice said:

"They 'll be going up stream presently."

There was again a pause, longer than the first. Then, "It 'll be sport to see 'um," came from a thin little man with a whistling voice, the whistle that comes through broken or absent teeth.

Another five minutes' silence was finally broken by a coarser, stronger tone, with solemn accent, as if there were something grim in the coming fun, —

"Yes, it will be thot."

Silence fell again upon the little group. Each man's gaze sank into the flowing river, as if to plunge anew into the depths of his own reverie.

"How a group of French peasants would have gabbled!" I said to Boston, as we strolled away to take a turn in the fields, determining, however, to return in time for the "sport."

"Yes; and how they would have spoilt it all! Their eagerness would have anticipated everything. Now we have something to look forward to. An Englishman's silence is dramatic; it is full of potentialities," replied Boston, sententiously.

When we returned, in an hour, the knot of villagers had not, apparently, so much as moved. No one stirred, or even turned his head, as we took our places silently, — no one, that is, except the thin little tanner, who readjusted his pipe to the end of his mouth farthest away from me, in the fear, presumably, that smoke might be used as a conversational medium.

In the river below, however, there was life and stir enough. The oarsmen were busy filling their boat with baskets of beer and luncheon. It required great care to adjust the baskets rightly; for the boat was tossing beneath them uneasily, as if in haste to be gone. In another moment the men were seated; a turn of the oars, and they were off.

"The other artch, sur, — the other artch," came from our neighbors lustily enough now, and almost in chorus; for the oarsmen had attempted to go in under the nearer one. In trying to obey instructions, they had struck against the stone abutment.

"Your hoar, sur, — your hoar," was again shouted from the bridge. But the oar was gone; and so were they, nearly, for the strength of the stream was crashing them against the abutment again and again.

"They hall does that, every one; they never gets clear, down yonder," was the complacent comment of my neighbor.

"Why not warn them in time?" I asked, a trifle indignantly, my sympathies stirred by the spectacle of the struggling crew.

"Why, mum, they likes it; it's what they comes for, to work a bit." And a laugh went down the fringe of on-lookers.

Well, if they liked it, they were having enough of it. All the pulling like madmen was not helping to clear them into mid-stream. Finally, as all pulled together with the force of young giants, out the boat flew, free and clear. The clever steering was resumed; they shot under the arch like a flying bird; there was a vision of a strong young arm waving a red cap in triumph, of a tawny mustache bristling in the sunlight, and they were far off and out of sight.

We ourselves crossed the bridge to gain the farther side of the river. In a few brief moments we were among the grain-fields and the farms. The object of our walk was to get a really satisfactory view of the castle. In our former walks about the town we had had numberless views of its walls, turret and tower studded, of bits of its huge façade and its venerable keep, fitting into the street corners or rearing their beauty above the low gabled roof-tops. But in the town, through the medium of enclosed streets or through accidental openings between chimney-pots, there had been no chance of seeing the whole in perspective, — as essential for a right viewing of such a vast architectural mass as Arundel Castle as it is wise, as a rule, to look on human greatness from an historical distance.

In looking up at the castle from the river, as a foreground, one has a lovely breastwork of trees, the castle resting on the crown of the hill like some splendid jewel. Its grayness makes its strong, bold outlines appear the more distinct against the melting background of the faint blue and white English sky and the shifting sky scenery. In the river that morning there were brilliant touches of color, — reflections of the houses, the castle towers, and the brown and gold of the meadow, here and there lit up with the flame of the poppies lining the banks. Beyond, toward the sea, was the long green line of the plain, the one line of rest and repose in the landscape. Over all was the rosy, calm, virile bloom of English health. The bloom looked out at one through a faint mist, like a rosy child in the midst of its bath. The entire scene was suffused with that delicate, vague, misty veil of light, which imparts to all English landscape a certain aqueous quality. It is this moist, ethereal aspect which gives to this scenery its note of individuality. Earth appears to be a more soluble fluid than elsewhere, its outlines melting more easily into the ether of the atmosphere.

The earliest Saxon who built his stronghold where the castle now stands must have had an eye for situation, pictorially considered, as well as that keen martial foresight which told him that the warrior who commanded the first hill from the sea, with that bastion of natural fortifications behind him, the Downs, had the God of battle already ranged on his side. The God of battle has been called on, in times past, to preside over a number of military engagements which have come off on this now peaceful hillside.

There have been few stirring events in English history in which Arundel Castle has not had its share. As Norman barons, the Earls of Arundel could not do less than the other barons of their time, and so quarrelled with their king. When the Magna Charta was going about to gain signers, these feudal Arundel gentlemen figured in the bill, so to speak. The fine Barons' Hall, which commemorates this memorable signing, in the castle yonder, was built in honor of those remote but far-sighted ancestors. The Englishman, of course, has neither the vanity of the Frenchman nor the pride of the Spaniard. But, for a modest people, it is astonishing what a number of monuments are built to tell the rest of the world how free England is. The other events which have in turn destroyed or rent the castle — its siege and surrender to Henry I., the second siege by King Stephen, and later the struggle of the Cavaliers and Roundheads for its possession, during the absence abroad of the then reigning Earl — have been recorded with less boastful emphasis. The recent restorations, rebuildings, and enlargements have obliterated all traces of these rude shocks. It has since risen a hundred times more beautiful from its ruins. It is due to these modern renovations that the castle presents such a superb appearance. It has the air of careful preservation which distinguishes some of the great royal residences, — such as Windsor, for instance, to which it has often been compared. Its finish and completeness suggest the modern chisel. It is this aspect of completeness, as well as the unity of its fine architectural features, which makes such a great castle as this so impressive. As a feudal stronghold it can hardly fail to appeal to the imagination. As the modern palatial home of an English nobleman, it appeals to something more virile, — to the sense that behind the mediæval walls the life of its occupants is still representative, is still deep and national in importance and significance. Pictorially, there is nothing — unless it be a great cathedral, which brings up quite a different order of impressions and sensations — that gives to the landscape such pictorial effect as a castle. It adds the crowning element of the picturesque, — that of elegance combined with grandeur. It also invests the land with the emphasis and the dignity of a purpose. English landscape, especially, owes much to its castles. The land, from its high degree of finish and the perfection of its detail, would produce, in the end, the effect of a certain monotony. There might come the sense of tameness, of too perfect a prettiness. But its castles are to its dainty beauty what the figure of a human being is in a parterre of flowers. The castle is the knight, mail-clad and with visor drawn, standing amid the rose-gardens of England. It adds the crowning dignity of a majestic historical completeness.

CHAPTER III.

SLINDON AND BOGNOR.

THE exact distance between the giving of advice and the possibility of following it has never, I think, been properly measured. I presume one of the reasons why the experienced only ask counsel in order to reject it is because they have tested the truth of the axiom that everything goes by contraries in this world.

How simple a matter, for instance, had it seemed to our charming friend in Kent, to say, with persuasive zeal and the assurance born of inexperience,—

"The best and easiest way is for you to depend on the local traps. There will thus be no responsibility, no going lame, and you will have no worn-out beast on your hands."

How could a man, whose own stables were always full, know anything of "local traps," indeed, except from the optimist's point of view, regarding them chiefly in the light of the roadster's facile conquest, as vehicles both easy and pleasant to pass on the road? But the driver and owner of the "local trap" naturally takes a much more serious attitude. Mankind, from his point of view, is divided into two classes, — the men who own horses, and those who don't. The latter are to be numbered among the dangerous elements of society. The logical inference deduced from the theory of the inherent total depravity of men not owning horse-flesh is so conclusive as to be irrefutable. The man who does not own a horse will quite naturally wish to hire one. He who hires, secretly hopes to steal. Every man therefore has in him the instincts of the horse-thief; hence ceaseless watchfulness is necessary on the part of the horse-owner. This is one of those cases in which it behooves every man to be his own vigilance committee, policeman, detective, judge, and executioner. Civilization has done much, but in the matter of horse-thieving the world may be said to be still in the dark ages.

Such were the conclusions forced upon us by our brief but vigorous attack on the hostlers and stable-owners of Arundel.

Boston returned from two or three interviews with the livery-men in town with the discouraging announcement that none of them would trust him with a horse and carriage. "We never lets out traps without drivers, sir," he reported as having been the universal but equally firm answer to his request for a trap without one. The unanimity of the response, he admitted, had alone prevented its wearing the front of a personal reflection.

Here was a difficulty no one had foreseen, yet it was one which threatened the very life and pleasure of our little trip.

Take a driver! Why not take the train and have done with it? With a driver, how could we be sure of having the tamest of adventures, — of losing our way, for instance, or of asking it of the people we met along the road, and hearing, instead, of the crops or the voting? Besides, the driver would do all the talking. He always does. (Both of us had secretly sworn to have a monopoly of that privilege.) A driver, in fact, represented everything from which we had fled, — the common-place, the conventional, the world, the flesh, and — that fiend called discord, that hated third in a duet of harmony.

As we were standing confronting the owner of a

pony and wagonette in the open square, — one who really gave signs of distress at not being able to oblige us, but who was as firm as he was apologetically civil, — an inspiration dawned on me.

"You, of course, or your man must go as far as Chichester by train to bring home the carriage. You shall take our trunks on with you, and that will be sufficient guarantee that we have no intention of running away with your horse and trap, will it not?"

The man laughingly confessed that it would. But before entirely committing himself, he consulted with half the town, who had come from the bridge to watch the proceedings. The town had evidently formed an estimate of our character, — to our advantage.

In less than an hour the trap stood in view within the inn courtyard. Our luggage, a few seconds later, was comfortably packed in the rumble, and we were off. The town idlers were still on watch, as if conscious of having vouched for our honesty and not entirely willing to lose sight of us. In view of the distribution of a few discriminating shillings, they relented their watchfulness, and melted a little later into the adjacent side-streets.

Our route lay first along the river, up into the hills at the back of the castle, then down again into the valley to Slindon, and thence toward the sea to Bognor. In all, the distance was not more than fifteen miles, and we had before us a perfect August afternoon.

After a half-hour's drive along the charming little Arun's banks, we turned with reluctance into the cool shade and greenness of the hillside road. Who ever likes to leave a river? A river in a landscape is its pulse, its arterial throb of life, the nearest approach to that ceaseless law of motion which informs man's own body with vitality. A landscape, however glorious, without a flowing river, always seems a bit of *nature morte*, — a kind of still-life nature, with no real life in its veins; it is a headless, heartless bit of creation, with no stir of pulseful energy which makes it a part of the active living forces of the universe. When a river has the order of attraction which this buoyant, coursing, turbulent little stream of Arun possessed, darting like a silver flame into the Down valleys, or leaping with the audacity of a full-fledged river into the very bosom of the ocean, it is little wonder that we stopped again and again before we parted irrevocably with its changeful aspects, its flowery banks, its castle-crowned heights, and its tall hillsides.

The instinctive reluctance with which a man exchanges even one delight for another, be it ever so lovely, argues well, I think, for the inherent constancy of human nature.

After a steep climb along the crest of a long and beautiful hillside, from which there was an enchanting series of delightful views, we came to an iron gate. Our pony came to an iron stand-still. Neither whipping nor coaxing proved of any avail. She was a sturdy little beast,—a "wee brute, sur, but strong, strong in the legs," her owner had said at parting, when I had expressed a doubt as to her capacity for speed under the heavy load she was to carry. The "wee brute" was strong in something else besides her legs. She evidently belonged among the strong-minded of her sex. That fine decision of character possessed by the owners of horse-flesh in Arundel appeared, by some occult means, to have been communicated to the horses as well.

"Perhaps she is used to the feminine spur," I said, as Boston laid aside the whip in despair. I took the reins, and administered that form of encouragement to the bit familiarly known as "nagging." But on this self-willed little creature this usually most effective method produced no more satisfactory result than, on occasions, has the same system when applied to the most perverse of men.

"She has such an air of being right, it almost seems as if we must be in the wrong," I argued at last. "Suppose this gate does lead somewhere,— where we ought to be going?"

"The gate was not in our list of directions," Boston replied.

"But since we are in search of adventures, why not see where it will lead us?" And we did. It led us into the prettiest bit of road we had yet seen in Arundel. The road was through the upper, remoter regions of the park known as the Deer Park. This particular portion of the vast estate lay at a distance from the castle. It was a great open, formed of a series of short hills, covered with thickets and noble trees and long stretches of grazing-ground. Herds of deer, hundreds in number, stood grouped under the trees, or, startled by our voices, bounded over the grass.

Distant as were these glades and silent bits of wood from the garden loveliness of the grounds immediately about the castle, the impression which the aspect of the landscape produced was unmistakably that of its being a great nobleman's park. There was visible none of that rank and lawless wildness and disorder one sees in our own great untrimmed, untressed fields and forests. There was about us the most penetrating solitude, but there was no touch of desolation in the loneliness. There could be no sadness where on every field and bush the evidences were so obvious of man's persistent efforts. Nature, in this remote and unfrequented region, had been carefully pencilled into beauty during the long centuries. The grass was still a lawn, although the castle was a mile or two away. It was, in other words, a king's possession, where even uninhabited and disused lands were kept as trim as a garden, lest by chance the monarch's eye should light upon it, and discover it *en déshabille*.

The deer were the only unconscious, entirely natural element about us. These delicate creatures preserve, even in captivity, their instinct of isolation and independence. Their solitude they consider is to be respected. There were hundreds of the slim, beautiful creatures, carrying aloft their coronal of branching horns, entirely at home in the companionship of the great trees and the solitude of the wind-swept Downs.

Leaving the Duke's park was only to pass from one nobleman's estate to another. Our road to Slindon took us past a procession of great gateways and stone-built porters' lodges. Now and then we caught a glimpse of a Queen Anne gabled façade or of a broad, low Georgian mansion. So jealously does the Englishman guard his privacy, that we had to content ourselves for the most part with glimpses, through the high hedge-rows, of the lawns and the flower-beds. Nature in England has been fashioned into a mask, behind which English reserve can conceal its features. When the convent wall was pulled down, the hedge-row replaced it. The latter is quite as high, and on the whole even more impenetrable.

At last, however, we were up on the hills, with neither hedge-row nor escutcheoned gateway to bar Nature out. The turf beneath our feet was as soft as velvet. It had, we found, on trying it, — a particularly fine and open hillside having tempted us to prolong the beauty of the view by walking,— that delightful quality of elasticity peculiar to English grass. It was both soft and firm beneath the foot. In our faces such an air was blowing over the hills as only winds that pass over a hill-country ever yield. These Down breezes have a particularly high reputation for softness. But they were blowing that afternoon as if they wanted to prove to two aboriginal Americans accustomed to the brutality of transatlantic winds,— winds that stab and sting and bite,— what a really well-behaved English wind could do when it had a mind to show off its paces. It even caressed us a little, as if in pity for the beatings we had to take at home.

Who is not cheered by being petted a little? Under the soft, caressing touch of that tenderhearted summer breeze we walked on and on. The more we walked, the better we liked it.

Nature is a coy creature. She is as hopeless a plebeian as she is difficult of approach. She insists on equality as the first essential of a true friendship with her. The walker, therefore, has a better chance than any one else of being, so to speak, on a footing of intimacy with her. She resents being looked down upon, from even so humble an eminence as the box-seat of a wagonette. For our pains she let us into several delightful little secrets that afternoon. She bade us stop and listen to the stillness, if one can listen to a thing which is not. How still it was!—so still that some sheep grazing two fields away made the only sound there was. We could hear their soft nibbling, and even the noiseless movement of their feet against the grass. A bell, a few moments later, deep-throated and richly sonorous, pealed out a chime or two at some far distance, coming up the valley from Slindon. The vibrations in the air seemed to stir the daisies anew,—tiny bells ringing in unison. The tasselled tops of the oaks above our heads made a rustle in the air that had something feminine about it. It was like the flutter of a woman's silken gown.

A brisk trot of two miles or more brought the roofs of Slindon within sight.

At Slindon we had been promised the spectacle of a model English village, with a model specimen of a Saxon-Norman church.

Slindon was even better than its promise. It was an ideal little village. It was the most beautiful collection of thatched houses, vine-covered, garden-enclosed, and dimity-curtained, we saw anywhere in England. The houses were so perfect, we suspected them of being on show for purely decorative purposes, rather than designed for human habitations.

"Slindon may be a rustic, but she is also a consummate coquette," exclaimed Boston.

The thatched houses had indeed taken on endless airs of refinement and knowing ways of adornment. The roofs were of just the right color, a warm gray turning to silver,— the color of all others to go with pink and white. The houses were built of brick, and then stuccoed a dazzling white. They had a complexion to make the eyes blink. But what with the rose-vines, the creepers, and the clematis, their white faces were as jealously guarded as a beauty's tender skin. Of pink there was abundance. Every tiny diamond pane was filled with roses and rose-geraniums, their petals all the pinker for being enclosed between spotless bits of white curtains.

Each little cottage stood, besides, in the midst of a blooming garden, a rose within a rose. What with the honeysuckle, the azaleas, the great Eastern lilies, the rose-vines, and the window-pots, the air was thick and luscious with the fragrance and perfume. Nothing at once more flowery, dainty, softly brilliant, and yet charmingly and harmoniously rustic, could be imagined than these two streets running at right angles up a hillside, which made all there was of the perfect little village of Slindon.

"If this be England, and I had been a Pilgrim Father, I don't think I should have troubled myself to move," exclaimed Boston, as he let the reins fall on the pony's motionless haunches.

"I doubt if even before they moved, the Pilgrim Fathers had a pronounced taste for gardening." Then we both laughed a little; for instinctively we contrasted the bleak, bold, barren New England farmhouse, its slovenly vegetation, and its hideous color, with this collection before us of ideal little cottages and thatched huts, all as daintily robed as a maiden in spring. Indeed, what did become of the Englishman's instinct for beauty when he transplanted himself across the seas? Was it the biting frost of Puritanism that killed his native taste? Or is it that even in two centuries the struggle to subdue a great continent to his needs and necessities has not yet given him time to set out the little garden in which he can take his ease? Together with the taste for gardening which the Pilgrim Father left behind him, we noticed other qualities this little village possessed, which it might have been wise to have exported,— its air of content, for one thing, thrift and a kind of mild-eyed prosperity seeming to look out of the window at us as we passed. This appearance of well-being may have had some indirect relation to the fact that the cattle seemed sleeker and the sheep fatter in the adjacent fields than those we had seen on the uplands.

The church we found to be less entirely satisfactory. It had certainly once been Saxon, and later on, Norman. There were two round-headed little windows a Norman would have scorned to build, and an early Norman doorway in the porch which the later early-English architects would have pronounced equally inelegant. But the entire little edifice wore a thoroughly modern and recently renovated appearance; so that it was no surprise to come upon the disenchanting and familiar date 1866, to attest the fact of its nineteenth-century rebuilding.

As we turned from the village towards the plain, there was a meeting of four roads.

"Which road to the Royal Oaks?" Boston asked,

in his dilemma, of a slim rustic who was leaning against a gate, with his eyes glued upon us as he feasted his curiosity.

"Straight ahead, sur, till yer come ter the mill, and then there's sign-posts," the boy had answered, and readily enough; but he remained motionless.

"He isn't genuine. A true rustic would have pointed," I said.

For his "straight ahead" left us bewildered; before us there were three "straight aheads." However, we plunged recklessly into the straightest. We were rewarded by soon seeing the four great white arms of the mill waving unblushingly in the sunlight. Beneath them the sign-post, with less manners but better judgment than our rustic, pointed the direction of our destination.

For several miles now our road lay through the plains, — flat, fruitful lowlands towards the sea. There was a succession of pretty hamlets and of numberless detached farmhouses, but no sign of human life, except the farmers who were busy in the fields carting or pitching hay. The huge hay-ricks, cone-shaped and green, were the only rivals, in these flat fields, of the hills beyond, now hazy in the dimness of distance.

We were in Bognor before we knew it. The fields led us directly into rows of neat, tidy little houses, and clean, well-swept streets.

A man in knickerbockers with a tennis racket, and a lady wearing a thin white muslin gown and a thick fur cape, announced to us that the season at Bognor had already begun.

Other signs of its activity greeted us as we proceeded on our way. Tennis was being played, with a zeal that made it appear to be a serious battle rather than a harmless contest about balls, in every square inch of green large enough to hold a court. The familiar London sign, "Apartments to let," hung above the tiny, dazzlingly clean doors of the little houses. The number of these signs was conclusive proof that Bognor's season was not as yet at its height. So frequent were these modest appeals to the unlodged, as to prepare us for the comparative quiet we found brooding over the little town.

At its best, however, Bognor could never, I think, have been anything but a dull little town. It was so decorous, so painfully clean, so oppressively self-conscious a prude, that dulness must have been as much a part of its being as were its demure little

airs of conventional propriety. What has the sea
to do with conventionality? Its merest ripplet is
Nature's indignant protest against too clean and
well-swept a beach. Here there was no beach at
all. Instead there was a brick sea-wall, which kept
the sea at a proper offish distance. The waves
broke a hundred yards out, as an English sea
should do when it is to serve as the tame and tepid
bath for an Englishman's wife and children.

The houses that fronted the water might have
been London houses, suburban London; there was
no holiday air pervading them. There was nothing even of the flowery, pretty picturesqueness
which had charmed us in some of the country inns
and taverns we had passed along our road. These
dull-brown and brick façades were the epitome of
British decorum. Even when off on a holiday, it
appears that the Englishman feels he must build
him a prison in which he can lock himself in and
others out.

"The Englishman can't throw off his social
straight-jacket even when he puts on his bathing-suit," I said in a fit of disgust to Boston. "Have
you noticed the bath-houses? The notices on the
doors are little chapters of autobiography."

"They are of a piece with all the rest," was Boston's answer. On the doors of several of the little houses were signs in large printed letters of " Elizabeth Primrose, aged fifty, bather from Teignmouth, where she had been bather for over thirty-five years."

" Even one's bath-woman must have a pedigree ! " we said, and then we laughed.

But we were the only laughers. No one else was gay. Holidaying at the seaside, it appears, is a serious amusement over here, to be enjoyed in a measured spirit of conscientious dulness. Even the children, who with their governesses were gravely walking along the sea-wall, were evidently far too well brought up to look upon the sea in the light of a playfellow. Other promenaders there were whose expression was familiar; it was the look we had grown to know in London, in the Row, — that of being bored according to the most correct methods of a well-bred ennui. A few very upright young ladies were sitting, alone or in pairs, under huge white parasols, on the little iron benches. They were looking out at the sea, staring at it as if they expected, if there was to be any conversation, the ocean would begin it. The only talking there was, was being done by several stately old ladies in bath-chairs. They were each accompanied by their upright handsome husbands,— or such we took them to be, from their air of indifference to the ladies' chatter and from their general appearance of command. Why is it that in England it is only the woman who grows old hideously? These fine old gentlemen were pictures of blooming old age, with their pink cheeks, white hair, and well-knit, erect, and graceful figures. It appears that one must cross the Channel to find the secret which woman holds there of growing old both wittily and handsomely.

It was with but little regret that we passed out of the long, stiff, straight little streets, noting, as we passed, the fact of how cheerfully many of the houses gave up half their façade to the great business of proclaiming their names. Where else except in a land of cockneys would a residence twelve by ten be dignified by a name, ostentatiously paraded, suitable only for a palatial dwelling? "The Elms," the "Albert Villa," the "Richmond Mansion,"— such were the pretentious signs painted in great flaring letters over every other house-door which we passed. For a modest people the English break out into astonishing vagaries of vanity.

It was a relief to turn away from the stiff, vain little town into the country road once more. It was a flat road. But there was no monotony in its flatness. Arms and branchlets of the sea swept up into the fields and meadows, making bright pools of light. In the air there was a delicious mingling of salty vigor and sweet earthy smells, and it was the loveliest, tenderest hour of the day. The work of the day for man and beast, and for the sun as well, was done. All three were going to their evening rest. Men with rakes over their shoulders were following wagons so plenteously laden with hay that they generously left tithes along the roadside for stray sheep. A boy with a sickle over his straight young back walked near us, whistling a gay little air. The sickle was repeated in silver in the sky, the dawning crescent of the young moon cleaving the eastern horizon. Cows in groups were moving slowly, in calm contentment with the day's bounty. Earth and sky, under the dying light, were changing from the gold of sunset to the violets and deeper purples of twilight; it was the feet of coming Night pressing out the rich wine of color from the fruitful land.

But the gift of sensibility to the beauties of nature had not been given to all three of our party; to our pony the charms of twilight proved no substitute for a good supper. The Chichester Cathedral spire, which had guided us inland with its tapering spiral beauty, appeared to grow no nearer for all our frequent use of the whip. Another hour of whipping, of desperate spurts of energy on the part of the worn and weary pony, of manifold losing of our way amid the tortuous streets of Chichester, which was a far larger city than we had expected to find, and behold us rattling within the brick courtyard of "The Bird and the Swallow."

CHAPTER IV.

CHICHESTER.

"THE Bird and the Swallow" was a wise little inn. It had known just where to place itself when there was a cathedral in town to be looked at. The next morning we awoke to encounter the charm of a surprise. Our windows, we found, opened directly on the cathedral. The whole of the beautiful western façade rose in noble dignity beyond the trees in the green close, whose branches almost rustled against our windows.

Our breakfast, that morning, promised to prolong itself into an indefinite feast. The *mise-en-scène* in our cosey little sitting-room was altogether perfect. "The Bird and the Swallow," we confided to each other over the crisp toast, was to be numbered among the ideal inns. That conclusion had been reached the night before, when a particularly pretty barmaid and the stout and matronly innkeeper's wife had preceded us to our rooms with flaring candles and a pot of hot tea.

"It'll warm ye, ma'am, and ease ye after yer long drive, ma'am; but the gentleman 'll have a toddy, now, won't he? — a drop of hot Scotch?"

Such delicate discrimination merited its just reward. Is it necessary to add that the stout landlady won our hearts at once? She had been the first innkeeper who had really appeared glad to see us. The "Norfolk Arms" was much too splendid an establishment to be moved by the coming or the going of travellers. Our waiter had preserved to the last an impassive composure and indifference, seeming to be fully conscious of what was expected of one who lived so near to the best society. But the Chichester inn was provincial, — uncompromisingly, unblushingly, avowedly provincial. The landlady was not above showing her pleasure at the coming of travellers the size of whose trunks and whose general air of fatigue promised a more or less lengthy stay in the dull season. She had bustled about our rooms as if she were doing the honors of her own house, — giving a twitch to the white chintz curtains, rearranging chairs to take the stiff look out of the room, and altogether behaving as a human being should whose business in life it was to make travellers comfortable and to make money out of them.

"I presume it will be charged in the bill, all this extra pains and extra cordiality, but I don't mind. One gets at least what one pays for; and, besides, she really works for it. See how hot and puffy she is getting!"

She was purple as she tried to lift one of the heavy hand-bags on the rack; but she was smiling as if she were enjoying it. The real misery would have been to be a degree less hot and less officious. Then we tried to picture to ourselves any American boarding-house keeper working herself into that crimson heat of active zeal.

"No American woman could, you know. Either she would be so thin and tired, she would n't have muscular energy to spare, or else she would be above it, — above waiting on her 'guests.' She would ring a bell, which no one would answer, and it would end in your carrying your own bag. There is nothing like a democracy for inuring the upper classes into doing their own work. I prefer a monarchy myself, where there is somebody left in the class below you who is willing, for a consideration, to wait on you."

Boston only laughed. He was too weary just then to reply. But I could see that the excellences of the English system produced their effect when, the next morning, we descended to our sitting-room to find a snowy table laid with bits of old china and silver, set close to a window, through which the sun was shining cheerily, with the gray and mottled cathedral mass uplifting its greatness beyond the tree-tops. We finished our meal, only to discover, as we leaned farther out of the window to gain a freer view of the spire, that beyond, at the right of the cathedral, rose a beautiful square tower. It was the campanile, — the only detached bell-tower adjoining a cathedral now existing in England. It was a rugged, massive structure, as different as possible from the slender, graceful campaniles that rise into the melting Italian skies; but its gray stones were full of color, and were peculiarly rich in shadows, which we found were perpetually haunting its fine octagonal crown and girdling its turrets.

At the other end of the street, placed at just the right angle to make it a perfect pendant to the campanile, was another structure,— one so unique, so unusual, and so altogether lovely as to send us forth into the street that we might gain a nearer view.

Was Chichester to be a series of surprises? Was the little city a museum of architectural masterpieces? We had expected the cathedral, but had been told that the town was dull. Yet here were three buildings, brought within the focus of our sitting-room windows, which merely to look upon would repay one for many miles of travel. Who are those ingenious ignoramuses who write the guide-books, whose dexterity for telling us the things we don't want to know about is only equalled by their criminal incapacity when dealing with the things which are really worth while? Perhaps, however, we really are more deeply in the debt of these self-constituted misleaders than we willingly own. How truly dull would travel be if all travellers were wise! If it be true that happiness lies more in acquisition than in possession, the truism must hold that in travel the chief charm is to be found in the act of discovery rather than in the enjoyment of the thing discovered. *Ergo*, a well-written guide-book would defeat the chief end of one's journey.

CHICHESTER. 73

The name of the beautiful structure we found, on consulting the Chichester guide-book, to be the Market Cross. There was certainly no appearance of any salable merchandise; nor, at a first glance, did there seem to be any signs to mark its remote resemblance to a cross. It was a perfect octagon, whose eight-arched openings made a circular arcade. In the centre of the little building was a massive pillar, from which, as branches grow out of a palm, the finely groined roof shot forth its thick ribs. Its exterior blossomed with ornaments, flowering into richly decorated finials and flying buttresses, and budding into a wealth of cusps. About the whole little structure there was a delightful luxuriance and efflorescence. It had evidently bloomed into beauty at a wonderfully perfect moment of the later Gothic inspiration.

The Cross being placed at the juncture of the four principal streets of the little city, its arcade formed the natural crossing for the street passengers. Beneath the vaulted roof there was a ceaseless patter and echo of passing footsteps, of broken speech and laughter,— the noise of people meeting, talking, and parting. It was as if a huge umbrella had been opened, beneath which all the townsfolk had come to take refuge for a moment of time away from the dazzle of the sunshine and the noonday glare.

It now serves, doubtless, as wise and admirable an end, we said to each other, as the original purpose which its founder had in view. It had been given to the city, in the latter part of the fifteenth century, by one of the artist-bishops of the cathedral, to the end that it might delight his own eyes by its beauty and relieve the city from an extortionate tax. The poor farmers of the neighborhood were here provided with a shelter where they might sell their produce — their eggs, butter, and other articles — free from toll.

We have changed all that in these days. The poor still pay toll, but we call it by a loftier name; and so the Cross is a market no longer, but the open-air lounging-chair of every weary or idle soul who cares to give his leisure an airing.

We were neither weary nor willingly idle; but we sat there, and still continued to sit, finding it too perfect a point of observation to leave. All the life and hubbub of the little city were about us. At least half a dozen streets were in full view. Instead of a dull city, as we looked out upon

CHICHESTER CROSS.
Page 74.

its busy life, we found it uncommonly sprightly. There was a brisk commercial stir and life bustling up and down its streets. There were so many shops, one was not surprised at the multiplicity of buyers. The women had the eager air common to the sex when there are plenty of shop-windows bristling with novelties. There was a modishness in their attire, suggestive of the significant conclusion that some of those tempting London fashions were being worn by the happy buyers with a genteel consciousness of an elegance superior to the prevailing provincial styles. There was another cause which awakened our suspicions that something else besides the natural instinct of the sex for wearing only the latest conceits of fashion may have inspired the smart costumes with which the streets abounded. Chichester, true to its ancient Roman origin, is still a camp. We had passed the barracks of the regiment now quartered here, the night before. There were brilliant dashes of color abroad this morning, — brave scarlets, and jaunty red caps, the latter tilted at the most extraordinary angle compatible with adhesiveness, worn by dashing young braves, who walked with the step of young giants off on a stroll.

The direct relation between a military button and the corresponding activity of a woman's vanity has never yet been satisfactorily explained. But we all know that the appearance of a single military coat has been known to change the millinery of an entire town from a condition of stagnation to one of frenzied animation.

Besides the red coats and the pretty, fresh faces, the streets were filled with numbers of traps and carriages, many of them, from the plethoric baskets strapped at the back, evidently having been driven in from the surrounding country. Gentlemen from box-seats were giving orders to fruiterers. Stout ladies were handed down from drags by their footmen, with an air of serious concern, to the level of the shop windows. One charmingly pretty girl rode up with her groom to a book-shop near us, and dismounted. She stood for a brief moment, holding her habit over her arm, as she looked in at the window over the titles of some new books. Her sweet, fine profile, her straight, firm figure, with its air of breeding and refinement, made a charming picture in the midst of the old street and among the motley crowd of passers-by.

Altogether, we repeated to each other, Chichester was a charming little town; were this to be taken as a typical English provincial town, the spectacle of its stirring life makes the secret of England's greatness the more understandable. Even these remote little English towns and cities, it appears, are centres of life and movement. Throughout the whole extent of this wonderful island there is the flow of quick arterial blood; its very extremities are replete with nervous life. There are no stagnant places, no paralyzed members, in its compact little frame. London is not the only head or the sole heart of this admirably organized kingdom. The pulse and throb of active life thrills to its remotest finger-tips.

From the picturesque point of view, the beauty of Chichester appeared to have been focussed in the buildings about us. The town wore a sufficiently venerable appearance to be in keeping with the gray and mossy fronts of the cathedral, the campanile, and the Cross. The houses were for the most part uninteresting. Commerce is as brutal as war, and defaces as wantonly as the latter destroys; and Chichester was, and is, distinctively commercial. It has been for many generations the great wool-fair of the kingdom.

From the historical standpoint Chichester may be said to have had a career replete with vicissitudes. For so small a city it has amassed a good deal of historical experience. Its origin was, of course, Saxon. No English city which respects itself but points with pride to its heathen ancestry, when its barbarous ancestors fiercely worshipped Thor and Odin. Chichester was Roman before it was Saxon, being one of the chief Roman settlements, known as Regnum. All these southern cities were for the most part Norman camps. They were on the high-road to the sea, and were the natural halting-places of the enemy or of the brave defenders of the soil. There is a temple just out of the city, at Goodwood, erected by the Duke of Richmond, containing a slab which brings Roman paganism wonderfully near. It bears the inscription: "The college or company of artificers, and they who preside over the sacred rites or hold office by the authority of King Cogidubnus, the legatee of Tiberius Claudius Augustus, in Britain, dedicated this temple to Neptune and Minerva, for the welfare of the Imperial Family; Pudens, the son of Pudentinus, giving the ground." Minerva and Neptune next gave way to Thor and

Odin; for gods succeeded one another, as dynasties did, on these ancient battle-grounds. The shrine was erected by the victorious, that they might have a deity to pray to after they had done with the killing. If all the warriors turned worshippers, the temples about Chichester must always have been full; for those old warriors had an appetite for blood which makes a modern soldier seem a very feeble production.

When Ælle and his son Cissa took Regnum from the Roman Britons, they "slew all that dwelt therein, nor was there thenceforth one Brit left," says the old chronicler. When there were no others left to kill, they slew themselves. After a long period of famine, the hungry Saxons, linking themselves in companies of forties and fifties, sought to put an end to their sufferings by throwing themselves into the sea. What a spectacle must that wild horde of undisciplined passions have been, dancing their fearless dance to the sea! Even in suicide, it appears, they chose to march bravely, in battalions, to this voluntary death. They knew not how to endure, but they still preserved their instinct of bravery. Christianity came at last to teach this brute force its own strength.

Hence the cathedral. The battle-axe was laid aside for the chisel. It is impossible, I think, to compute the tremendous influence which the building of these great cathedrals must have exercised on the mediæval character. Much stress has been laid on the enlarging and civilizing uses of the Crusades. The Crusades unquestionably made experienced travellers of the mediæval ascetics; but a cathedral was a finer experience than a crusade. It developed the humanities. It kept men at home, and taught them the sweet uses of sympathy, of interest in a common object, and brought near to them the experiences of self-sacrifice. It developed the yearning faculties, the longing for the exercise of taste and skill, into trained talents which could be consecrated to the highest achievement.

What a stirring fire of enthusiasm, for instance, kindled the builders of the great Chartres Cathedral! Powerful men, proud of their riches and accustomed to a delicate and luxurious life, harnessed themselves to the shafts of carts to convey stones, lime, wood, and every necessary material for the construction of the sacred edifice. "Sometimes a thousand persons, men and women, are harnessed to the same cart, so heavy is the load; nevertheless such a profound silence reigns, that not the least whisper is heard. When they stop on the road, they speak only of their sins, which they confess with tears and prayers. Then the priests make them promise to stifle all hatred and forgive all debts. Should any one be found who is so hardened as to be unwilling to forgive his enemies and refuse to submit to the pious exhortations, he is at once unharnessed from the cart, and driven out of the holy band." This is quoted from an extremely interesting history of Notre Dame de Chartres, written by Abbé Bulteau.

No record brings to us any such account of the pious banding together of English nobles and peasants for the dual purpose of purging their souls by penance and hastening the completion of their grand cathedral. The Englishman's enthusiasm is colder, even when under the influence of the deepest emotion. His piety is never a sensational debauch; he is under no such dramatic necessity for the display of his sensibilities as animates the excitable Gaul, to whom the experience of emotion is misery unless it can be enacted before an audience, however small. And thus, I fancy, the patience and self-denial and the hard-won triumphs over rebellious spirits and haughty souls lie buried in the silence of the sculptured stones, whose enduring beauty is the nobler record.

As an eloquent instance of perseverance, Chichester Cathedral may be said to be unequalled. Its existence is proof of the indomitable energy of man in restoring what the elements destroy. Heaven itself appeared to be in league with the force of the winds and the fury of the flames. What fire did not consume, the winds wrecked. When the battalions of the skies had ceased their pillaging, the soldiers of the Commonwealth took possession with their swords. But in spite of revolutions, of wind-storms, and the scorching breath of fire, the beautiful cathedral, with its lovely spire, wore a wonderfully complete and serene front as we walked towards it on that bright summer morning. It is set in the midst of its close, a little apart from the main thoroughfare. A fringe of trees separates the brisk step of the passer-by from the silent footsteps, forever stilled, which lie beneath the old gravestones. Once within the iron gates, one feels the influence of that peculiar hush which the nearness of God's temple always brings.

CHICHESTER CATHEDRAL. *Page 82*

Who has not felt this peace and quiet in the air as he has stepped aside from the bustle of the busy world into the still, calm burial-ground surrounding some old church? It is only a distance of a few yards, and yet how remote the world seems, after a few moments alone there! One may be neither Christian nor believer, neither communicant nor worshipper; and yet such is the deep tranquillity of the place, such the sweet and restful peace beneath those cool aisles of the overshadowing trees, that unconsciously the heart becomes stilled, the soul is eased of its burden, and life, for a brief moment's space at least, is lived softly, peacefully, lovingly. A blessing seems to be abroad in the air, and to have alighted for a second's space in our bosoms.

This feeling is intensified in English churchyards. A beautiful fashion of appropriating a large space of green is one of the peculiar charms of English cathedral buildings. The velvety lawn and the grove of trees are an essential part of the English builder's plan, in the arrangement of his architectural effects. The cathedral is thus preserved against accidental surroundings. It is set apart, away from the disturbing influences of incongruous buildings. Unlike the great continental cathedrals, an English cathedral is neither hidden among the slums of an old market-place nor barbarously exposed to the inclemencies of the weather on a barren hill-top. Sheltered amid its well-wooded paths, the entire mass of the beautiful structure rises unencumbered and unobstructed.

Apart from the admirable advantages gained by such a wise combination of the beauties of nature and of art, there is an added charm, — the cathedral appears to have an ideal poetic isolation, the effect of its separateness as a temple being thus the more fully emphasized.

It would have been impossible, for instance, for just the effect which the exterior of this cathedral produced on us, as we approached it, to have been wrought by any continental cathedral. The deep shade of the trees, the thick sweet grass, the quiet pathways, and the shadows resting on the gravestones were the prelude to the deeper sensations the interior of the church itself was to awaken. We were keyed into an emotional feeling before we entered the temple. It is scarcely a matter of wonderment that men in the worst times of Anne and the Georges, when the most exquisite Gothic carvings and altar-pieces were destroyed, should have spared the grass and the trees. An Englishman is a nature-lover even when he turns iconoclast.

Entering the low portal, we discovered with delight that we had the interior of the church to ourselves. Not even the flutter of a verger's gown was to be discerned. We could sit down unmolested on the little rush-bottomed chairs, and enjoy the beauty about us without feeling that our sensations were to be summoned up to order.

Our first impression was one of bewilderment. The interior of Chichester appeared to be three or four churches made one; not because of its size, but because of its extraordinary architectural variety of design. Imagine a Norman nave, so massive that it appears to grow out of the earth, with square-capped columns and round arches rearing their sturdy strength up into the roof beyond, tier on tier. This massive nave is flanked on either side by two slender, graceful Gothic aisles, as light and delicate in their lines as the branches of so many young trees. As if this, as an architectural shock, were not sufficient to have satisfied builders in pursuit of novelties, a walk toward the south transept and the Lady Chapel introduced us to the fantastic elaborations and rich traceries of the fourteenth-century workers. Beyond, out among the trees and grass of the cloisters, the upright perpendicular lines of the still later Gothic showed that in this most curious and interesting little cathedral one could trace the growth and flowering of the English taste in architecture during those five hundred years when the pre-eminent qualities of its excellence and beauty made England take its place among the two or three great and original masters in the art. In no other English cathedral, perhaps, can the transition in styles be so distinctly traced. Chichester, considered from this point of view, may be said to be a mosaic of English experiments in cathedral building.

The result as a whole is more interesting than beautiful. The absence of a distinct unity of plan or design makes one tremendously conscious of the effort there has been in it all. The Norman bishops planned one thing, which the Early English and later Perpendicular architects did their best either to obliterate or to destroy. But strength is more persistent than grace; and so all through the charming geometric lace-work the rugged massive ribs and round-arched vertebræ of the Norman structure protrude their giant strength.

A certain coldness and want of color, and also a sense of the loss of that contrast that comes with prismatic light, made these effects and this architectural diversity even more conspicuous. The whole interior was as gray as a convent. There was none of that beautiful, mysterious cloistral twilight which pervades the atmosphere in continental cathedrals, — an atmosphere that makes their dim aisles as shadowy as if enveloped in some delicately tinted fog. Here the pale sunlight brought the colorless pallor of this interior into almost cruel relief. The absence of glass would account for something of this defect, there being only a few modern stained-glass windows in the entire edifice. But even where deep shadows were made by some architectural feature, the contrast they brought to the whole was sombre. In the Norman triforium the shadows were black; it was the blackness of the dungeon rather than the rich depth of blended shade.

We did not escape the verger, after all. He discovered us just in time to prevent our making the complete tour of the cathedral. We had not seen the tombs, of course, having neglected them for the above less important features. But the little verger was a man of determination. He had had to deal with indifferent and rebellious tourists before. He soon brought us round to the correct sepulchral attitude; not a mortuary urn was allowed to pass unnoticed. He presented us first to the bishops, as they lay in state, with mitre and crozier and archiepiscopal hat. Each had his history, of which only the commendable features had evidently been confided to the verger. One must go to Froude's profane pages for the scandals which made the lives of some of these blameless gentlemen such a curious mixture of piety and immorality. Their frailties live on in history; their virtues appear to have been infolded within their august robes of state. The recumbent figures of the knights in full armor were more to our taste; there is something honest in men who go to heaven armed cap-a-pie, as if they meant to fight for their rights even at Saint Peter's gate. By the side of one of these warriors, apparelled in the stiff narrow gowns of the fourteenth century, lay the effigy of his lady. The knight had taken off his glove, and held in his own the slim, tapering fingers of his calm-browed spouse. The couple are Richard Fitzalan, Earl of Arundel, and his Countess. The former was beheaded by reason of too great fidelity to the Duke of Gloucester, in King Richard's reign. King Richard was not a man to be stopped by too nice a feeling if he had a purpose to accomplish. After the Earl's interment, "it having been bruited around for a miracle that his head had grown to his body again," that thorough-going monarch ordered the tomb opened. Little wonder that the poor gentleman wanted the cold comfort of holding his wife's hand down through the ages, after such a double indignity!

Our verger was filled with grief over the fact of the loss of the fine old brasswork,— the crosses and the shields inserted into the stone slabs. They had all been stolen or destroyed by the soldiers of the Commonwealth. The pillaging and desecration in this little cathedral were riotous during the Revolution. Sir William Waller's troops "ran up and down with their swords, defacing the monuments of the dead, and hacking the seats and the stalls." These Puritan warriors must have been connoisseurs as well as iconoclasts. They knew just what to smash and to steal. They stripped the cathedral as bare as only an educated eye could have directed.

"Yes, ma'am, they smashed all the old glass, and they stole all our brasses. The jewels in the sculptures, did you notice, ma'am, they was stole, I fancy," was our guide's mournfully resentful summary of those old days of pious pillaging. He could not have been more indignantly melancholy had he held his office during the Puritan raid. The sculpture to which he referred was some most interesting old Norman work, of which we were to see more at Salisbury. The stolen jewels, which formed the eye-sockets in the faces of the rude figures, had left holes that looked like deep wounds. This early Norman sculpture is strangely like early Assyrian and Indian work. All archaic work has a more or less close resemblance; for it corresponds to the primitive art impulse, to the period of the beginning of a nation's art. The verger, we noticed, drew his finger over the stiff draperies lovingly, as if he wished to smooth out some of their rigidity. It was when the sad-faced little man, however, came to the recital of the falling of the spire, that he touched the apogee of his dra-

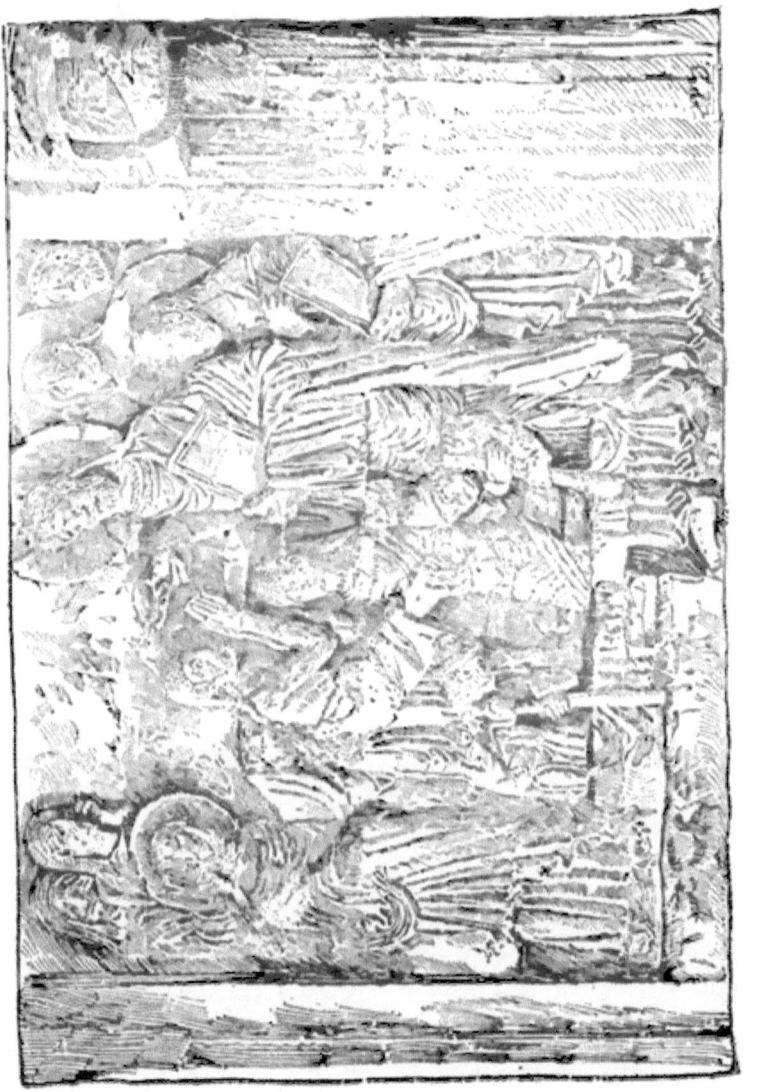

OLD SCULPTURES, CHICHESTER. *Page 90.*

matic capabilities. He drew us into the choir, above which soars the present lovely and modern spire. He assured us that long before any one else had suspected the old spire of weakness he knew that it was doomed.

"Why, ma'am, the fissures was in the walls as big as crevices. The sides 'ere of this 'ere arch was as wrinkled as an old shoe. It wasn't any use patchin' of such walls as that. No spire was goin' to set firm on them rickety legs. All the workmen in the country couldn't make an old man stand straight; and that was what these walls was, hold men that 'ad got tired. They couldn't 'old themselves hup, much less a big tall spire. Well, the cathedral was full of workmen who done their best. They was a-workin' and a-workin'; they done their best, I will say, and when the storm came, they was like giants,— they never gave hup night nor day. It was an April storm, and every time the wind 'owled every man in Chichester trembled. There wasn't a closed hi in Chichester that night. Why! every one on us, men and boys, 'ad grown hup under that hold spire. We loved it as we did our own. But it 'ad to go. When mornin' broke, the storm was a tempest.

We could almost 'ear the great spire a-rockin' in the wind. And then it fell. We was all out in the streets, bareheaded, when it caved. It fell, sur, just like it was a telescope, a-falling into itself. It did n't do no harm to nobody nor nothin' but just itself. It was just God's mercy that watched over it, and when it was gone a prayer was on every lip, and a tear in every hi; and, sur, oh, sur, but was n't the dust awful? It was weeks and weeks before we was clean and to rights." And the little man began furtively to dust a near choir-stall, as if the memory of that time had brought up the old habit.

The cathedral guide-books tell the story of this famous falling in of the old spire in 1861 with more elaborateness of detail, but the old verger's account we found quite as accurate and far more picturesque. After the débris had been cleared away, designs for the rebuilding, based on the old models, were immediately begun. The result is the present beautiful structure. Many authorities prefer it to its famous Salisbury rival; and, indeed, in its aerial lightness and grace and its perfection of proportion, it would be difficult to conceive a spire more pleasing. It possesses that genuine soaring quality without which a spire always seems to miss its intended effect. It is little wonder that the inhabitants of Chichester loved their spire; for Chichester, a flat city in a flat country, would be as unnoticed as featureless plainness ever is. This lovely arrow shot into the sky makes the city as conspicuous as some old veteran who, ere he launches his weapon, takes a fine and noble attitude.

CHAPTER V.

GOODWOOD.

THE next day an important transaction was to take place. We were to hire another horse. This ordinarily simple matter had come to assume serious proportions. The Chichester mind we found even more obtuse in the recognition of honesty — that apparently rare virtue in rural England — than Arundel. The town, as one man, had refused to trust us with even so much as a she-ass outside its gates. Three carriages and as many horses had been stolen within the memory of the oldest inhabitant. The most credulous believer in mankind among the Chichester inhabitants refused to add a fourth to such a list.

Clearly something must be done. We could hardly proceed on our tour subject to such repeated suspicions of our honesty, and continue, conscientiously, to call it a pleasure-trip. It would be almost better to elope with a horse and a suitable trap, and have done with honest dealing. I wonder if such be not the origin of half the wickedness of the world! Every one suspects every one else; and some among us, not being able to make a stand against public opinion, end by becoming that which it is expected we in reality are.

We bethought ourselves, however, of a compromise with villany. A London friend had given us a letter to a gentleman living in Chichester; we would present it in the hope that he would help us in our dilemma. He did better; he solved the whole difficulty.

"Why not hire a trap out and out? You will be far more comfortable, and then you won't be having this wretched bother," he suggested. "I know an excellent man."

The man, we discovered on a visit to his stables, had an excellent horse. Such at least we divined the latter to be from a rather fragmentary review of his hind quarters and his glossy coat, as he stood quietly in his stall during our brief inspection. It was only when he appeared, an hour later, in the brave livery of a bright new harness, with fine gold mountings, that his admirable thorough-bred ancestry, though somewhat remote, declared itself in the tapering legs, the small sensitive ears, the intelligent head, and the straight horizontal back. He was a beauty, in a word. The only doubt which a survey of his apparent perfections suggested was whether he would be quite up to his work. Could he carry the weight for six successive weeks of the pretty T-cart, brilliant in its fresh green and yellow varnish; of ourselves, who were not cast in a liliputian mould; and of our luggage, consisting of two small trunks, two valises, and several hand-bags?

"No fear of that, sir. He's up to twenty miles a day, week in and week out. And it's mostly parties we take, sir, and he never minds how many it is."

If the owner didn't doubt his steed's capacity and endurance, why should we? So the bargain was concluded, with the reservation, however, that if, after reaching Winchester, we were not entirely pleased, we were to return the trap by train. This would give us several days' trial of the qualities of our new companion.

Happily unconscious that he was under inspection, our new steed in the subsequent two days' drive made a most frank betrayal of his character. I am not sure, on the whole, however, that he had as much character as he had nature. The pony, for instance, had possessed in an eminent degree those qualities which distinguish the former, but she was lamentably deficient in the latter essential. This horse, on the contrary, had more temperament than character. He possessed less mind and far more intelligence than his predecessor, — two qualities only too rarely seen in combination in either men or animals. He had too much intelligence and not enough mind, for instance, to oppose to our own. He responded to command with the docility born of an enlightened acquiescence in the right. With such high qualities he would have been really insufferable, if only by sheer force of contrast, had he not been veined with a certain feminine timidity; his shying made him human and endurable. As this fault appeared to be a latent susceptibility to what may be termed the accidentals of travel rather than an active habit, it could hardly be looked upon in the light of a serious objection. He possessed one admirable qualification we discovered, which was of inestimable value to us, with more than a month's driving ahead: he was one of the best walkers we had ever seen. His was a long, even, slightly quickened step, that got him over the ground in capital time, making him a really exhilarating companion. Altogether our star of luck had been in the ascendant when he joined the party. At Winchester we promptly proceeded to engage him by telegraph for the remainder of our journey.

"What shall we call him? We ought to have asked the hostler his name. A horse without a name is as bad as an unchristened infant. We can't go on calling him plain 'horse' for six weeks."

"Why not call him Ballad? That was his owner's name. It strikes me as an eminently proper one too. We're off a-holidaying, and Ballad is suggestive; it is suggestive of glees and things, of the poetry we shan't write and the songs we can't sing. Besides, he is a merry creature, and deserves a merry name."

And so Ballad it was. Inside of a week he knew his new name quite as well as we.

From Chichester we were to go early the next morning to Goodwood, the famous race-course grounds which lie within the Duke of Richmond's estate. Later on, towards the afternoon, we were to start on our regular route as far as Fareham, a little village half-way between Chichester and Winchester. In all, the day's journey would include about twenty-five miles, in which Ballad might show us his metal.

Hardly two miles out of Chichester, and we were within the grounds of the great estate. Once within the park gates, and we were again struck with the fact of how the character of the land changes in England when it ceases to be the property of the people and becomes the property of one man. It is like exchanging the plough for the senate. Every great estate, no matter how vast, has an administered look, as if it had ceased to be vulgarly used for purely agricultural purposes and had passed into the aristocratic stage of being just so many ancestral acres. Goodwood, for instance, which was enormous in extent, far larger than Arundel Park, had the patrician air of doing nothing in particular, except to be beautiful. We passed several miles of turf, of lawn, of grassy, clean-shaven mounds, which appeared to be laid out as so many grand spaces wherein the great and splendid trees could grow to enormous size, and whereon they could cast their resplendent shade.

"What trees they do grow in this country! Look

at those oaks! Don't they look as if they were conscious that they had a constitutional government and a secured law of primogeniture to grow up under?"

"Well," replied Boston, smiling, "I suppose that does have something to do with it. They don't look as nervous and shivery as some of our trees."

"And haven't you been struck with the appearance of calculation there is about it all? It seems to me as if there were a kind of destiny presiding over the trees in English landscape. Only just so many seem to be permitted to grow. Their quantity appears to be gauged by the amount of good they will do. So many trees, so much timber, so much good drainage, so many crops; it all seems based on the multiplication table, a kind of moral multiplication table."

"Yes, perhaps there is something moral even in their landscape-gardening. An Englishman wouldn't be happy, I suppose, unless he had a law behind him for every action, however trivial," said Boston, as he whipped a fly off Ballad's back, who, resenting the familiarity, dashed off with a spurt, and brought us quickly to the top of the hill overlooking the race-course.

The Goodwood track is noted the world over for the beauty of its situation. It is on an upper table-land, and overlooks a lot of pretty hills which appear to be tumbling into one another's laps. It might not be inaptly described, indeed, as a paradise of hills framed about with sky. The course itself is an elongated ellipse, whose curved lines dip slightly as they rise and fall along the slope of the hill-top on which the track is laid out. The sides and crest of the encircling hills form a natural amphitheatre not unlike the great theatres of old, where each man had an equal chance at the play on the stage below over his neighbor's head. It was easy to picture the sight of the breathless thousands peopling those hillsides, and to imagine the swelling chorus of their deafening cheers and roars, making a thundering music, as the sounds rolled out through the length and breadth of the great, roofless, unenclosed amphitheatre. What a spectacle to see and to have missed seeing!

"Can't we wait for them, — wait for the races? They are only two weeks off," I asked Boston, as the prospect warmed before us.

"And in two weeks'· time we ought to be in

Devon; yes, we can forego Devon, and have Goodwood if you like."

Is it the mission of husbands in this world to carry about buckets of common-sense, that they may always be in readiness to extinguish the follies of their wives? I suppose the reason why nations are always so well governed who have women as sovereigns is because these latter are under the subjection of not only one man, but many. It is the ministers who keep their queen, by sheer force of numbers, from committing errors, by reducing her to the proper feminine attitude of incapacitated energy.

Such a spectacle as Goodwood presents does certainly suggest a lesson in the uses of sovereigns and ministers. One is willing to forgive a country its constitutional monarchies in view of such a result as this. England, after all, is the only country which still provides splendid outdoor festivities for its people, which are both pure and healthy. There is no such democrat in his pleasure as the Englishman. On the turf all men are equal; all that the nobleman has is none too good for the peasant on the fête-day, when he opens his gates and bids the latter come in and take possession. It is true the nobleman does n't go to the extreme of allowing the peasant to remain long. But during the remainder of the year it is the titled landlord who really works and plans and spends his money that he may keep the playground in order till the people come again to be his guests. On the whole, the English yeoman gets a great deal out of his aristocratic class. He gets a country lovelier and more beautiful to look upon and to walk about in than any other on the round earth; he gets great and splendid belongings which supply him with a perpetual round of spectacular pageants and excitements; and he gets such public pleasures as no other nation save the Greeks and the Romans have ever managed to supply to a people generation after generation. And now I suppose socialism has come to end all this. It will issue its commands; and England, the last of the people's great stage-managers, must chop up its lawns into cabbage-beds and harness its hunters to the plough.

We had been walking in the meanwhile along the crest of the race-track, examining the Grand Stand and the adjoining stables, when we stumbled on an adventure. It met us in the shape of two frank, boyish blue eyes, that seemed quite as much surprised as we were startled at confronting them, as we turned the corner of one of the larger buildings. The owner of these blue eyes was a slim, but beautifully erect boy in white flannel knickerbockers, who was walking about, swinging his jersey cap in his hand. As he had his cap in his hand, he couldn't lift it; but the instinct of good manners was in the charming little fellow, for both cap and hand went up, after his first start of surprise.

He was alone, and apparently was indulging, like ourselves, in a survey of the surrounding buildings.

"This is the way out, is it not?" asked Boston, more for the purpose of having a word with the boy than really because he was in need of the answer; for there was something immensely taking about the little fellow. As we approached him, I saw that he had the fresh, clear English skin, the straightforward, honest, and brave English eyes, and just that touch of correctness in his bearing, that nameless moral rectitude which seems to have worked itself out into square shoulders and stiff back and firm legs, — a bearing which distinguishes an English-bred boy as unmistakably as the Jesuits' training leaves its brand on the French stripling.

"This goes into the royal enclosure, sir," he replied without a moment's hesitation; then he added after a moment, as we both smiled down on him: "There is the Royal Stand, sir, where his Royal Highness always is. Would n't you like to see it? I can take you in." And he fumbled a moment in his deep pockets, out of which came a knife, a small apple, a bunch of raisins, a quarry of marbles, and one large key. He blushed now for the first time; it must have been at the raisins, which, presumably, he was surprised, and a little annoyed, to find still uneaten. They were quickly slipped into the other pocket. Then he opened the door of the stand, and ran up the steps to the corner of the huge building. He appeared to be entirely at home in the great empty building. He led us to the southern corner, which was partitioned off from the rest of the house and was enclosed in glass. It was like a great proscenium-box overlooking the stage setting. The prospect was glorious; all the lovely hills lying in full view, with wide horizons beyond. At this elevation the whole track lay beneath us in all its length and breadth. There was also the entire sweep of the grounds to be taken in at a glance. At one side, the side nearest the gate entrance, was a lovely bit of shade, — a velvet carpet of the greenest turf, with noble trees at near distances.

"That's the Lady's Lawn, ma'am, where the luncheons are spread," said our charming little companion, as he saw we were looking down into the coolness and the green. "The ladies sit down there or walk about. Sometimes her Royal Highness goes down. Then over there, over yonder, is where the coaches and drags stand, and over still farther is the place for the carriages and for the carts. Have you ever seen the horses run, sir?"

"No, my lad, I never have, here; but you have, I presume?" It was delightful to see the boy's eyes flame out, and his red cheeks grow redder yet, as he answered quickly, —

"Oh dear, yes, sir, over and over again. Last year I lost, but this year I shall win. I've bet on the favorite," — with tremendous earnestness.

He continued to do the honors of the place as if he felt the pressure of the true host's instinct of hospitality.

"Did you notice the road on the left as you came up, the road that goes through the woods? That's the road the Royal Party take to come here on race-day. The other roads are free; but that one is reserved for the Duke and the Royal party. And did you see the wood, sir, the birdless wood? It was on the right near the top of the long hill. No birds are ever found there, and they die if they build their nests there. Did you notice how still it was? It's nearly a mile long. I don't like it, it's too still; it's like Sunday. I always run past as fast as I can, and the deer always run through it too. Did you see the deer? There! there go some now, over there,— and there's my mamma. I must go now, please, sir. Good-day, ma'am."

He shook hands with us both, taking plenty of time for his pretty, boyish civilities, and then he was off like a shot. He joined a lady who was standing on the lawn, and who appeared to be searching for some one.

We passed them both a few moments later, as we drove down the road on our way out. The lady was holding the boy by the hand, and he was talking away as hard as he could, looking up at her with swift glances, and dancing along as boys do when they are talking about what interests them. The two made a pretty picture, walking along the smooth white road under the great dark trees, the lady's muslin gown fluttering in her grasp as she held above her head a white muslin sunshade. She was bareheaded, and the sunlight caught every once in a while in among the blond braids and beat a tress into gold. She had a noble carriage, and walked, as all Englishwomen of the upper class do, with the dignity and flexibility of women who, even when they sit or stand, seem to be still in the saddle. The lady's bearing has something soldierly in it, with an added grace and elegance, however, that no soldier can ever hope to possess.

As we drove past, they both looked up. The boy smiled, and his Jersey cap was waved at us as if we had been old friends. The lady smiled too, and bowed very prettily, the pink in her clear cheek flushing a shade deeper.

"For a countess she has uncommonly good manners, and so has her son. On the whole, I approve of the aristocracy."

"How do you know she is a countess? She may be a housekeeper or—"

"Are n't you ashamed? When she was so pretty, too! Well, she was a lady, whoever or whatever she was, and I'm glad she came out this lovely morning to add one more picture to it all. How her grace and refinement fitted into this delicate background!"

"Yes, I'll admit that an Englishwoman crossing an English lawn is about as complete an *ensemble* as one can hope to find anywhere on this round earth; and she *was* pretty," admitted Boston.

The memory of her refinement and beauty went with us into the dust and heat of the highway on our road towards Chichester. It comes up to me now, as I write of her, with vivid keenness and revived pleasure. I hope she still sometimes walks about bareheaded, on summer mornings, with a muslin sunshade over her head and that smile on her sweet face.

CHAPTER VI.

FAREHAM.—WALTHAM.—THE VALLEY OF THE ITCHEN.

OUR drive to Fareham was, after all, postponed until the next afternoon. There was just enough drizzle and mist, which came from no one knew where, to make the prospect unpromising. It was no part of our plan to wait for an English sky to make up its mind to stop raining; but we thought we might arrange it with the barometer, if it were in even a moderately accommodating mood, not to force us to start out on our day's drive in the rain.

The following afternoon, to repay us, the sun came out in really radiant glory, for an English sun. Sometimes it seems as if England were a little misty universe all to itself; as if the skies were so full of teary stars, and the weeping moon and the sun were so consumed by some hidden grief, that they had neither the strength nor the courage to shine as they do elsewhere. On this particular Wednesday the sun had concluded, apparently, to forget its particular sorrow and to shine as if it were off a-holidaying, like ourselves. Its brightness and radiance made our roadway brilliant in beauty. The golden light was everywhere: it was in the air, woven like a tissue in among the trees; it sparkled in diamond showers on the roof-tops, and turned, with its Midas touch, even the wayside stalks into " weeds of glorious feature."

We were still in the flat country of the plains; a few miles away from Chichester, however, glimpses of the sea became more and more frequent. A continuous chain of villages, hamlets, and farm-houses skirted this coast of the sea, and followed us as we turned inland. It was the most thickly populated region we had as yet seen. Most of the villages we passed were separated by a few farm-lands only; as we clattered out of the cobble-paved streets of one, we could see the roofs of the next, just beyond, thickening behind the trees. This procession of villages gave us a vivid sense of the fact that so small an island as England should yet have a population of fifteen millions; the fifteen millions live under their English sky as others live under the roof of a house, in adjoining rooms.

The houses, even here in the open country, appeared almost to touch one another.

The villagers bore a striking resemblance to one another. Their only distinctive difference appeared to be a discriminating taste in dirt. All were dirty, — houses, streets, children, and shops. Some were superlatively and others only comparatively filthy. The absence of gentlemen's seats in this neighborhood doubtless accounted for the slovenly appearance of these otherwise somewhat pretty hamlets and villages.

Wealth refines as much as it tends to mitigate the miseries of the lower classes. The human animal is an imitative creature. A tradesman learns to bow when he has a gentleman to deal with; but he is as unmannerly as the rest of the village if he has only villagers as customers. All the little shops looked mean, and all the shopkeepers frowsy and slatternly, as we passed them swiftly, as if the latter had no ambition in life which made neatly brushed hair and a clean shirt seem worth while.

There was a blot on the landscape that was neither these dirty villages nor the frowsy villagers; the blot was the number of tramps we kept meeting.

Every half-mile or so, there were two or three of these poor and wretched-looking wayfarers. They toiled, in pairs or in groups of four and five, along the dusty highway, dragging their rags after them in an aimless, hopeless, despairing kind of way. Who does not know the tramp's gait, and his uncertain, shiftless, going-nowhere-in-particular air? The manner in which he wearily lifts one foot as the other falls, tells his story. He is society's outcast, and wears the fetters of his own degradation. The English tramp adds viciousness to his despair. Most of these men whom we met had a dangerous, sullen growl on their sodden and bloated features. Their capacity for villany had a ripened expression, we noticed, which had stamped itself, like a brand of infamy, on their hardened faces. Their being all more or less drunk doubtless emphasized this vicious aspect. Some few had the look of predestined sots, and others appeared to have added drunkenness to the list of their vices, as they had the other accomplishments necessary to the equipment of their career of crime.

Among the sots the women far outnumbered the men. We passed several groups of these poor, shameless creatures, seated or lying on the roadside grass. One among them usually held a dark, evil-looking bottle, which was passed to the others and from which all drank without even the thought of shame. Their all too frequent stopping at the tap-houses along the roads apparently had not been enough to satisfy their demoniac thirst; they could not wait for that slower process of intoxication. There was no appearance of gayety or merriment in the demeanor of these poor creatures; they seemed to be possessed solely by the hideous determination of their vice. It is only the Englishman, I think, who proceeds to get as drunk as possible without mixing a little enjoyment with the act.

This was the blot on the landscape, — these poor drunken wretches and the many taverns and tap-houses we met at every turning. Every ten minutes or so, we would see the familiar sign, " John this, or Fanny that, licensed dealer in beer and spirits." The women behind the bar, as well as those the other side of it, appeared to do the most flourishing trade in these licensed demons. In more than half of these wayside taverns and beer-shops the bar-tenders were women, most of them rosy, healthy, and fresh-looking, as conspicuously free from the taint of the vice they dealt in as their frailer customers were branded by its unmistakable signs. It was the only refreshing human spectacle we saw during the first miles of our day's journey, — the sight of these hearty, strong, active barmaids, who during the intervals of trade could be seen easily enough through the wide-open doors and windows, going about numberless domestic duties. It is a characteristic of women shopkeepers, the world over, that they always appear to be doing several things at once. These barmaids were shopkeepers, but they were also mothers, housekeepers, gossips, and disciplinarians. Knitting and whipping their children were evidently the occupations only of the idle moments, when customers were loafing over the counter until the moment came to order a fresh glass. The more serious duties of sweeping, dusting, running sewing-machines, dressing and undressing their numerous offspring, were faithfully and efficiently performed in the slack periods of business hours.

It was good to leave it all behind us, — all the wretchedness of the vice, and even the thrift and energy which made money out of England's curse. It was good to get at last into the broad open country, and to have the last miles of our journey lead us up a gentle hill or two, into ripening grain-fields and among the wide meadows.

A long line of chalk cliffs defined themselves above the meadows. Disposed at regular intervals along its length were several large forts. These we knew must be the famous Portsdown fortifications, and that Portsmouth itself must be near. A few moments later, a dark mass against the southern sky resolved itself into tall black chimney-pots, a forest of masts, and an indistinguishable medley of dusky buildings. This was Portsmouth.

The sight of a city and especially of a seaport town in the distance seldom fails in impressiveness. Its size is doubled by the illusion which atmospheric effect creates. Portsmouth, as we passed it slowly, might have been London itself, so vast and huge it looked, as it loomed forth from its misty gloom of smoke and sea-fog. Only the mast-heads and the steep chimneys, like the radius of a crown, lifted themselves up into the clear light. A fine noble castle towards the farther end of the town, we knew to be Southsea Castle. From the tower of the castle the British lion was flying with a more than usually belligerent aspect, as if inviting the world to mortal combat. Here on his own ground, with that mass of forts behind him, armed to the teeth, ready to fling the foe his iron gauntlet, there did indeed seem little doubt as to the result of any foreign attack. Coming thus suddenly out from the sylvan calm and repose of those meadow-fields which we had left behind, into this bit of country bristling with fortifications, gave us a very realizing sense of the causes that have insured England's meadows having been free for so many centuries from the heel of the foreign invader: she has been careful to preserve her reputation of being armed cap-a-pie; and she has had a very ugly way of showing her teeth through her visor at the slightest provocation on foreign soil.

The remainder of the road to Fareham was rurally pretty, with hedge-rows untrimmed and a trifle straggling, — farmers' hedge-rows, we concluded, because only pasture-lands and farms were to be seen amid the gentle slopes that gradually gained *crescendo* enough to become hills.

It was at the top of one of the longest of the hills that the opening in a large-arched bridge presented to our delighted eyes, as if Nature had been in a generous mood and had come out to give us a picture, our first glimpse of Fareham. A green lawn-swept street, with charming little houses masked in vines; a small inland lake or pond, with drooping willows leaning sentimentally over its banks; a wagonette full of children with a fair-haired mother driving under the trees to one of the larger houses facing the pond; and a huge hay-cart filled with village youngsters pelting one another with poppies, — such was our first introduction to Fareham.

When we drove up to the low, broad, bow-windowed inn, we knew we had committed no mistake in judgment when we had decided to stop at Fareham. There might be better inns and prettier inland villages in England, but Fareham we were entirely willing to accept as a specimen and model of what rural England possesses in the quaint, the comfortable, and the picturesque.

A tall handsome woman, still young and modestly but prettily dressed, stepped out to greet us with a smile, and in a pleasant, courteous tone asked if we would like to see our rooms; that was the landlady. A fine-looking man, with straight clear eyes, also smiling, came a moment later, and took our hand-bags; that was our landlord. A bell was rung, and a grinning hostler appeared, who took possession of Ballad, stroking his wet coat as if he looked forward to rubbing it down as a matter of personal satisfaction; that was the stable-man. We saw him a few moments later from our bedchamber window doing it, the rubbing down, as if our getting Ballad into his heated condition had been a special favor to him. A waiter next appeared, also smiling, and a be-ribboned chambermaid, both of whom, with the landlady, preceded us to our rooms. They all stopped smiling only to begin it again when fresh orders were given. The rooms were in perfect order, yet the landlady bestirred herself to readjust a vase on the mantelpiece; and the chambermaid shook out the snow-white curtains as if to display their purity. The waiter was too absorbed in undoing shawl-straps and dusting the luggage to give himself up to decorative embellishment. The rooms were perfect in the dainty completeness of their outfit. There was a sitting-room, with a broad bow-shaped window fronting on the wide village street, a table with writing-materials at just the right angle in that pretty crescent, really comfortable chairs, and a reading-lamp. For "dumb companions," on the wall were some quaint old prints. The bedchamber was as pure as a virgin's bower, — a high four-post bedstead with cotton hangings, a dressing-table in white curtains, and pale faded blue walls with the print of last-century designs on them. About the whole establishment, indeed, — about the little inn, the rooms, and the village street, as we looked out into it, — there was this old-time air, as if the comfort and the purity and the courtesy had not been thought of and arranged yesterday, but had slowly grown during the long, quiet generations, and been patiently and lovingly added to, until this modest, tranquil, and altogether charming perfection had been attained.

On the whole, we concluded that our waiter was the most complete, as a product, among this assemblage of perfections. Perhaps it was because we ended by seeing more of him than of the others in the little inn. He served all of our meals, of course; and he was so genially, courteously garrulous it was impossible not to become more or less acquainted with him. There was an air of past acquaintance with gentility about Brown, as he told us to call him, which assured us that he had not learned his manners even in this perfect little inn. He had ways of passing a plate and of filling one's glass suggestive of a certain distant familiarity, as if family secrets in a remote past had found their way to his ear and he had not been found unworthy of the trust. His glance was beautifully paternal; and there was a general benedictory appearance about his somewhat fat and flabby person which, to a watchful eye, carried with it a vague conviction of his having frequently played the part of a good Providence to young lovers and to wayward youth. The smile he wore — the sweet, bland, mildly gleeful smile — could only have been acquired in a life consecrated to secret conspiracies against something which ought not to be found out. We attributed something of his interest in us to the fact that he appeared to entertain a veiled but vigorous suspicion that we were on our wedding journey. He had for me a specially protective and tender manner, which was occasionally illumined by a pregnant smile that seemed to promise an understood compact of secrecy.

Like most conspirators, Brown had himself evidently fallen a victim to his own talent for intrigue. The color and size of his most conspicuous organ, his nose, betrayed his all too frequent stealthy dealings with his master's port.

His respect for us began with the inspection of the wines Boston ordered. His friendship for me dated from the moment he learned that I took no champagne; regard deepened into admiration when he further was ordered to water my glass of claret — he was certain now that the bottles would outlast Boston's thirst. He next devoted himself to the satisfying of another appetite almost stronger than the vinous habit. He was too complete a provincial not to be curious.

"Brown, how far is it to Winchester?"

"Twenty miles, sir, — a fine drive, sir." And then discreetly, a second later, "A long ways, sir, from the North too, sir."

"The North?"

"The North of England. I took you for a Lincolnshire gentleman, begging your pardon."

"We didn't come from the North; we came from London."

Surprise tempered by a vague incredulity was

to be read in Brown's respectful glance. But his sense of decorum was too strong to embolden him to make further inquiries.

"London is a fine place, sir. I've been there in my time."

"Yes, London is a fine city — as is New York. We come from New York; we are Americans." Boston had taken pity on him, his disappointment was so visibly poignant. But the effect of the revelation of our nationality appeared to bewilder Brown to the point of rendering him speechless. He feebly repeated "America," and began eying us furtively, as if he expected us suddenly to break out into some strange antics of behavior. He made an errand immediately after into the hall-way, where the ribbons of the chambermaid were fluttering behind the door.

The chambermaid peeped at us through the cracks of the door. A few moments later, the landlord made an excuse for taking a more thorough and satisfactory inspection of our appearance by entering after dinner to ask if the trap would be needed early the next morning. We even suspected that some of the travellers in the inn had been taken into the landlord's confidence; for the family next door to us, whom we had seen grouped about a pretty tea-table in the adjoining bow-window, manifested great interest in our incoming and out-going. They filled the broad windows, craning their necks over one another's shoulders to get a better look. Even the handsome landlady stared after us as we passed out into the street.

"Don't let us do it again,— don't let us say we are Americans; it makes us so conspicuous. They are always expecting us to do something queer," I said, as we strolled out.

"That is the reason I do mention it. I want them to see we don't do anything queer. I'm giving them a little lesson in the manners and customs of an unknown country. There is no better way to prove that we are like all other civilized people than by being like them."

"Well, if you want to turn our pleasure-trip into an illustrated lecture, you can do so; I prefer to travel *incognito*. They may take me for a chimpanzee if only they will not stare."

"That they can't help doing, my dear," was Boston's gallant rejoinder; but I observed that to keep his conviction up to the level of his gallantry, he was obliged to light another cigar.

From a woman's point of view, a twilight walk is the best known substitute for a man's meditative after-dinner cigar. Walking abroad is at least an escape from the brooding melancholy which twilight breeds in-doors. The after-dinner hour in rural England is perhaps the only really trying one of the tourist's day. The tempting *al-fresco* arrangements which one finds in almost all continental summer inns or hotels, — the cosey, charming gardens, the shrubs in pots, and the bits of foliage under whose shade are placed the little iron settees and tea-tables so subtly suggestive of *tête-à-têtes* and prolonged starlit confidences, — these are unknown in England. The national standards of reserve and decorum forbid the traveller's enjoyment — unless taken in conformity with English notions and ideals of propriety. Rigid seclusion is the first of the Briton's canons of good travelling-behavior. An English inn is built on the plan of a series of separate fortifications; each traveller must be as unapproachable from inspection or intrusion as four walls can make him.

Even a balcony with an awning is a combination of the picturesque and the comfortable that no English inn has yet dreamed of adding to its list of luxuries. There are but two refuges, — the coffee-room, which is English for our American dining and reading room in one, or one's own private sitting-room. In the coffee-room commercial travellers and business men are to be found reading the papers or writing letters; but even their presence the waiters seem to look upon as intrusive. All Englishwomen who respect themselves dine and sit in their sitting-rooms. This latter custom we had ourselves adopted as by far the more comfortable as well as the pleasanter way of travelling in England. With the national habit of and delight in personal privacy come many compensations; for surely no other mode of inn or hotel life, in spite of pretty garden-beds and *al-fresco tête-à-têtes* on hard little iron chairs or settees beneath the shade of trees, is comparable to this cosey, home-like English fashion, which insures privacy and at least some semblance of home quiet, repose, and security. I know of no sensation more soothing, no simple delight more complete, than that of toasting one's slippered feet over the fire in the pretty sitting-room of some old English inn, while the noiseless waiter brings the five-o'clock tea; or later, when he spreads the dining-cloth the repast is accompanied with the luxurious sense of the stillness and the peace about one, with no flare of gaslight nor stare of curious-eyed fellow-travellers. It is this feeling of security and exclusiveness which turns an inn into a temporary home.

That our little inn was looked upon in the light of a home at certain hours by various dwellers in this Fareham village, was proved to us during the evening. There came, towards nine of the clock, a sound of footfalls along the little hall, the opening and shutting of the dull green baize door which screened the room directly behind the small office. Tones of deep voices and of pleasant chit-chat echoed through the resounding little house, which, with its well-seasoned walls and timbers, was as resonant as an old violin. A sound of hissing boiling water, the click of glasses, and the unmistakable rattle of the spirituous artillery of a bar became more and more frequent.

"Where are you going?" asked Boston, behind his newspaper, as I started towards the open door.

"I am going to see how the village looks by starlight," I replied, with the miserable duplicity common to our sex.

"Nonsense! you can see it just as well from the bow-window."

But I was already half-way down the broad stairs. An instant later I was out upon the little street. Starlight was certainly very becoming to the rural little town. The trees and the low houses seemed to coquet with the darkness. But what I had come to see, of course, was the picture the other side of that green baize door. Had I been a man, with a man's propensity for being the other side of green baize doors, I should long ere this have gone there honestly and straightforwardly. Being a woman, with a hopelessly incurable and unconventional taste for looking at that part of life which is hidden away from us, I must needs intrigue to gain what was, after all, a very innocent pleasure. At last, a somewhat late but most obliging tapster turned in at our door. He made straightway for the green baize door. He opened it wide, and I, close upon his heels, saw the picture I had come to see. There was a long bright-red covered table, with two or three shaded lamps upon it. At the head of the table sat the handsome landlady, looking handsomer than ever now; for she was an evening beauty, with tawny tints in her eyes and hair that needed a wealth of light to bring out all their hidden depths of color. Her husband was moving about, filling glasses and passing pipes around. There were fifteen or twenty men seated in large comfortable chairs. There was no noisy talk or loud laughter. It was, I should say, a rather exceptionably well-bred gathering for any part of the world, — a gathering of men in whose society no woman need be ashamed to sit. Perhaps the woman's being there was the cause of the good manners, of the quiet, and the orderly self-restraint. Whatever the cause, it all made a very comfortable, cosey, home-like English scene.

Our twilight walk through the Fareham streets had proved it to be a dull little town, with only a few fine old houses along its principal thoroughfare; so the next morning we were off early on our way to Winchester.

The road from the start was enchanting. It lay between fields and meadows brilliant in harvest-ripening grain, and there were farms dotted among them at just the right distances to make dark, rich bits of color in the landscape. The whole country breathed the peace of agricultural activity, with enough variety in outline to preserve it from monotony. A charming bit of country three miles from Fareham we knew to be Waltham Chase, famous among mediæval sportsmen for its deer. Henry II. and Cœur de Lion had come, a few centuries ago, to pursue this sport and to partake of the gay and splendid hospitality of the bishop's palace, the ruins of which we came upon a few miles farther on.

A few straggling houses and a church made a bit of a village. Then, at a sharp turn in the road, we drove past the magnificent ruins of the old palace, close beside the roadway, with a little lake on our right. The blue sky was framed in a dozen great arches, and the grasses and ivy had taken permanent possession of the grand halls and the roofless chambers. In its days of glory the palace must have been a kingly dwelling. The size and extent of the ruined arches, and the extensive walls were still suggestive of noble proportions, while the carvings over the windows and doorways were of lovely delicacy of workmanship. One could well believe that this palace must have been one of the finest examples in England of fifteenth-century domestic architecture.

Bishop Henri de Blois, who in the intervals of king-making turned to the fine art of building as his favorite pastime, certainly achieved one of his finest masterpieces in Waltham Castle. Mediæval architect-bishops were artists as well as inspired builders; for none but an artist would have built a great palace beside this lovely little lake, the former abbot's pond, once noted for its stores of fish, now the haunt of swallows and meadow-larks, who fluttered amid the tall grasses, singing their little hearts out as if conscious that they were the only live beings amid all this débris of dead greatness. To have looked out into this silent lake from yonder palace casements must have been like suddenly confronting Nature's quiet eye in the midst of the stormy conflict of the human passions shut up within those stately walls. What ideal surroundings for the Court and the great prelates to take their pleasure in! — the country overrunning with summer and fragrance, as rurally rustic as the palace was magnificently splendid; Waltham Chase as their happy hunting-ground; and Winchester within easy distance, if there were pageants or councils or tournaments in the day's round of pleasure or duty.

I presume it is as well, from the progressionist's point of view, to have been born as late as possible; but there are weak moments when History runs her fingers lightly over those forgotten notes of gay and debonair pleasures, when one would willingly forego many of the advantages which we of these later centuries so serenely enjoy, to have lived in those fine old days, when the gayer delights of life were pursued as ardently as leisure and culture or money-making are now-a-days striven for, when life was not all a tragedy, and comedy tripped its light measure across the field of existence, flecking it with brilliant, *riant* dashes of color and joy.

These reflections were doubtless suggested by the fact that our afternoon's drive bristled with historical associations. After leaving the palace, with its dead-and-gone company of pleasure-loving bishops, we passed close by Avington House, once the residence of Charles II., and still more famous as the property of that luckless member of the Brydges family who, marrying the Countess of Shrewsbury, came to that sad end of unloved husbands by the sword of his faithless wife's lover, the Duke of Buckingham. The picture of that intrepid and audacious lady, apparelled as a page, calmly holding her lover's horse while the duel went on, that comes down to us in our garrulous friend Pepys's diary, fitted in as a companion portrait to those of the gay bishops who were so sure of heaven that they could afford to indulge in endless bouts of pleasure while on earth.

Ballad, not having the wickedness of others to enliven his journey, gave signs of drooping just as we drove into the lovely valley of the Itchen, along the banks of the famous little river that makes this stretch of meadow-land one of England's most picturesque bits. Its beauty was even greater than its fame; it was a divine little valley. The road wound in and out under avenues of noble elms and oaks, between gentle slopes covered with golden grain; there were sleek cattle standing up to their middle in the flower-banked river; there were odors in the air so luscious that the whole valley seemed a garden of perfume; the grass was thicker, the trees were taller, the meadows were fairer, than we had yet seen elsewhere; and the whole valley, its sweetness and plenty and peace, was delicately lighted by a rosy glow which made earth and sky seem quivering in a luminous pink bath.

At a turn in the road we saw a city's roofs and spires glistening on the sides and summit of a hill directly in front of us. This city was Winchester.

CHAPTER VII.

WINCHESTER.

"I AM glad Ballad is tired and hot; we can go as slow as we like," I said, as we began to mount the hill.

"You mean as slow as he likes. He is, as you have justly observed, an admirable walker. As a walker I think he would bear off the prize in any slow go-as-you-please gait; and like most of us, what he does best he does oftenest."

"Now, I call that ungrateful. He's done particularly well to-day. Just think how quick we've come! And all those hills!"

"Which we've walked up, all three of us."

"And who liked the walking, pray, and would get out again and again to see views and things?"

"Well, never mind Ballad; he's done well enough. But this is pretty jolly, is n't it? Ballad *may* walk, the slower the better."

I should hardly have selected the word *jolly* to describe the scene about us; but men have a constitutional distaste for forcible or pictorial phraseology. I suppose the superlatives came in when women began to talk.

The prospect was, in truth, enchanting. We were slowly making the ascent of a hillside which, at first an elm-shaded country-road, became gradually a city street. Above, glistening in the pink sunset, were a mass of red roofs and a tall tower on the summit, the latter rising into the sky like a tinted plume on some warrior's head-gear; for the city, in spite of its rosy light, looked gray and armor-encased. There were bits of old walls and ancient towers and turrets, with lancet loop-holes, to remind one of mediæval contests. The jagged teeth on the crenellated towers were set against the pink sky, like lion's claws on velvet.

Of the general topography of the city we could only be certain of a few conspicuous features: first, that it was built along the banks of the Itchen, watering its feet pleasantly in the pretty stream; then, that it took an upward bend along the steep sides of a long hillside; and finally, that it cooled its brow on the summit, after its tortuous climb. Opposite, on the other side of the river, was the famous St. Catherine Hill, a long line of chalky ridges. Our own way led us more and more into a series of thickly settled, picturesque, but citified-looking streets. The bustle and traffic of a busy town-life were besetting our ears as we drove under the arched doorway of our inn.

Three waiters in white ties helped us to descend. A vision of a French cook coifed in his white cornered hat, seen through the vines that screened the kitchen from the courtyard, assured us that the *cuisine* felt it had a reputation to sustain.

"Winchester has, I believe, always had the reputation of living well," remarked Boston, complacently, after we had ordered a dinner designed as a delicate compliment to the only nation that understands making good soups.

"Yes; a city of bishops may be trusted to do that much. I suppose they imported their French cooks along with the taste for Norman arches. But do look at those chairs and at all the furniture! Has n't it a preposterously ecclesiastical air?"

Boston laughed, and said he should be mistaking the buffet for an altar-piece and the bed for a chantry, he was certain, now that I had suggested the resemblance.

There was, in truth, an absurdly impressive appearance about the furniture of our two stately rooms. All the furniture had a high-church, episcopalian aspect. There appeared to have been a pronounced taste for Gothic chairs and severe perpendicular outlines in the tables and sofas selected. No prints more profane than an assemblage of celebrated church councils or cathedral interiors adorned the walls. It was just the sort of room in which a bishop might rehearse, with suitable gravity, scenes to be enacted later in the chapter-house; he need not look in the mirror to see a reflection of his own dignity.

The soup and the entrées were up to the approved ecclesiastical standard; they were also worthy of the nationality of their maker. Only an Englishman, however, can be trusted to cook Southdown mutton, we regretfully confided to each other as we looked upon the joint done to a crisp.

Better than the French soup was the view from our windows. We were in luck again. The windows of our sitting-room opened upon the city's chief thoroughfare.

It was a beautiful and perfect little jewel of an old street. It was delightfully irregular, wandering up the hill with the undulatory, uneven progress we had noticed as a characteristic of the Arundel High Street. It began its existence, as we found on a later inspection, at a bridge which covered the little river near an old mill. At the top of the hill it was crowned by a noble gateway and a fine mass of famous old buildings. The bustling, gay street had retained its mediæval aspect in a wonderful degree. It had the bulging façades, the projecting casements, and the gabled roofs which the earlier builders knew so well how to combine. They had divined the secret that the beauty of a street, like the charm of the human face, depends more on expression than on any mere perfection in symmetry. The street is lined with palaces, shops, hospitals, gateways, a sixteenth-century piazza, beneath whose open arcades nineteenth-century citizens still lounge and gossip, a market cross, and the old-fashioned open butchers' stalls, whose warm meats communicate a pleasant culinary odor to the atmosphere. The western gateway at its summit seems to cut off Winchester from the rest of the world, as it did in reality of old when it had its own private little sins to commit. The Itchen, at its feet, is still the slender umbilical cord connecting the city with the rest of the kingdom, on whose destiny Winchester has had so powerful an influence.

To write the history of this street would be to write the history of most of England's stirring events.

It can be, indeed, with no ordinary tourist's set of commonplace emotions that one wanders about Winchester. The city is as full of historical suggestiveness as any in England. It has made enough history to suffice for a very respectable national career. It is an epitome of all the English virtues, and has possessed its share of English capacity for crime. It has been murderous, treacherous, imperious, dictatorial, tyrannical; it has founded some of the finest charities, has built some of the noblest buildings, and perpetuated some of the most admirable educational systems in the world. While its murders have left a brilliant stain on its palace steps, and its lighter crimes have peopled its halls with a whispering-gallery of ghosts, in the midst of its wickedness Winchester experienced brief returns to virtue, when enough good was done to make the blot on its escutcheon seem dim by comparison.

Winchester could not have been English if it had not conscientiously erected buildings enough to commemorate its goodness, knowing, with the prescience of a bad conscience, that its wickedness could safely be left to historians. It is the office of history to be the embalmer of human frailty. The passion for building was doubtless invented when the great found their virtues were in danger of being buried with them.

"I think, on the whole, architecture and the virtues have the best of it here in Winchester," remarked Boston, as I propounded to him the above conclusion.

"Wait till you re-read its history."

"I don't intend to. Virtue and beauty are good enough for me. After all, why should we care how wicked they were when they've left us this?" — with a comprehensive sweep of his hand.

The gesture included a distant group of turrets, the gateway at the top of the hill, the King's Cross, a great iron arm stretching half-way across the street holding the town clock, and a beautiful old arched doorway, which was too tempting not to end by luring us to pass beneath it; for we were out once more to take a twilight walk about the city.

The archway led us into a quaint, perfect little bit of a street. It was filled up at one end by a curious old church, which we learned later was named St. Lawrence, whose portal was almost hidden out of sight, tucked away amid a lot of tiny shops and queer low-browed houses. In the half-dusk of the twilight hour there was something indescribably mysterious about this assemblage of closely packed old buildings. They had the air of conspirators. The silence added to the secrecy of the effect; the archway seemed to separate this retired little corner from the bustle and activity of the broader thoroughfare.

A rustle of trees in the sweet dusky air made us hasten our steps. The little street ended as abruptly as it had begun. We had soon passed into a large open space. Then, directly in front, at an oblique angle, there loomed up into the gloom of the coming night a superb avenue of elms. Beyond them loomed something else so vast and stupendous it could be nothing save the great cathedral itself.

We passed under the green arch of the elms, over the short sweet grass of the close. Gravestones were dimly glistening here and there in the

OLD HOUSES IN CLOSE, WINCHESTER.

fading light, while the delicate mystery of twilight melting into night was thickening about us. A few steps farther on, the green arch above us came to an end, and the huge façade of the cathedral rose into the sky. In the rich gloom its stupendous outlines seemed almost to touch the stars that were coming out to light it. All details were lost; only the mass as a whole was defined for us by the mingled play of the gloom and the tender glow. A splendid sweep of shadowy light swept the length of the long nave, girdling it with darkness, — a darkness which had deepened in the great buttresses till they looked like fissures in a hillside. All the light there was in the sky had focussed itself on the southern transept and the low square central tower, beating the marble into a dulled jewelled iridescence. The sloping roof, as it rose into the light, looked like the pyramidal line of some great mountain ridge, tenderly etherealized as it neared heaven.

It was not its size which made this first view of the cathedral so penetratingly impressive. It was the grandeur and the unspeakable majesty which the influences of the hour bestowed. The silence, the quiet stars, the dark mantle of the night, made an isolation as remote from the profane surroundings of the outer world as if the great cathedral had been transported to some Egyptian desert and were resting on those silent sands.

If the modern sight-seer fails to be impressed by some of the great spectacles of the world, and finds his emotional activities but feebly stirred before some of the shrines of beauty the world holds sacred, I am convinced it is because the moment of observation is rarely rightly chosen. Art, like Nature, has her poetical moods, when she can be studied under perfect conditions. The artist comes to learn the workings of these rare and fitful periods. If he sees deeper into beauty and lives nearer to it, it is because he has grown to know intuitively this moment of its tenderest, loveliest bloom.

How different, for instance, would have been our impressions of this famous cathedral had we seen it first under the disenchanting influences of our next morning's approach! The broad sunlight made the conspiracy of the little old buildings a very prosaic array of bric-à-brac shops. On the greensward of the close, among the gravestones,

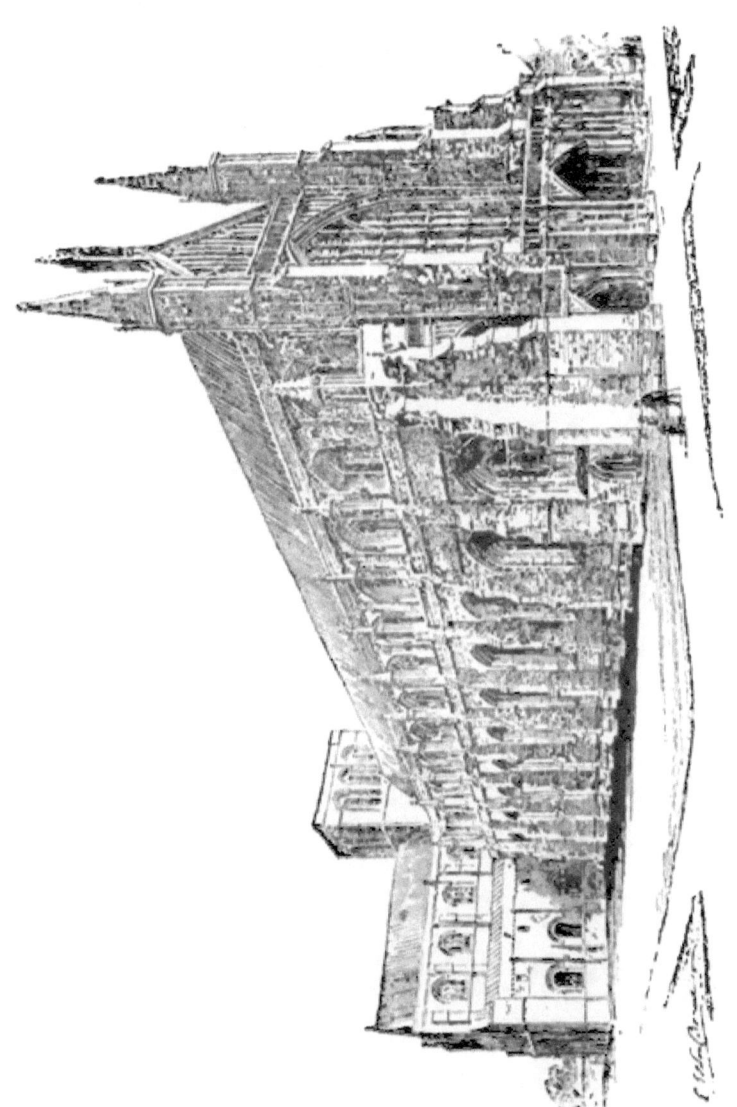

WINCHESTER CATHEDRAL. *Page* 144.

on a very cheerful footing of intimacy, apparently, with these solemn reminders of death, were some children and goats playing at hide-and-seek. At the rear of the cathedral, near some rather shabby-looking buildings, hung some washing,— irreverent garments fluttering their new-born whiteness in the very face of their magnificent neighbor.

Even the cathedral partook, at a first glance, of the general disillusionment. It was great, it was magnificent, both from its size and because of its noble proportions. But at first, and before one comes to the period of accepting its defects and looking only for the beauties which end by making one oblivious of the former, a vague feeling of disappointment ensues; it comes from the sense that the vast mass is lacking, as a whole, in those qualities of the picturesque which are among the pre-eminently essential qualifications of an impressive architectural *ensemble*. The eye unconsciously searches somewhat restlessly over the huge pile for a finished tower or for some imposing turret or spire, whose spring and lightness will float the mass and lift it into the sky.

Once within the cathedral, however, one is only conscious of an overwhelming delight and admiration. The fact that the entrance through the western front had seemed insignificant as the approach to so splendid a building, is forgotten now. The glorious flood of light pouring in through the great western window, to which the entire façade was sacrificed by Bishop Edington, renders one oblivious to all else save the sense of the splendid lighting that makes the farthermost perspectives clear as a noonday forest. It is due to this famous Edington window that the cathedral, the largest this side of the Alps, is the least gloomy in all the world. It has an open-air, sunlit atmosphere I remember in no other of the great English or continental cathedrals.

A curious story is told of the glass in this window. After Cromwell's soldiers had run their swords through each jewelled figure that filled the splendid old windows, some industrious and painstaking citizen went about collecting the broken fragments that lay on the floor. These were by him carefully preserved; and after the restoration had made it safe for them to be produced, this discreet and far-seeing preserver returned his valuable collection to the cathedral. The bits were carefully arrayed in a heterogeneous mosaic, and now form a kind of crazy-quilt pattern in the traceries of the huge window. The rich reds, the deep purples, and the golden ambers gleam with all their old famed jewelled lustre. The sunlight, imprisoned in those nests of color, escapes to carry the secret of its luminous brilliancy into the farthermost shadows, tinting the dusk under the great roof, and flecking in "patterns of fine gold" the uneven tomb-paved floor. Through the maze of that prismatic morning light we passed slowly down the great nave under its glorious perpendicular archings; we lingered for a long half-hour in the rough, unfinished Norman transepts, remains of the Cyclopean work left by the early Norman bishop-builders. The warrior has left the impress of his military taste on all these early Norman cathedrals. It is easily seen to be the work of men who were accustomed to build fortresses as well as cathedrals, when the cathedrals, indeed, were fortresses and must be strong before they could be beautiful. These grand old transepts might have resisted any number of sieges. There are centuries of significant change in manners and in men to be read in the tremendous contrast afforded between those delicate, perpendicular, branching traceries out yonder in the nave, and these giant fortress-like transepts. Think of the audacity of the man who should dare to transform those stern features into the elegance and symmetry of the later Gothic! The man whose genius and daring made him divine that such a transformation was possible, was William of Wykeham. His predecessors, in order to complete the beauty of the great cathedral, had added either entirely new portions, such as the Lady Chapel, built by Bishop de Lucy, or the original Norman structure had been taken down and entirely reconstructed, as was done under Bishop Edington in the presbytery, the western portion of the nave, and the triforium. But it was reserved for the original genius of Bishop Wykeham to deliberately change the old Norman work to the soaring perpendicular into which the Gothic of his day had only just begun to bloom. So triumphant was the success of this stupendous venture that not a trace of the Norman structure in the long nave, the most beautiful in England, or in the aisles, is to be discovered. This triumphant feat probably stands unrivalled in the history of architectural transformations. The three great features of the interior of Winchester — the elaborate perpendicular nave and side aisles, the rude colossal Norman transepts, and the lovely Early English of De Lucy's work in the presbytery — combine in producing such an *ensemble* of striking architectural contrasts as makes this interior perhaps unrivalled in interest in England. It would certainly be difficult to conceive of a result more remarkable in the union of the grand and the picturesque. Part of this picturesqueness is due to its being so richly furnished with tombs, chantries, statues, monuments, and banners. The chiselled monuments and stately airy chantries branch in their upshooting lines towards the great roof, like slender tree-trunks beneath the shade of loftier forest-heights. Under one of the stateliest of the throne-like chantries we came upon William of Wykeham's tomb. Only some semblance of a throne would have sufficed to enshrine the memory of so autocratic a spirit. He was one of those magnificent prelates who during his life "reigned at court," according to Froissart, "everything being done by him, and nothing without him." With such superlative pre-eminence during a long and triumphant earthly career, when he "reigned" as courtier, wit, engineer, architect, bishop, and chancellor, he would hardly have been human if he had not wished to carry something of this state with him beyond the shades of death; so that it is no surprise to learn that between the busy hours of so varied and brilliant a career Wykeham found time to arrange it with his architectural genius to raise a monument in his own behalf. This chantry, with its rich and yet regally majestic elegance and severity of style, was designed by him and built on the spot where, as a boy, he had been wont to offer up his childish prayers to the Virgin. One can forgive much of that foolish yet harmless human frailty, the vain longing for eternal remembrance, to a man whose transcendent genius peopled England with some of its noblest buildings, and who, it is supposed, was the real inventor of perpendicular tracery, that last and richest fruit to bloom on the lovely Gothic stem.

Chantries, tombs, monuments, and mortuary urns succeed one another in such bewildering variety, blazoning forth such a wealth of virtue, such a multitude of military achievements, such an inexhaustible array of talents and capacities, that genius and goodness and greatness come to appear as commonplace here as mediocrity elsewhere. Winchester has, indeed, been so rich in great men that even the largest cathedral in England is found none too large in which to bury them. Greatness under its aisles dwindled into such dwarfed proportions that in the presbytery yonder, above the screens, in those quaintly curious mortuary chests, the bones of Saxon kings and bishops lie comfortably mingled together.

King Rufus might himself be in very grave doubt as to the authenticity of his own osseous framework, since what are supposed to be the royal fragments of that monarch were picked up after the fall of the tower, and somewhat promiscuously handled later by irreverent Parliamentary troops. Verily the wearing of a crown has not been found to be the most stable performance even in an English burying-ground.

Some among the wearers of ecclesiastical crowns have been suffered to lie in more comparative peace. Even in death the hand that carries the pastoral staff seems to hold within its grasp heaven's hidden thunderbolt of vengeance. To connect the staff with any idea of spiritual guidance in the case of some among these bishops would be to demand some very athletic gymnastics on the part of one's imagination. With Henri de Blois, for instance, — that fine old martial prelate who " wore arms, mingled in war, and indulged in all the cruelties and exactions of the time;" who, when he was not fighting or king-making or stealing benefices or castles, filled his leisure with the refined amusements of building; who also could found the noblest charities as easily as he could " convey," in Pistol's phrase, a foot of Saint Agatha or the thumb of Saint James for his cathedral when the latter was in need of some really notably holy relics, — one would hardly go to such a middle-age combination of ferocity, genius, and unscrupulousness for a delicate adjustment of one's spiritual relations with Deity.

Under the masses of the stone embroideries which cover almost every inch of the great Beaufort's chantry yonder, lies the stately recumbent figure of the Cardinal, whose portrait Shakspeare has immortalized with even more vivid force than the sculptor's chisel. It is a dark portraiture, with Rembrandtish shadows of iniquity in it; but that picturesque mingling of the good and the bad there was in the all too "rich Cardinal," the stately Beaufort, will survive all attempts of the historian to produce a more faithful and lenient delineation.

It was a relief to turn away from the vices of the great, and even from the magnificence of the state in which the dark glory of their achievements lie buried, to the unostentatious, simple tombs about us, — to those poorer tablets and monuments which commemorate the gentler lives of some whom we have all grown to love — as one loves the nobler, sweeter influences.

Under a white tablet, as pure and snowy as her spirit, in the north aisle, lies the body of Jane Austen. The inscription is characterized by a directness and simplicity so admirable she herself might have been the writer thereof: "Jane Austen, known to many by her writings, endeared to her family by the varied charms of her character, and ennobled by Christian faith and charity, was born at Steventon, in the county of Hants, Dec. 16, 1775, and buried in this cathedral July 24, 1817. She openeth her mouth with wisdom, and in her tongue is the law of kindness."

A soul as gentle, and one whose delicate genius for discovering the hidden joys that dwell in the world has made him the immortal companion of every lover of the woods and streams, is buried in the opposite transept. Izaak Walton, that " prince of fishermen," lies under a plain black marble slab, as humbly as he doubtless walked among his inferiors, in his shabby hose and neglected wig, during his peace-loving life. As he is known to have died in the house of his son-in-law, who was a prebendary of Winchester, all the streams and river-banks near the city must have been the scenes of his sylvan experiences and the inspiration of that genial philosophy which has made the delicate flame of his genius light up so many of our dull hours.

But with the best disposition in the world to linger among the tombs of these lesser great ones, whose immortality has been won by the more plebeian birthright of genius, so richly incrusted is this cathedral with the memorials and reminders of those whom destiny and history in combination have crowned with fame, that one is confronted at every turn with some new name or device which arrests the eye and stays the step.

We had turned into the Lady Chapel to look at some particularly lovely bacchic ornamentation on some of the capitals, — vines, grapes, leaves, and tendrils as tenderly carved as if meant to crown a god instead of a column, — when we chanced on a faded chair. The chair in itself was not remarkable either for beauty or grace; but in that moon-shaped curve and on that now worn and faded velvet Queen Mary had sat when in this chapel she gave her hand to Philip of Spain. It was the wickedest hand-clasp ever interchanged; for it was the pledge of those two cold-blooded fanatics to make English heretical blood flow farther than English rivers run. English beauty, however, as if foreseeing its decimation, had, at this wedding ceremony, a moment of brilliant triumph before the lights were put out and the fagots were fired; for the historians of the period tell us that the English court beauties put the darker olive-cheeked Spanish women under a total eclipse in the beautiful little chapel. Their fresh complexions made their Southern sisters look sallow. They completed their revenge later at the marriage banquet and ball, where their stateliness made Spanish grace seem wanting in elegance.

Even a little persecution could be endured with equanimity after such a triumph. A few years later, the Gallic saying " Il faut souffrir pour être belle " needed, presumably, no translator.

In spite of this unhallowed association, it is impossible not to return again and again to this apsidal portion of the cathedral. The wealth of ornamentation and the inexhaustible variety of beauty in the choir, presbytery, chapels, and chantries, together with the marvellously lovely lighting, or rather darkening, from the effect of the deep shadows, make this eastern end full of peculiar fascination. In the choir one lingers longest, perhaps, over the carved stalls, whose delicate foliaged ornamentation seems to have been carved by the sun and the wind rather than by the chisel. Beyond is the magnificent reredos, so ingeniously elaborate as to make the minutiæ of lace-work insignificant by comparison. Behind this great altar screen-work of embroidery is a series of shrines known as the *feretra*, or shrines, of patron saints. Here the glory of workmanship has given place to the strictly professional necessities of the place; for here, in early superstitious days, sick persons, awaiting

CHANTRIES, WINCHESTER.

Page 156.

some miraculous cure, were allowed to remain over night, that they might the more obstinately wrench their salvation from the saints enshrined above, — from Saint Swithun, Saint Birinus, and other sainted workers of cures.

With the superstition something also of that olden talent for religious enthusiasm has vanished. Those ardent troops of pilgrims, who were so sure of their saints, are now replaced by pilgrims bent on a very different mission. The pilgrims in search of the picturesque, who level opera-glasses at the stone effigies whose feet those earlier pilgrims bathed with the passion of their believing tears, are more numerous now, on week-days at least, than the worshippers. We came again and again, at all hours and at all seasons, to morning and evening service, in the hours when the whole of the vast interior should resound only to the echo of devout footsteps, and it was always the tourist, rather than the worshipper, who formed the conspicuous plurality among the visitors. The Englishman and the Englishwoman (who is the better saint) do not go to church to pray. The closet is a place more in conformity with the national reserve and the abhorrence of emotional parade. Thus these great and magnificent cathedrals are as empty and as silent as deserted palaces. At evening service, it is true, dark drab-colored figures, old ladies with sweet pious faces and an air of subdued provincial calm, a few younger women, among them sometimes a lovely fair-faced girl, and a child or two, passed within the choir screen and formed the little band of worshippers, for whom the long line of deans, choristers, and vergers, with their elaborate vestments, seemed a useless and wasted pageant. One misses the troops of beggars — the squad of the ill-clad, the cold, the hungry, and the homeless — who flock under the great roofs of the continental cathedrals as to a natural refuge. One misses also the earnest passionate faces, the lips moving in half-audible prayer as the fingers slip over the worn pater-nosters, the bowed forms, and the bended knee of those more spectacular-loving worshippers who love to make their piety a public thing.

Here, on the contrary, there is the dignity of reserve, there is order, there is the holy calm of silence. Even the chairs under the great aisles are placed in precise lines. They can safely be left there; none will come to disturb them. The priests issue from their vestry clothed in the majesty of their dignified calm; the lessons are intoned with beautiful but cold correctness; the boy-choristers' voices rise up under the great arches with sexless purity and unimpassioned accent; the prayers are whisperingly responded to by the little group of the devout; and then all silently rise and pass out, and God's temple is as silent as a tomb.

One must come to England to see what Protestantism really means as a religion,—how deep the religious feeling may be, and yet how calm and unmoved, almost to the point of seeming indifference, the outward bearing remains. I have sometimes wondered if the tenacious English reverence for decency may not be a strong and potent element in their religious observance; if in the logical make-up of even the dullest and poorest there may not be some vague notion of the relation that ought to exist between a clean shirt and a conscience pure enough to approach its Maker. Certain it is that one rarely if ever sees a tattered worshipper under these vast aisles. It is a pity, because, once within, the beggar would find himself in a company of his fellows. The saints wear their rags and ruined draperies very complacently. But then they were canonized for it; and enforced impecuniosity, in search of eleemosynary pennies, cannot always be sure of earning an aureole to make its poverty glorious.

CHAPTER VIII.

A COLLEGE AND AN ALMSHOUSE.

NO little city ever lent itself so admirably to the innocent designs of two tourists bent on the capture of every hidden secret of its ancient charm and antique beauty, as Winchester. One may almost count on an adventure with the picturesque at every turning. A surprise appears to lie in wait for one at the corner of each of its perfect streets. Gateways open at most unexpected angles, beneath which one passes from the bustle of its lively old streets into the cloistral calm of some ancient convent or palace; or one confronts the crenellated tops of mediæval walls to find within such a nest of old houses, in so perfect a state of preservation as to make it appear that the enclosure had been built for the sole purpose of affording a fortified protection against decay and ruin.

The contrast presented between such model specimens of antique life and the active, stirring, every-day modern living invests these old towns and cities with their perfect quality and charm. In spite of its venerable and austerely remote age, Winchester ends by impressing one with its having already included the nineteenth century among its collection of historical periods. The bargaining, for instance, which we could not fail to notice, from the quite audible tones in the little open shops, gave us a very realizing feeling that if time was fleeting, trade at least was long. The Winchester buyers and tradesmen have not lost all their ancient talent for investing the simple act of buying and selling with those difficulties which raise it into an art. Its citizens have had a long tutelage in trade. From the time of the early Norman kings to the reign of Henry VIII., its great annual fairs on St. Giles' Hill, just outside the town, attracted the great merchants from Flanders and France and Italy, who came to buy English cloth. The little city still retains some pretty customs and habits as a legacy of that lost glory of commercial supremacy. We chanced to prolong our stay over the market-day, which, in England, is still held on Saturday. Early in the morning strolling venders and pedlers erected little booths and improvised gay holiday shows along the undulating High Street. All day the thoroughfare was thickly packed with a swarming mass of humanity,— with farmers and their wives, the latter in wonderful poke-bonnets of the last century, and their more modern daughters in the modified French poke of our own decade; with townspeople and county squires, who crowded about the shops, the booths, and the gayly decked carts, thronging into the middle of the street and filling the air with the noise of their bargaining. There were brilliant dashes of color among the dull blouses and the flimsy printed lawns, contributed by the numerous red coats of the soldiers; for Winchester is a brigade station, and we concluded that the entire brigade had assumed, as part of its military obligations, the duty of lighting up the sombre nineteenth-century dulness with the brave splendor of its fatigue-coats and gold lace.

We followed, at a discreet distance, a group of these sons of war on their stroll through the crowd, up to the top of the hill. It was partly with the desire to learn whether the day's unwonted animation had spread up and beyond the imperial crown of the great gateway, and also because we were in search of a palace and a fountain. The sons of war deserted us before we had discovered either. They passed, in a body, beneath a swinging open door near the gateway. The door remained open long enough for us to catch a glimpse of a charming pair of blue eyes, a mass of curly hair, a trim jaunty figure, and a row of shining glasses. We were no longer in doubt as to the cause of the brigade's unanimous preference for beer a mile away from the barracks, even if to drink it they must climb the long steep hill.

The fountain lay so close to the little beer-shop that we could hear the click of the glasses and the short bass notes in the laughs that went up within. The admonition contained in the lines cut on the stone pedestal of the fountain seemed curiously ineffectual and meaningless with that rival establishment and its potent magnet so near. Who would even stop to read the appeal on the old fountain? —

"Stop, friends, and drink your fill,
And do not use my fountain ill."

The thin stream of water trickling into the open basin seemed of a piece with most of the wise counsel in the world,—a slender treble of warning drowned by the loud chorus of the unheeding.

The mass of gray shadow which filled up the foreground directly in front of us, as we turned to the right, could be nothing else save the palace which we had come to find. If it was a palace it had so very pronounced an ecclesiastical aspect as at first to lead us to infer it was a church. But as we had been told to find in this ancient palace of Henry III.'s reign one of the most perfect examples of domestic architecture of that palace-building period, the fact of its interior being divided into aisles by pillars, and its long church-like windows, that further served to emphasize its religious character, proved the deficiencies of our own architectural standards. The series of murders — which historians, with more amenity than veracity, call executions — that have taken place in the courtyard of the castle make it, on the whole, much safer for the tourist at once to establish its identity as a palace. The Church has had so many such dark stains to hide within its own mantle, it is but generous to allow the State to stand sponsor for a few of those bloody necessities. The luckless Earl of Kent came to his execution here; and in the seventeenth century several priests marched wearily up the long hill to look their last on earth over the stone parapet which crowns the hill, and beyond which lies such a glorious prospect of the city, the cathedral, and the sloping hills.

The least depressing association with this palace is the fact that to its keeping has fallen the honor of preserving a rare and singular painting. It is so old that its history is lost in conjecture. The painting represents King Arthur's Round Table; the gallant king himself in the centre, wearing his crown, the twenty-four radiations of which bear each the name of some famous knight. The severe, upright-looking monarch, with his grotesque limbs out of drawing, and his strange history-flowering crown, seemed admirably in keeping with the solemn cathedral-like interior, the heraldic bearings on the old stained glass, and the air of brooding silence we had left behind us. It was the ghost of the past come to take possession of this ghoulish palace.

Our walk that afternoon did not end with our discovery of the castle. We descended the hill by making a detour among a number of little streets, avoiding the more thronged thoroughfare. We were rewarded for our temerity in plunging into these unknown labyrinths by stumbling on a number of little adventures. We learned, among other things, that all of the Winchester inhabitants who were not shopping on High Street were very busy doing nothing, unless lolling out of narrow casements and leaning against door-jambs, exchanging the small pence of conversational amenities, may be termed a form of industry. It was quite evident that market-day in the little city was looked upon as a *quasi* holiday, — a time for a loosening of the moral tension and for an unwonted indulgence in the breaking of the eternal English silence. We might almost have thought ourselves in some French town, such was the din of the voices and the clatter of heavy-booted feet over the rough stones. The faces could. never have been anything but English, with their fresh high color, their calm and immobile expression, and the soft liquid eyes. Beauty among the women in England appears to diminish in proportion as the rank in life increases. These streets were filled with charmingly pretty girls and fine-looking women, whose type can only be classed as rustic, because the word seems best to describe the delicious quality of their freshness and *riant* health. Two girls standing in an open doorway, with close little English hats and white netted veils, made a charming little picture for us as we passed down one of the wider streets. Their air of simple unaffected naturalness was rather heightened than otherwise by the fact that they were both munching tarts; and this proof of their hearty and unabashed young appetites reminded us forcibly that a two hours' walk up and down crooked streets would make the sight of a cake-shop a most welcome spectacle.

At the turn of the next street, as if in answer to our wish, we stumbled on a really astonishing collection of pastry. For nearly two streets, on either side of the way, every other shop appeared to be a cake-shop. Every variety of jumble, muffin, tart, seed-cake, plum-cake, and turnover, known to the inventive mind of cake-making man, was arranged in such multitudinous confusion and profusion that nothing but a proximity of boy could possibly explain so many rival establishments eying one another so complacently.

"I have my suspicions that we are nearing the college; only a college could eat and pay for so much pastry," I remarked to Boston, as we stood making our choice of the several shop-windows in front of us.

The suspicions were entirely confirmed by the appearance of two dashing young fellows, carrying the train of their black gowns over their arms, and wearing the well-known three-cornered Wykchamite hat. They were of stalwart build, and both boasted a very perceptible growth of virgin mustaches; and they were engaged in no less serious an occupation than the eating of two large seed-cakes. Age in this case, it was quite evident, had nothing to do with an appreciation of tarts. The shops, we discovered as we strolled past them, were peopled with numbers of young gentlemen of similar tastes; however grown up their appearance might proclaim them to be, their capacity for devouring unlimited cakes proved there was nothing venerable at least in their fresh young appetites.

College Street, which ended by leading us directly to the college, is flanked on the side nearest that famous collection of buildings by a wall so high and so formidably protective as to suggest its capacity for withstanding a very respectable siege. Doubtless the wall has served this very obvious purpose in the defence and security of the buildings; for these latter date back to a time when every house needed to be a fortress. In Saxon days Winchester had already gained its reputation as an educational centre. King Alfred and Ethelwold were sent here to be under the influence of the learned Saint Swithun. Five hundred years later, when William of Wykeham raised the present noble buildings on their ancient foundations, the system of education which he established increased the fame of the college to such a degree as to make it stand among the first in the world, — a pre-eminence it maintains until the present day.

As we entered the courtyard, we seemed all at once to have entered into a different climate. There was something peculiarly soft and sweet in the air. It was more than sweet; it was sweetish. The air was heavy with a fragrance which appeared to penetrate into all parts of the grounds and the buildings. When we learned later that the college still brews its own beer, the mystery of this rich soft odor was revealed. It is the distilling that makes the college appear to have a climate of its own. William of Wykeham had presumably some relish for the good things of life, although doubtless his taste did not take the now classical Wykehamite preference for tarts over other dainties. He made very ample provision that his boys should not suffer for the essentials of life. Beside the brewery, which is close to the street, there stands a building, now empty, where until very recently the college did its own beef-killing. With an abattoir, a brewery, and the college bakers and cooks, the institution was as independent of the rest of the world as all self-respecting institutions should be.

That a man's stomach was of far more importance than the condition of his skin in those old days before the fine art of cleanliness was discovered, was very forcibly proved by the contrast presented between the grand old mediæval kitchen, of the proportions of a palace audience-chamber, and the washing apparatus of the same period. The latter is now shown among the curiosities of the college. In the courtyard was a low arched recess, within which stood a moderately-sized square stone trough. This, we were assured, was the primitive lavatory, bath and basin in one, of those less scrupulously cleanly days. It was assuredly most complete in the economy of its equipment. No Yankee invention for supplying an entire college with an apparatus of that nature, one which should combine simplicity with cheapness, could hope to equal so perfect an arrangement. Imagine the spectacle of seventy or eighty boys in line on frosty mornings, awaiting their turn at that ice-cold basin. Such a reminder of past sufferings makes one's sympathies with the great mediæval unwashed very active. The only wonder is, since English boys have grown up under influences so adverse to the development of a love of personal cleanliness, how it comes that the daily bath has now become the sign by which, the world over, the Englishman betrays his nationality. In keeping with the Spartan severity of the washing-trough was the primitive character of the dormitories. A still more eloquent reminder of the discipline maintained in those ruder, hardier days was the warning mottoes on the walls of the big school-room, — " Aut disce aut discede: manet sors tertia cædi," — and the various devices illustrating the same; one of the quaint paintings being a vivid portrayal of the meaning of "sors tertia" — the birch. The old oak forms, on which the boys sit astride, and their "scots" still remain; both bear the hieroglyphic writing of which every boy appears to have the secret.

Architecturally one's interest centres in the college chapel, which is of great beauty. It bears evidence, in all the features of its refined and perfect proportions, of the genius and taste of its builder, William of Wykeham having built it in 1387. It is the more interesting as proving that wonderful architect's versatility in dealing with different styles, the severe simplicity of the Early English interior of this delightful little chapel differing as widely as possible from the more ornate perpendicular of his work in the cathedral. The cloisters are in an equally perfect state of preservation, with some rare and charming traceries in the arcades. Here, in the cool sweet damp of the summer-time, the Wykehamites in olden days came to walk or to sit as they conned their lessons. The stone benches are as worn as if they had been made originally of more impressionable wood. They are as scratched with names and dates as only school-boys and glaciers know how to scratch. Many of the names one reads over the archways or along the cornices are among those now great and famous. Among them the initials "T. K." are a reminder of Bishop Ken, that courageous churchman who, as Prebendary Ken, refused to allow the gay wanton Nell Gwynne to enter the deanery on the occasions when her lover Charles II. had the impulse to lodge there during one of his flying visits.

Another kind of hand-writing still more eloquent than these scrawled great names is written on the tablets and brasses in the little open arcade adjoining the chapel. Here, as well as in the chapel, are memorial tablets commemorating the bravery and gallant deeds of those Wykehamites who have fallen on the battle-field in defence of their country. Some bore very recent dates. The Zulu and Afghanistan wars have mown down many a Winchester hero: and here was the record of their glorious courage blazoned in gold and black on the shining brass tablets. There is something stupendously fine in this speedy recognition of heroism. In England, if a man loses his life for his country, at least he may count on her not forgetting the sacrifice. This admirable and hearty recognition of a man's services must breed the very heroism it commemorates. There can be no more stirring appeal to youthful imaginations and to young courage than just such eloquence as this, — the eloquence of heroism aureoled by death and crowned by public recognition.

It was impossible, however, to entertain such a sombre assemblage of departed heroes in the company of the very lively young gentlemen who were engaged in cricket and ball matches in the playground at the back of the college buildings. These grounds are of great extent, ending only with the river, which makes a silver thread of gleaming light in among the more distant meadows. There were a number of the boys crossing the river, on their way up towards St. Catherine Hill, a favorite playground on a still wider plane of extension. It all formed a charming, brilliant prospect, — the green fields, the splendid trees, the soft summer sky, and the added animation of the romping, ball-tossing, fine young English lads with their bats and their cricket.

Their holiday gayety was infectious. In spite of our long walk we did not feel in the least inclined to go back into the narrow, close little streets of the city. These soft, brilliant meadows and the flowery river-banks were altogether too tempting company to forsake on such a golden afternoon.

Our stroll took us along the very edge of the river, under noble trees, with the full breadth of the hills on the opposite side, on which the afternoon shadows were sleeping as if on a mother's breast. We traversed several fields, green, star-gemmed with the trefoiled buttercup, and behold! again more ruins. A noble mass sprang up, as if magic impelled, at a sudden bend in the road.

In taking the most innocent walk about Winchester, bent only on pastoral pleasures, it is not safe, apparently, to venture forth without one's guide-book and an exceedingly alert imagination.

Our memory and our imagination served us admirably that afternoon in establishing the date and the history of this beautiful crumbling pile of buildings. We knew the ruins could be none other than those of Wolversy Castle, formerly the great and splendid Bishop's Palace. It was demolished in the time of the civil war, and never entirely rebuilt, the bishops having taken refuge in Farnham Castle, Surrey, which latter seat has since been the Bishop's Palace. Nothing more admirable could be conceived than the taste of the Commonwealth troopers in making such a superb collection of ruins just here. The river, the surrounding green fields, the tender protecting foliage, and the delightful grouping made by the crumbling castle in the foreground, with the little modernized perpendicular chapel, and beyond, the square mass of the cathedral tower, made as complete a picturesque *ensemble* as the most fastidious tourist's eye could desire. Even Henri de Blois, who built the great Bishop's Castle, would have forgiven his iconoclastic countrymen who destroyed it, if he could but have seen how charming a picture it made under the soft haze of that August afternoon. Unquestionably the bishops made the best builders; but Cromwell's troops made the best ruin-makers, and I am not quite sure that, in the end, the ruins of a country do not become even more famous than its buildings. A ruin is an appeal to the least gifted, architecturally, to do a little building on their own account.

With the ruins, our discoveries had not come

to an end. Just beyond them, a fine square tower amid a mass of foliage began to grow nearer and nearer. It grew also more beautiful. A few steps farther on, and we saw that it was attached to a massive old Norman church. A long high wall seemed to shut it off from the surrounding fields and the cluster of houses immediately about us. Soon we discovered a fine arched gateway, of remarkable beauty, with a square octagonal turret, which we had no hesitation in approaching, since the door stood invitingly open. Having passed within the portal, we found ourselves in a small quadrangle, whence issued a porter with a black hat and a demand for sixpence apiece. To our inquiries as to where we were to go, after having crossed his hand with the required stipend, he waved us towards another gateway. Here we stepped into a larger quadrangle, within whose broad space was a group of wonderful buildings. Directly in front was the church, whose tower had led us hither. At the right a row of the quaintest, primmest, whitest, neatest little houses formed two sides of the angle of the bright green square of grass-plot that made a dazzling spot of brightness in the midst of the open court. In front of each house was a gay little garden, and up the façade of each house-front ran a tall straight chimney. It was so entirely obvious that there being just so many chimneys, so many gardens, and so many little houses concealed some intention in the mind of the builder and designer, that I proceeded at once to count them. There were just thirteen.

"I know what this place is," I cried, in the delight of my discovery. "It is St. Cross. Those are the thirteen houses of the thirteen old brethren, and this is their church; and — and there comes one of the old men out to meet us." For a gray-haired upright old gentleman had appeared all at once in one of the doorways of the little houses. He wore a black gown with a silver cross on his breast, and that we both knew to be the dress of the St. Cross Brethren.

We had been reading only the day before of this beautiful old charity, one of the oldest and most famed in England, — how that Henri de Blois, in the midst of his fighting and palace-building, had found time to think of the poor and the aged. He founded St. Cross, in 1136, as a hospital, designed as a retreat for thirteen old men who were unable to furnish means for their own support. There were to be also daily doles for many who resided outside the hospital. Under Cardinal Beaufort, it was made more of a conventual establishment. This great churchman changed its name to "The Almshouse of Noble Poverty," and added priors, nuns, and brethren. During the troublous period of the Middle Ages, St. Cross was enabled to keep its endowments, although many abuses crept in. Its original purpose has gradually been restored, however, and now it is admirably administered by trustees, the former number of thirteen inmates and the "Wayfarer's Dole" being retained in virtue of its founder's original intention. The brethren come from all parts of the kingdom, the only eligibility being their inability to earn their own livelihood.

"It is as well, assuredly, that the number *is* limited to thirteen. If inability to earn one's own livelihood be the only test, the hospital would otherwise be as crowded as a Roman amphitheatre. I know a good many who would be eligible. I am not sure that I myself would be above submitting my failures to the test, if I could end my days in such a retreat," said Boston, as we had strolled out

St. Cross Hospital. *Page 180.*

to meet the little old gentleman who was coming towards us.

The place did, indeed, breathe the most tranquil, peaceful, unworldly calm. It was so still that our footfalls on the gravel walk made resounding echoes. It was so neat, so bright, so exquisitely dainty, with its clipped lawns and trim gardens and spotless houses, that one became insensibly possessed with the longing to become a part of the noiseless, spotless purity.

We had been joined by our old gentleman, who asked us, as he gave us a beautiful old-fashioned bow, adorned with the cheeriest smile, if we wished to be shown about. He preceded us, after our reply in the affirmative, with so brisk and firm a step that, in spite of his silver hair, we classed him as among the younger members of the little fraternity. He was beautifully erect, with such a rich blue tinting his eye as bespoke the vigor of his health. His whole personality diffused an air of singular simplicity and contentment, such as only cloistered seclusion appears to breed.

Convents and institutions create a distinct type of face — the visage of those who live untouched by the worry of the world and remote from its activities. It was such a face as this that this Brother had. It was serenely calm, with a childlike simplicity and credulity. What he had been when he was an actor in his little world's drama, it would have been impossible to conjecture. Neither his troubles nor his disappointments, had he ever had either, had left their mark on him. Even the memory of his past appeared to have been left behind, with his relation to it. Now he was only a Brother, — one of the little family who receive their daily bread from the hand of charity, and who, in taking it, have parted forever from the outer world, from its battles and its contests.

His pride in the fine old buildings was beautiful to see. It was with an air of most satisfied proprietorship that he pointed out the chief architectural features in the charming group of quaint and rare structures that fronted on the two quadrangles, — the church on the left, the cloisters leading from it to the gatehouse above the former nuns' old chambers, the kneeling figure of the cardinal above the gate-arch, and the charming background made by the great trees beyond in the open fields. Later he led us into the fine old hall which contains the offices, the old kitchen, and dining-hall.

His pride was tempered by the cheeriest good-humor and a certain boyish light-hearted gayety. A little fountain of inward merriment appeared to be perpetually playing within; it leaped out in his kindly old eyes, and curved the sweet wrinkled corners of his fine old mouth. He grew merry, indeed, as he was showing us the old kitchen, its great roasting-apparatus, the huge spits, and the quaint old ovens. To our inquiries as to whether cooking was still carried on here, he gave a gay little laugh as he answered, —

"Oh yes, indeed, ma'am, there is cookin' still done here. We have hot joints four times a week; an' on those big spits there's still whole sheep roasted on our gaudy days, as we call them."

"On gaudy days?" I asked, a little wonderingly.

"Yes, on festivals, ma'am, on holidays an' the like, — on Whitsuntide, Michaelmas, Easter Sunday, and other great days; these are our gaudy days. Then we eats the sheep, all together, the whole thirteen on us, over yonder in the old dining-room, just to keep up the good old customs."

The dining-room, which we entered a moment later, retains with a startling degree of preservation its mediæval character. The high-pitched timber roof, the minstrels' gallery, the upright little stairway leading to the muniment room overhead, even the black jacks and the quaint tall and narrow tables, remain to impart to this beautiful old room the most completely fourteenth-century air conceivable. In the centre of the room the primitive brick fireplace is preserved, with its iron railing. The brethren still make a fire here on those famous "gaudy days," of a kind of prepared wood, instead of those great logs that formerly burned there, that blackened the room with their smoke, and turned the rafters to the deep hue which still makes their shadows so rich overhead. Even now it must be a goodly sight to see the thirteen gathered here, even about a nineteenth-century compromise of an open fire. But the picturesque still lies in the dimmer perspectives of the past, when a group of minstrels overhead, in buff jerkin and leathern breeches, breathed music out of their horns and quavering flutes; when the old gentlemen sat at the deal tables yonder, while a rude stone lamp, such as are shown us in the cases now, and the great fire blazing away on the bricks, filling the air with the sweet perfume of burning wood, made the flaring flickering light;

when the great and heavy leathern jacks — the beer jugs — were passed from one shaking old hand to another; and as the fiddlers took up the jig measure, one can fancy the feeble, cheery old song that broke forth as the little company of jolly old brethren filled their glasses anew and drank to the health of the oldest.

The guide-books and the reference-books on architecture will tell you that the church of St. Cross is one of the most interesting of the style known as the transition-Norman, although it also possesses several Early English and Decorated features of unusual beauty and distinction. The first impression is certainly less Norman in character than early Gothic; for the nave, which dates from the twelfth century, with its remarkably massive columns and heavy pointed archings, belongs among the most admirable specimens of Early English work. The choir is a superb example of transition-Norman, with exquisite zigzag mouldings, and is further enriched now by the polychrome decorations which were intrusted to Mr. Butterfield. This decoration is as exact a reproduction of the old work (all church interiors being profusely decorated and colored by the mediæval architects) as it was possible to make it. Some faint bits of the older work are still to be traced over one or two of the arches and along the mouldings. The new painting produces very brilliant and rich effects. At the first, indeed, one is impressed with the sense that it is all a little too brilliant, the strong colors interfering with the effect of the simple massive richness of the architectural details — a gaiety that offends, so to speak. Doubtless time will soften these rather too intense purples, reds, and blues, and fuse their now somewhat obtrusive garishness into a more complete harmony with the architectural *ensemble.*

With an air of its being a personal grievance, our conductor pointed to the vacancies left in the floor and on the walls by the stolen brasses, and also referred in a melancholy tone to the fact that all the glass was modern. While the nineteenth century cannot hope satisfactorily to replace the beautiful old brass-work, the fine memorial windows in this perfect little church prove that the old art of glass-making is not wholly a lost one. They were very beautiful in color, and equally strong in design.

We had gone to the rear of the church to look out upon the fields and the noble trees. As we stood for a moment, our eyes resting on the tranquil rich pasture-lands, and the admirable grouping of the buildings behind us defined against the sky-line, a man crossed the lawn within the quadrangle. It was a beggar with a pack on his back. He was turning towards the porter's lodge.

"Is he going for the dole?" Boston asked our little old gentleman, who was placidly eying him out of the corner of his kindly blue eye.

"Oh yes, sir, that's what he's come for."

"Are they always the same beggars, the same wayfarers — or are they sometimes genuine?"

"Well, sir," the brother replied, with a little ripple of laughter, "some does come every day in the summer-times; but for the most part it's poor men going along the road who stops for the beer and the bread. Many of them comes a long ways out of their road to get it; it's known, you know, sir, and my good lady, all over the kingdom."

In his character of wayfarer, Boston concluded that he also must test the quality of the hospital beer. He declared it excellent, and avowed himself quite ready for a second glass. The porter and the brother both laughed, the former saying that even the Prince of Wales himself could not be given double measure. The porter further hastened to assure Boston that that particular mug was the one from which his Royal Highness had drunk on his recent visit to the hospital; at which excellent invention the old brother kept an unmoved face.

A few seconds later he had bloomed into his habitual wreath of smiles, as he bade us farewell, when Boston had left a bit of shining silver in his pink old hand. He stood, hat in hand, under the great archway, bowing us out, his black gown making a dark mass of color against the bit of sky that was framed in the arch. His kindly, smiling old face seemed the epitome of the content, the peace, and the calm that make this hospital one's ideal of a home for sheltered old age.

"What a place for them to do their dying in!"

"Hasn't it seemed to you as if we had strayed into a little paradise of noiseless, restful calm? It's like a bit out of some other planet, before worry or dust or nerves were invented."

"Or dying, you might add; for it appears they live forever. The porter told me that very few die before reaching the nineties. One of them, who is still alive, has been here over forty years, and as yet gives no hint of dying."

" Why should he? I would n't if I were he. I presume if none of us ever did anything in particular except to make a business of growing as old as possible, we should no doubt find it beset with difficulty. It is n't so easy as one thinks to die just when it is expected one should."

" Well, it appears these old gentlemen surmount the difficulty by dying as infrequently as possible. And now which way home?"

" By the river, by all means, and then we can face the city and the sunset."

We journeyed towards a golden city, through golden fields, under a golden tinted sky. Even the river had changed to a rich amber. Each blade of grass in the dying sunlight looked like a golden dagger freshly unsheathed, and the trees appeared to have absorbed the tinted light into their remotest depths of shade. No hour, I think, reveals the splendid luxuriance and perfection of English foliage and verdure as does the short — the all too short — golden sunset, which, like a torch, lights up for one brilliant glorious moment into fullest splendor the riches of English efflorescence.

CHAPTER IX.

HURSLEY AND ROMSEY ABBEY.

IT was on the afternoon of the following day that Ballad trotted up the steep hill of High Street at a brisk speed, passed under the great gateway, and hurried us away from the beautiful old city. Of the three, Ballad was the only one who carried a light heart and a merry spirit out of the city. Evidently the Winchester oats had been of an excellent quality. Both Boston and I were under the influence of so poignant a regret that only the importance of a mail which had been telegraphed to meet us at Salisbury on the following morning could have had the power to force this decision of leaving on us. Soon, however, the fresh sweet air, the stretch of wide horizons, and the sense of that quickened, more vivid life which the excitement of going forth to meet new scenes awakens, stirred our pulses into more responsive pleasure.

If one is forced to leave a city which one has

grown to love, to be able to view it again and again from some commanding height tempers at least the poignancy of the parting. It is like the sweetened grief of holding a dear face between one's palms and scanning each feature anew before the wrench comes. Winchester, as we rose along the crest of the hill behind the city, appeared to us this last half-hour in a series of dissolving views. As the hills grew steeper, the proportions of the wonderful old city seemed to shrink away, leaving only its nobler and more stupendous features to rise into a worthy rivalship with the encompassing hills. The huge, uplifted mass of the cathedral, as we looked down upon it through a green valley of curving fields, seemed not unlike some mountain in stone carved by those master architects, the storm and the tempest. The houses near it were dwarfed to the proportion of huts. It was a prospect that led us to reflect that such indeed had been, in the disproportionate mediæval days, the true relation existing between the Church and the world, when the former looked down upon mortals only in the light of so much material for the furnishing of the necessary pence with which to rear its temple of holy scorn.

Ballad, not being given to philosophic reflections, took a much less sentimental view of the hills. They were, in truth, seemingly unending. It had been one long continuous climb from the courtyard of the "White Swan" up to this breezy eminence, at least two miles distant from the city gateway. Among the admirable qualities which we had grown to admire in Ballad was his talent for remembering a promise. They were, it is true, always promises which, in moments of weakness, we had made to him. But his tenacious memory of the same pleased us, as proving the extent and variety of his capacities. It was in virtue of a covenant we had entered into along some of the longer Fareham hills, to the effect that we should walk up the longest and the steepest ascents, that now, with the most confiding faith in our honor, he appealed to us to redeem those pledges. He stopped again and again, turning his deep brown glance backward upon us, speaking, as only dumb brutes can, with mute but eloquent entreaty. I, for one, could resist no longer.

Boston soon joined me along the roadside, swinging himself out of the low box-seat. But Ballad's demands did not cease with having merely forced us to lighten his load. He possessed those refinements of taste which characterize every true walker. First of all, he loved companionship. He loved best to have one of us on either side, so close that the tip of his forehead or his long nose touched our elbow as he plodded along. Neither was he adverse to more caressive advances, when either one of us, with an arm about his glossy neck, would the better keep pace with his long swinging gait. If we stopped to examine the landscape, he improved the moment to test the quality of the roadside grass. But he was rather a *gourmet* than a *gourmand;* one succulent taste of the good roadside fare appeared to satisfy his delicate but fastidious palate. The length of such a meal was the most flattering proof we needed to assure us of the richness of the soil.

It was in such amity of friendly companionship that we all three toiled up the steep Winchester hills. Once at the top, however, of the steepest, and the splendid prospect made us stay our steps. Far as the eye could reach the country stretched itself out like an unrolled carpet at our feet. Hills dipped into valleys only to rise again into hills, till they and the far edges of the horizon were merged into one indistinguishable blue. There were several miles of driving with this great prospect before us, changing in some of the nearer details, but the vast panoramic aspect remaining the same. The county of Hampshire appeared to lie beneath and out beyond us, as if, like some conscious beauty, she were bent on displaying her charms on this last day of our drive among her hills.

Hampshire is hilly, as Sussex is rolling. She is a wild beauty, with a touch of unkempt disordered loveliness about her, strange enough to find among these Southern counties. Our journey through the heart of her forest and in among her rude hillside-villages was a revelation of the store of surprises reserved for those who seek them out in this compact and wonderful little island. Here was a bit of country almost as wild as some parts of our own transatlantic continent. Instead of the park-like meadows of the Surrey downs, their trim garden finish, their sleek parterre perfections, these hills and fields had a touch of nature's more abandoned freedom. The trees were true mountaineers, growing on perilous heights or where best it pleased them, that they might prove their hardihood in facing the elements.

Of course, wild as was the aspect of the country, there were still hedge-rows, or it would not have been England. A roadway without hedge-rows, from an Englishman's point of view, is only conceivable in a country whose government is either unconstitutional or in sad want of political repair.

These upland Hampshire hedges were quite unobjectionable. They were charming in their reckless disorder. They strewed the grassy roadside, in their gay abandonment, with the loose petals of the wild white rose and the honeysuckle. Their dense shade was the home of the robin. We startled one of these crimson-liveried gentlemen as we leaned over the top of a particularly odorous hedge to catch a glimpse of a little old farmhouse perched on the edge of a tiny precipice. We startled the robin, but we had very little effect on the musician. He had begun his song amid the honeysuckle. Finding himself in good voice, he continued his *roulades*, when we came to disturb his serenade to their perfume. A shower of thrilling notes descended as he whirled himself into the upper skies. It was the revenge of the musician in showing us how easily he could wing himself into aerial spheres.

His song accentuated the stillness, the absolute quiet, and the forest-like remoteness. There was not a sound except the nibbling of Ballad in among the grasses, those now sky-distant robin-notes, and the crackling amid the trees made by unseen insects or squirrels. It was such a moment as lingers afterward in the memory with the resonance of a full rich chord.

In the midst of the hills was an ideal little rustic. We had been driving for several miles without having seen even so remote a sign of civilization as a distant church-spire. But at the bottom of a series of hills we drove straight into a little village which might have posed as the nymph of the woodlands. It was Hursley, a village with as wild a grace as the roses which covered its gabled and thatched old houses. Almost at the entrance of its wide straggling little street was set a beautiful ivy-grown church. Its round Saxon-headed windows told its age and history. Our guide-book had already furnished us with the secret which explained its admirable and perfect state of preservation. The pious John Keble was vicar here for many years, and generously gave the money derived from the "Christian Year" for its restoration. There were some admirable brass tablets to be seen in the church, erected to the memory of his wife and himself, as well as an interesting monument to Richard Cromwell. But we did not stop to enter, as the congregation were just about dispersing; for it was Sunday, the first of our drives on that day.

No time could have been chosen to see this bit of English rustic life to better advantage. The little congregation, as it came slowly forth in groups of twos and threes from beneath the low church portal, stood about on the green, or wandered quietly up the village street into the open doors of the thatched vine-covered houses. It was strange to see the attempts at London fashions in the women's dressing as they walked along the little rural street; they were the London fashions of several seasons ago, so that their modernness was not too startling. The men had the look of discomfort and awkwardness common to the sex when wearing their Sunday broadcloth; some of the older farmers, however, wore their corduroys and faded pink and yellow vests and great neckties, in defiance of the modern modes. In spite of the freshness and fairness of the younger women, it was these latter — these fine, vigorous, sunburnt, last-century faces among the old farmers — who bore off the palm of beauty. Some among them were superb types of English strength of build and sturdy mould of feature. There was hardly a weak face among them. But strong and robust as was their general aspect, these farmers had a look peculiar, I think, to an English farmer. It was the look of mingled simplicity, honesty, and peacefulness, which no French, German, or American agriculturist ever successfully combines. It is such an expression as can only come from long descent and heredity, — from men who for generations have lived on the same soil, have thought the same thoughts, have had the same simple ambitions, and yet whose intelligence has been of an order which enabled them to take an active personal interest in their contemporaneous political surroundings. The French farmer, if he be intelligent, is too shrewd to be simple; the German is too stolid to be intelligent; it is only the English yeomanry who are at once industrious, intelligent, and still rurally simple.

The younger men, we noticed, accompanied their wives to the cottage or the farmhouse doors. They picked up a child or two who had run out to meet them to joy in the unwonted Sunday delight of indulging in the happiness of a father and the sport of being trundled by strong arms. But the older men passed on farther down the street, with a group of younger lads, embryonic young men, at their heels. These turned with simultaneous accord into a little tavern at the farthest extremity of the village, — as far as possible from the church at the other end and the omniscience of the vicar's eye, we said to each other. They took their seats about the long narrow tables in the little inn. The orders for the evening toddy were given audibly enough for us to hear as we stood without in the courtyard; for Ballad had not been proof against this example of profane Sabbath-breaking. He had walked deliberately up to the village trough, and had drained its contents. It was presumably, also, purely in the interests of his character as a student of rustic habits and customs, that Boston was suddenly inspired to swing himself off the box-seat and to declare that he was consumed with the prevailing thirst. The noise within the little tavern stopped for a brief moment as he stepped into the low room; but the strong rough voices broke out again a moment later. Only seven of the tapsters followed Boston to the door to look inquisitively at our trap. Ballad was evidently an unknown acquaintance, although each farmer did his best to identify him.

"'Ee's frame Winchester, I tell 'ee.'"

"Naw, 'ee's naw frame Winchester; 'ee's frame deown yander, frame Salisbury."

"Naw, mon, 'ee's cum naw so fur; 'ee's frame Winchester."

"You're all wrong, — all of you; he's from Chichester," I called back at them, as we drove off with a dash. It was sport to see them scatter like affrighted geese, and fun to hear the mocking laughter of the men within, which greeted the astonished questioners as they ran back into the inner tap-room.

The discovery of two or three lawn gowns and smart bonnets, each attended by a village swain, in among the adjacent fields and woods, was proof that not all the Hursley males were left behind in the tap-room. These more sentimental villagers were employing this classical courting-hour in the useful purpose of inducing their lady-loves, doubtless, to be the presiding rustic divinities of their hearts and homes. These, once safely insured, could then comfortably be left for the tavern. It is a law of sequence not wholly unpractised among what we are pleased to call the upper classes.

The road to Romsey, the little town where we were to sup and rest ere we pressed on to Salisbury, was almost as picturesquely wild as that part of it which had led us to Hursley. The prospect was, however, not nearly so large and open. The dense shade of the woodlands made the views of the outlying country less frequent. The breaks in the thick foliage only served to make such glimpses the more interesting and admirable.

There were five miles more of delightful driving through the woods, past the hedges and the quiet grassy slopes, and we were rattling over the cobble-paved streets of Romsey.

We count Romsey as among the discoveries of our trip. We had only been told so much of the charms of the little town as that it contained an excellent inn where we could break our fast, and that near it was Lord Palmerston's beautiful seat of Broadlands. But it is due to neither of these attractions that Romsey remains to us among the most perfect and complete of the little towns we encountered on this charming tour.

The pearl of our discovery lay in the fact that Romsey boasts of an abbey, which from its beauty and its unique architectural features should be counted as among the chief architectural Meccas of all lovers of fine and rare old Norman work. We classed ourselves amongst such lovers; yet it was only by a happy accident that we made the discovery of Romsey Abbey's surpassing beauties.

We owe our seeing it at all to the landlady of the "Deer Hound." She had stepped out to meet us as we drove in under her cosey little brick courtyard. After greeting us with a courtesy which was almost formidable in its ceremoniousness, owing to the emphasis of her large and somewhat obese person, she ordered the hostler to unstrap the luggage. We protested, explaining that we had stopped only for supper and to water our horse. Had I foreseen how keen her disappointment would be, I fear I should have weakly yielded and have stopped over night; but she rallied almost instantly.

"Ho, very well, sir, we'll try to make you as comfortable has possible, although most every one stops, has they all goes to see the habbey. You'll go to see it, sir; it's the finest church in Hingland, an' I'll make the lady a nice cup of tea while the gentleman steps over and rings for the verger; he's opposite, an' 'll show you everything."

Her garrulousness was too good-natured to be resented, although a trifle overpowering. Boston broke the torrent of her talk by retreating under cover of an excuse for looking after Ballad; but he did not escape without binding himself to look up the verger. She then preceded me up a creaking winding flight of worn steps, leading me into a large upper room evidently used as the inn coffee-room. She lost not a moment in placing me in a chair, in pouring the water into the kettle, in giving a multitude of orders to a sweet, fresh-looking country-girl who obeyed them in silence, all the while continuing one of the longest, most endless, wandering, and inconsequent monologues it has ever been my punishment as a listener to endure. Yet she was well versed in the history of her native town, and she gave me a not uninteresting though somewhat discursive synopsis of its existence.

The tea equalled her promise of its excellence. I sat and sipped it as the stream of her talk poured on. The room was fine and large, with rich old mahogany cupboards and buffets, high straight-backed chairs, and a mantelpiece with some lovely old Tudor carvings. Its ample proportions and air of prosperous antiquity matched well with the appearance of its owner, whose generous outlines, dimpled rosy cheeks, and glittering gold chain bore evidence to the successful business done at the "Deer Hound." Her father had kept it before her, she said. And did I know how old the old house was? Almost as old as Romsey itself, and the town dated back to Alfred the Great. For the "habbey" was built by Edward his son, as a convent, and the Nuns' Garden was still shown, and the Nuns' Door. The convent had been a rich one in its day, but all that had gone with popery, and now it was only the parish church. And we must look in the choir for the tombs and monuments of the Saint Barbes, the original owners of Broadlands, and for the splendid windows put up in honor of the great Prime Minister, and also for the tomb of Sir William Petty, who had been the son of a Romsey clothier, but who was also the ancestor of the great Lansdowne family.

"An' you must see the cloisters, — or rather where they was, for there ain't no trace of them left, — an' you must see the nun's 'air; it's the beautifullest an' the loveliest color — an' now there's your good gentleman and the verger, an' mind you ask him for to show you the nun's 'air."

I joined the "good gentleman" and the verger at the bottom of the creaking flight of steps. We proceeded at once, without further delay, to thread our way through the streets of the silent little town to the abbey. The silence had a drowsy, brooding quiet in its stillness, as if centuries ago there had been a lively stirring time among these quaint sad-faced streets, and ever since the little town had lived on the memory of it all. Not a soul was astir; not a footfall save our own resounded on the clean cobble pavements, and no voices save ours broke the silence, which might have been under the spell of a charm, so complete and so profound was its slumber.

This drowsy quiet may perhaps have served to enhance the effect which the striking unmodernness of the abbey produced. It needed this emphasis of unreality, this suggestion of a shadowy, dim, and hazy remoteness, to touch us with its wand of illusion, and prepare us for the surprise which the strange and yet lovely structure was to produce. The surprise lay in the abbey being at once so venerable and yet in such a perfect condition of preservation. The discolorations on its façades, the mosses, the leaflets, and the few wild-flowers which had intrusted their delicate existence to the few inches of earth along the cornices and in among the window-ledges, were trustworthy proofs that there had been no modern renovations. Yet with the exception of some traces of crumbling and decay in the toothwork over the beautiful arched doorways, the fissures and the rain-stains, the grand old church must have presented the same appearance to its Norman builders that it did to us on that still, sunny August Sunday. The interior we found no less exquisitely beautiful. I use the word *exquisite* with deliberation, and chiefly because no other word would so well describe the delicacy, the high degree of finish, and the supreme elegance of this wonderful interior. The style is Norman, but it is the Norman of that later, more refined period when the natural elegance and taste of the Norman builders had come to demand something more than strength from their rounded arches and a more ideal massiveness from their structural

ROMSEY ABBEY, TRANSEPT AND NAVE.

Page 206.

solidity. Here each archway, each string-course, and each cornice had been made to bloom under the inspired chisel into rhythmic waves of ornament,— that wise linear restraint which preceded the moment when the poetry of tracery was to break forth into the efflorescence of the Gothic.

Grace had been the guiding divinity of the architect's inspiration, until the grandeur of the Norman had been transformed into something of that soaring quality of lightness we are wont to associate with the later Gothic. The eye wanders in enraptured ecstasy over these towering arches, up into the rare and original two-arched triforium, and down the shadowy length of the noble little nave. It is the most triumphant union conceivable of grace and strength.

The verger was at infinite pains to explain to us at just what precise points in the transept, the choir, or the nave the Norman became transition, or the latter changed into early English. But it was the admirable harmony and beauty of the interior as a whole which chiefly charmed and interested us. There was a richly ornamented door opening from the southern transept, called the Nuns' Door, formerly used by the sisters as they passed to and fro into the cloisters and into the old gardens. Both these latter are now part of that shadowy time when the old interior was full of the white-capped, black-gowned nuns. It was the memory which the thought of these silent saintly-browed women brought up to our minds, that served to remind us of the covenant we had made with our kindly and garrulous landlady. We proceeded at once in search of the remarkable hair, which the verger assured us was as genuine as it was ancient.

"It's a thousand years old if it's a day, mum," he said, with the severe accent which is wont to accompany conviction; "and it's as perfect as any lady's in the land."

He thereupon proceeded to uncover a semicircular box with a glass top. Through the glass we looked down upon a bit of a wooden log, on which lay evidently a woman's scalp, depending from which was a mass of golden brownish hair, carefully braided. The log, the verger explained, was the cushion used in those ancient times as the rude head-rest of the dead. The "relic" had been found years ago by some workmen while digging up a grave. It was an interesting, but on the whole not a cheering or inspiriting sight, although there was a certain glimmer of ghoulish fascination in watching the threads of gold, which the stray sunshine lit up these hundreds of years after the owner of those fair locks had crumbled into nothingness. It was a relief to turn away to the beautiful lancet windows put up in memory of Palmerston, and even the tomb of the Romsey clothier seemed to make death and decay more decently remote and unreal.

The landlady, however, was troubled by no such dismal sentimentalities. Her first question, as she stood awaiting us on the doorstep, was whether or not we had seen "hit." On assuring her that we had, she added with cheery blitheness: "Beautiful specimen, is n't it, an' such a lovely color has it was; there was no dye about that, was there, an' so neat as she was,"— in full confidence, apparently, that it had been the custom of the dead of old to do their own hair-dressing.

Half an hour later, after supper, we clattered out of her hospitable courtyard. Her farewell speeches pursued us down the street. But the town was evidently familiar with the sound of her strong voice; for although it started a number of slumbering echoes under the old doorways, it appeared to arouse no fellow-townsman's interest.

Our glimpse of Broadlands came just after we had crossed the clear little river Test, over which sprang a pretty two-arched bridge. A rise on the hill just outside the little town gave us a commanding prospect of the great premier's former seat and of the adjoining lands of the estate. The house stood in the midst of emerald lawns which swept, by a series of gentle declivities, down to the river-banks. There was a dim vast perspective beyond, of meadows, trees, and bushy banks. In the immediate foreground some fine cows were standing in the clear stream up to their middle, making, with the noble colonnaded façade of the dignified and somewhat severe-looking stone mansion, with the turf and the great trees, an immemorial picture of tranquil and yet stately beauty. It was a prospect which fulfilled one's ideal of the perfect blending of the pastoral and the majestic. Such a grouping as Broadlands made, with the rustic charms of the old town, the mediæval sanctity of association clustering in the tightly-knit Norman abbey structure, and that note of rural loveliness struck by the meadows and the river,

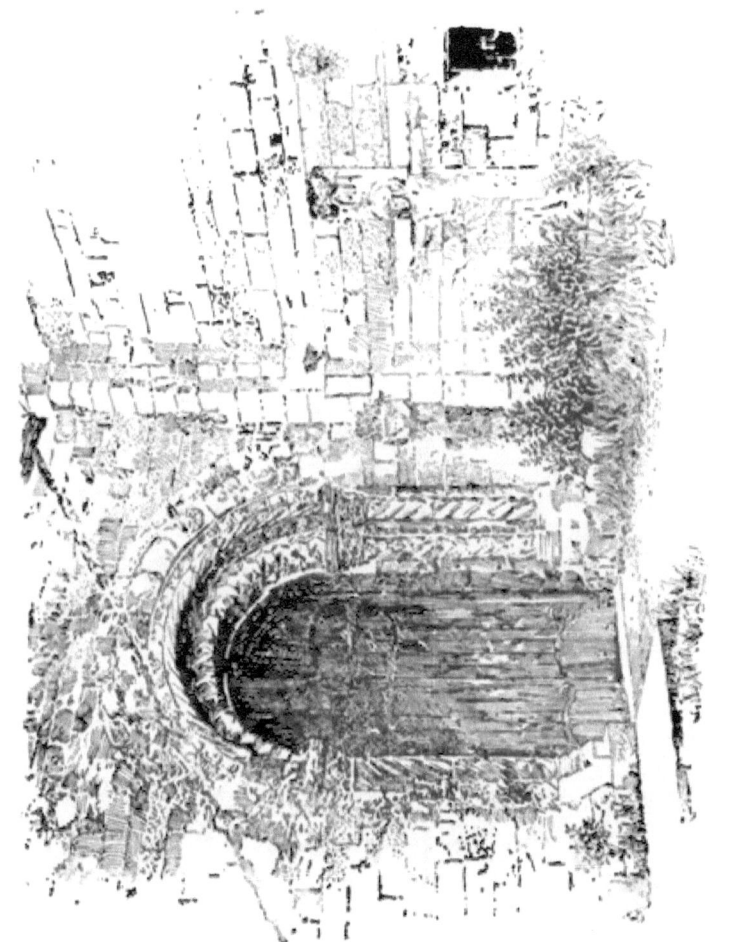

NUNS' DOOR, ROMSEY ABBEY. *Page* 210.

was such as completes one's ideal vision of a fine old English seat. No spot could be imagined more conducive to repose, from a weary statesman's point of view; and no surroundings would be more certain to awaken and to stir anew the fire of an ambitious devotion to one's country, to its interests and its welfare. It is ever the homely sights and sounds of nature which tend to nourish best the clinging tendrils of affection, and stir the profoundest chords of a vibrating patriotism.

It appeared as if it was destined, on this particular afternoon, that we should have vouchsafed for us a very complete series of revelations,— of the sources, for instance, whence spring English love of, and English delight in, her rural landscape. From Romsey to Salisbury our road led us into what must have been the very heart of England's richest and most vernal loveliness. The wildness of the Hampshire hills had become tamed into the gentleness of pretty, approachable undulations. The verdure was greener with the thickness of sweet grasses; the trees were fuller and taller, like all things that have plenty of space and light in which to grow. The roads and lanes were such as the poets have sung since

Chaucer's Canterbury Pilgrims took their pleasure along them.

Imagine a road lined as with velvet, with broad grassy strips growing into a maze of flowering hedge-rows; overhead an unbroken arch of elm, under whose cool green aisles we drove and continued to drive for miles. As the road dipped and rose, we caught glimpses of hills distant as the horizon, with gleams below of ponds and pools, the liquid eyes of this fair-featured landscape. The houses, thatched and vine-covered, and the larger farmhouses made brilliant flowery little groups in the vernal picture. Children whose cheeks were redder than the pinks ran out to peer at us from the rustic gateways; women and girls with bright kerchiefs were busy milking in the barnyards; and men, with serious Sunday aspect, in their shirt-sleeves were solemnly leaning over the fence-rails surveying them, their pigs, and their sheep, true to the farmer's habit, the world over, whose rest is always consecrated to doing sums in arithmetic over his cattle and his lands.

This was the England we all know and have learned to love since we were old enough to love any land or nation; whose greatness has always been allied to a certain grave simplicity, whose best poets have sung the natural joys of rural life, and whose heroes' passion and fire have ever been tempered by the taste for temperance and justice. It is from English soil that have sprung the true sources of English strength and greatness, — from that healthful fountain of her rural life and her rural loveliness, which, like the eternal springs that flow around Hymettus, are immortally fresh and life-giving.

CHAPTER X.

SALISBURY.

THERE is a peculiar charm, in an unknown country, in watching the daily miracle of day giving way to night. Twilight invests all landscape with a fresh meaning. English landscape particularly gains by the transformation of this hour of mysterious charm. Details are lost in the twilight blur; they are merged or obliterated by the long finger of the deepening shadows; outlines etch their indistinctness against the sky, and the landscape can be but dimly divined through the dense masses of shade.

It was through the rich gloom of such an hour that, as we skirted the crown of a steep hill, we looked down upon an outstretch of country not yet so lost in the dusk of the night that we could not distinguish the arrowy flight into the sky of the great Salisbury cathedral spire. Only the noble outline of the encompassing hills, the foliage massed

SALISBURY.

in the valleys, through which the light of the scattered villages glittered like tangled fireflies, and that upshooting tapering spire, could be seen in the thick richness of the coming night.

Our road into Salisbury led us from the brighter light on the hill into the darkness of the valley. The villages were in shadow. Even the lights were out in the little cottages and taverns. Not a tapster seemed astir. The hush of an early Sabbath sleep appeared to pervade each one of the hamlets we passed.

Salisbury, we found, was by no means such a rustic as her country neighbors. On entering its thickly built streets the lights were ablaze on the street corners. The taverns, apparently, were still doing a lively business. There were any number of friendly vagrants, with no other ostensible occupation, an hour before midnight, than to continue the day's work of diligently keeping their hands in their pockets, readily willing to show us our way to the "White Hart" inn. A formidably realistic figure of that anomalous member of the animal kingdom, surmounting a portico which projected over the sidewalk, proved that our idle guides had dealt fairly with us.

We were received with that air of unmoved calm and that appearance of impassive interest characteristic of good English inn-manners. Our coming at nearly midnight from nowhere in particular, with a horse that gave every evidence of having found the way long, — ourselves and luggage covered with dust, proving the length of our journey no fable, — appeared to arouse no more concern or curiosity than if we had come at midday by train.

"Do you really suppose it is genuine, this indifference, or is it put on?" I queried of Boston, when the last dusty bag had been deposited in the pleasant lamp-lit sitting-room.

"My dear, human nature is n't as varied as it might be; it has a way of repeating its types. I presume curiosity in Salisbury is as lively and active a faculty as curiosity in a New England town; only, in England it has learned the good manners of repressing itself."

"There's something deeper in it than that, I think; it's the reticence which rank imposes upon its inferiors. Fancy a peasant asking a lord where he has come from, and imagine a Yankee refraining because of any such reason. But here's supper, and it looks as good as their manners are perfect."

To the respectful attention of the waiter who served us, was added, we discovered, another quality of excellence. It was that of thoughtful considerateness. The discretion of the man's silence was suddenly broken by what appeared to be a spontaneous impulse. He was on the point of withdrawing with the tray, at the end of our repast, when he stopped a moment at the door, turned towards me with a little bow, and said,—

"I hope, ma'am, as ye won't be troubled by the noise in the mornin', ma'am, after your long drive, ma'am."

Before we could ask a question he was gone.

"What does that mean?" exclaimed Boston.

"It means that something is going to happen,— a procession, or a country-meeting, or it may be the advent of Royalty. But whatever it is I shall take the precaution to get my forty winks immediately."

It was well that I did; for before dawn the "noise" had begun. Our first impression on awaking was that a menagerie and a circus in combination had been let loose.

"The yearly tiger has broken out of his cage," I said conjecturally to Boston, as I went towards the window.

Light hoofs were striking the pavement, and the tread of heavy-booted men and boys. But as I opened the shutters, there came other sounds, — the pitiful bleating of lambs, the neighing of horses, and the lowing of cattle; so the circus theory had to be abandoned.

Looking forth into the faint bluish gray of early dawn, I saw that the street, as far as the eye could penetrate its length either way, was filled with great droves of sheep and cattle.

Teamsters were driving huge wagons and carts, the latter filled with calves and kids. There were groups of horses tethered to one another, led by farmers' boys riding one of the leaders bare-back. Many of the horses were tricked out with ribbons and straw trimmings in their manes and tails. The teamsters also wore a festival appearance, with gay little knots of colored ribbons fastened to their coats and large hats. The noise and the tumult were indescribable; there was the barking of the shepherd dogs as they plunged madly after stray sheep, the yelling of the teamsters to one another, the shouting of the boys as their horses reared or struggled, and, piercing through the din like some flageolet note of pain, was the pathetic bleating of the sheep and the groaning of the calves. Naturally, with such a chorus of sounds in the air, sleep was out of the question. Shortly before six we rang for breakfast. In just fifteen minutes it appeared, borne by our waiter of the night before. His unexampled promptness he at once proceeded to explain, deeming, doubtless, that a haste so contrary to the provincial habit rendered some form of apology necessary.

"I knowed you could n't sleep, sir, what with the noise and the uproar, an' so I got your breakfast ready in case it was ordered, sir."

"What is it? — what is all this noise about?"

"It's the sheep-fair, sir, — the sheep, horse, and cattle fair, as takes place once a year."

"Is it held here in town?"

"About a mile out, sir, down in the meadows. But the city's full, — full of the gentry and the farmers come in to buy. We've been up nearly all night a-waitin' on 'em, sir. You ought to see it, sir, begging your pardon; it's a grand sight."

"See it? I wonder what he takes us for?" said Boston, with more emphasis than elegance as the waiter closed the door behind him. "Not go to a sheep-fair in England when it's at your very door? As well go to Rome and not see the Pope, should he pass beneath your window!"

"I suppose, then, we'll postpone the cathedral."

"The cathedral, my dear, having been here some five hundred years, will presumably be in town at least till to-morrow."

"We can't drive Ballad out; he's too tired."

"We don't want him. It would be better to go as the rest do, — as those people are going now in those queer-looking traps; don't you think so?"

We were looking out of the window again. The droves of cattle had given place to multitudes of people, — to farmers, country-looking gentlemen, young and old, to tradesmen and their wives, — a motley anxious crowd, standing about on street-corners waiting for seats in some one of the numerous passing vehicles. But not a seat was to be had, apparently. Every species of cart, wagon, trap, and vehicle which the surrounding country contained had been put into requisition. Drivers plied their whips, speeding along in clouds of dust to the fair, returning for fresh passengers; yet the crowds never seemed to thin.

It was nearly midday before we ourselves were in possession of a broken-down phaeton and jaded horse, whose owner, at a preposterous price, consented to our occupying the vehicle, without the addition of the dozen or more fellow-passengers usually crowded into it.

The mile, what with its dust and thronged thoroughfares, and the curious mixture of the human and animal species, we found just a mile too long; but the first glimpse of the fair grounds made these discomforts more than endurable.

In a wide stretch of rich meadow-land, with fringes of trees and bits of wood for an enceinte, with gently sloping hills towards the west, where the flags and the bunting would show well against the sky, lay the fair grounds. The scene, as we entered, was brilliant with life and movement. The wicker pens were packed with noble-looking sheep and rams, crowded together so closely that their backs looked like an unbroken sheep-rug. Under the trees, and in the open, were grouped the horses and cattle. Some jockeys, in brilliant tweed vests, and farmers' boys were riding stallions and half-broken colts, while the mares and still younger colts were tethered to the tree-trunks, contentedly nibbling the short grass, as if a change of masters were among the things to be accepted with philosophy in a life of vicissitudes.

The ceaselessly moving throngs of people filled the alleys between the sheep-pens, crowded about the auctioneers' stands, and packed the narrow strip allotted to spectators about the horse enclosures. The crowd had the instability of a mercurial stream; now conjoining into groups to halloo and hurrah over some feat of horsemanship; or dissolving like quicksilver, only to meet again at the improvised booths and *al-fresco* restaurants which countrywomen and gypsies had erected under the belt of the more distant trees. The scene, teaming with life and replete in contrasts, was set, like a picture in its frame, in the emerald meadows and the tender foliage; all the outlines were softened and harmonized by the rich verdure. It was a Teniers framed in velvet.

The dominant note in the scene was its dead earnestness. This was no make-believe fair,— a Frenchman's gala-outing or a Spaniard's *fête*, where barter and trade were only to serve as the mask of revelry. This was a camp of traders bent on business. There appeared to be little or no loitering under the great trees, among the buyers, in wait for any chance pleasure or gayety to which the occasion might give rise. In trade an Englishman is as serious as he is when at his prayers. He would as soon think of play as an accompaniment to the one as to the other.

The absence, presumably, of any coarse gayeties accounted for the presence of so many sons of the Church. They were quite as safe here from the profane vulgarities of the world as in their pulpits. The curate's innocent round-eyed face, the rector's more worldly figure, immaculate in linen, with severely cut garments, were in amusing contrast to the knowingly tipped nose of the pervasive jockey, who cracked his short whip and uttered a joke in the very teeth of these gentlemen. Among the crowd sauntered swells in perfection of riding-gear. Stolid-looking country squires and every variety of farmer were inextricably mixed in the mass of the moving, jostling multitude. Here and there a swarthy-skinned gypsy-girl, with gleaming teeth and glossy hair, shot through the crowd like a darting bit of flame, focussing all eyes upon her as she smiled boldly back. At the outskirts of the grounds some noisy flirtations were in full swing between some of these gay-kerchiefed gypsies and the plough-boys and farmers' lads who had been left to guard the wagons and teams. The sound of their broad coarse laughter was like the introduction of an opera-bouffe aria into the midst of a grave cantata.

Such pleasures as the fair offered were concentrated about the eating-booths. It was rather a solemn company of feasters that we passed, crowding about the little tables. The English farmer has never learned the art of seasoning his food with laughter. The cattle feeding out yonder, and these silent farmers who gave out a monosyllable or two between the beer-draining, both brought to their meal the same Egyptian gravity and dignity. One admirable little rustic scene greeted our eyes on our way out. It was an old barn filled with long narrow tables on which was placed a profusion of coarse homely fare. Farmers and teamsters crowded the barrels, casks, and broken stools, — the only available seats. Their strong sunburnt faces loomed out of the dark. The steaming food, the coarse textures of the farmers' coats and capes, and the serving-women, who now raised a beer-jug, now planted their arms akimbo on their wide hips, throwing back their full strong throats, as they joined in the occasional short laughter that went round with the beer, made a very complete picture of rustic life and manners.

Just outside the barn a trade was being struck. The buyers were two gentlemen, one of whom had taken off his riding-glove and had thrust his richly jewelled hand deep into the nearest sheep's thick coat. The sellers were two farmers. The elder was a noble-looking old man, of the last-century type, whose frugal savings had written their obvious balm of peace and content on his rugged unworried face. Next him stood a thin nervous younger farmer, whose premature lines of care were tell-tale proofs that American beef and American wheat were harder competitors to fight than his Georgian grandfather had found the American Rebels.

There were but few words interchanged, but the gentlemen handled the sheep with the air of connoisseurs. Finally the elder gentleman turned to the younger farmer, and said,—

"We'll take them. Have them driven over directly, will you?"

The farmer nodded and whistled; a lad appeared in response; the sheep were driven out of their pens, and all started forward.

"Is it a long bit?" the lad asked of the gentlemen as they mounted their horses at the gate.

"Not so very,—about eight miles or so."

The boy grasped his stick more firmly, turned, made a half-moon of one hand against the side of his mouth, and shouted down into the hollow,—

"Father, don't ee wait dinner; it's a long bit, eight mile or more. Don't ee wait." He then resumed the guardianship of his sheep.

"It's a primitive way of doing one's shopping, but it has the advantage of appearing to insure speed and an honest delivery of the goods," said Boston, as we proceeded leisurely to follow the sheep and the two men, but at a distance, because of the dust raised by the sheep in the open roadway.

A short drive soon took us into the heart of the city. The streets, as we drove back, seemed strangely still and deserted. All the stir of life had evidently localized itself in the fair grounds.

The character of the streets, we noticed, appeared to be a curious mixture of the old and the modern. Salisbury, having been built so recently as 1220, failing to be as old as possible, was probably bent on being as modern as is compatible with the national conservatism. In proof of this latter ambition there were so many structures, brave in fresh paint and in modern complexity of design, as to make the still remaining older houses appear out of place.

Perhaps it was the intrusion of these modern buildings that made us suddenly dismiss our lumbering vehicle, and decide to walk into the darkness of one of the older narrower side-streets. A really experienced traveller never looks for the picturesque on the main thoroughfares. The true antique spirit of the past is usually to be found lurking among the less pretentious streets; for the antique spirit, like all other decent ghosts, prefers darkness and secrecy to the glare of daylight, knowing full well the advantages to be gained by the jugglery of mysteriousness. Thus the true beauty of old towns is to be looked for among the sunken narrow sidewalks, among the rickety houses and the little weedy gardens, — parks and terraces once, perhaps, but which the poor of the town have no time now to plant or to weed. All this we found as true of Salisbury as we had of many another city, whose fresh modern main streets had sent us home with a chill of disappointment.

The narrower, the meaner, the poorer the streets, we found as we walked along, the prettier the town grew. No one had found it worth his while to pull down these half-decayed old houses, or even to repaint them; so the tiny casemented windows, the carved Tudor pilasters, and the rare old doors and entrances had remained unspoiled. In color, two or three of these streets were lovely in their dulled prismatic hues. The crumbling façades had the softness and mellowness of old ivory. Their faint yellows and pale grays made some of the carvings look like bits of tattered rich old lace. The only conspicuously modern element was the filth; but as dirt seems everywhere the true and necessary concomitant of color of the best sort, we were disposed to regard the sloppy sidewalks and the reeking alley-ways with a lenient eye.

A girl with a red kerchief pinned across her bosom, and a pitcher in one hand, suddenly appeared from beneath one of the arched doorways. Instead of proceeding down the street, she turned at one of the corners of an alley-way, and went towards a path that led into the open meadows; for the outlying fields straggled with comfortable assurance close along the edges of the streets.

"She is going for water, and probably to the river; I mean to follow her!" I exclaimed.

"How absurd! We shall only lose our way!" protested Boston, who, after the fixed habit of men, always made a point of distrusting an impulse.

"Nonsense! we haven't any way; besides, we have discovered before now, that the true method of finding it is to lose it. Come!"

I started down the alley-way in pursuit of the red kerchief. Boston followed, but at a distance; for a man at all times has a certain respect for the varnish of his boots, — a respect which is apt to be accentuated when he is following his wife into paths not of his choosing, and which in this case, at least, were uncommonly slippery.

The reeking alley-way soon became a path along the river-bank. It had turned at a sharp angle, and lo! almost at our feet stretched the low, sweet, straggling river. I was right. The girl, our guide, had come for water. She stooped over the bank, filled her ewer, and then rose slowly, its weight bending her over as she walked back along the path. Her red kerchief and her frowsy reddish hair made the scene seem less brilliant when she had disappeared behind the corner of the first house.

We continued our walk along the river-bank. Each step brought a fresh revelation of beauty. First of all, there was the charm, which every one knows who has tried it, of following an unfamiliar river. One never knows just where an unknown river may lead. As a guide, a stream or a little river is far more interesting than the most entertaining of streets. It is more talkative, for one thing. Its babble and its ripple, as it flows gently over the sedgy grasses, is at once new and familiar. It is like the tones of some old friend's voice sounding in our ears, rendered strange only because he is clothed in unfamiliar garments. So this low-toned Avon sounded delightfully friendly, as it chatted to the weeds and the tall grasses growing along its straggling banks. It led us almost unconsciously along, as we travelled in the company of a number of wonderful old houses, whose decrepit appearance told us how long they had been standing here, watching the river flow on. Here, at last, was the ideal Salisbury. This maze of soft foliage, these odorous river-banks, these rows of tottering buildings, long since fallen out of the perpendicular, made a rich harmony of architectural adjuncts to the natural rural note of the meadows and the waving tree-tops.

There was a bridge, I remember, which we crossed, and on which we stood for several moments, watching the picture as it focussed into new outlines. Suddenly we lifted our eyes; and there upward soared the giant spire of the cathedral. It shot its tapering spiral into the dizzy ether like a thing of life.

There could have been no better point of view than this from which to gain one's first glimpse of this great spire. Subsequent observations taken from the cathedral close diminished very sensibly the effect of its incomparable grace and its majestic symmetry. A spire, more than any other architectural feature perhaps, demands a certain distance and the advantages of perspective. Seen at near range, neither its true height nor its just proportions can be properly measured. Here, in the midst of this rustic setting, with only the trees for rivals and to serve as aids for measurement, the noble spire rose toward heaven in all the fulness of its perfection. At first its true height is scarcely appreciable, so symmetrically proportioned are its four hundred and four feet. After repeated and careful examination, the wonder still remains that this tapering angle, lanced into the sky to such a daring altitude, can, at the last as at the first view, appeal to the eye rather because of its surpassing lightness and grace than merely as a triumph of height. This latter glory it leaves to its two rivals, to Strasburg and Amiens. It still remains unequalled in the higher beauties of true grace of proportion and in simplicity of design.

The note of contrast between such a noble architectural feature as this spire and this smiling pastoral setting was touched again with singular felicity, we found, in the first full view we had of the cathedral, set in the midst of its beautiful close.

In our subsequent walks about the little provincial streets of the city the presence of one of the greatest cathedrals in England would be scarcely suspected, so concealed is the magnificent structure behind its ramparts of walls and trees. Salisbury

SALISBURY CATHEDRAL, FROM THE CLOISTER.

Page 232.

is, I believe, the only walled cathedral in England. In the reign of Edward III. a license was granted for an embattled wall to be built around the enclosure, which contains the cathedral itself, the Bishop's Palace, the broad sweep of turf, and a number of smaller houses belonging to the cathedral. The walls are pierced by four gateways. The cathedral enclosure is in reality a city within a city. Once past the formidable-looking St. Anne's gateway with its quaintly ancient chapel overhead, one has the sense of treading consecrated ground.

The cathedral rests its grand base on a clear, wide sweep of turf. The velvet of the lawn runs close to the roughened edges of the foundation stones. The trees are removed at wide distances, and form no part of the immediate surroundings; so that the wonderful structure stands clear and free. From its base to the diminutive apex of its spire there is nothing to break the fulness and grandeur of the effect of the structure as a whole.

Next to the completeness of the genius which could conceive and erect such a building, is the talent which knew just how best to place it. Salisbury is as perfectly placed as if Phidias had had a hand in it. There is much, indeed, in this cathedral to remind one of Greek workmanship. Its supreme air of high finish, the perfection of its proportion, its aerial grace, and its ideal symmetry all recall the greater works of those masters whose creations must forever remain the models of the world. One is under the same stress of necessity to view this cathedral from all sides and from every point of view as seizes upon one in gazing at the great statues of antiquity. The cathedral may be said to be as complete as the most perfect Greek statue. Much of the same airy grace, the lightness, and, more than all, that bloom which the best Greek work irradiates, belongs also to this cathedral; the bloom that is only to be found at the most perfect moment of the growth and virility of an art. Salisbury was built at the most fruitful period of England's building era. Its inspiration came when architecture had attained the meridian of its technical skill, and when the art had been domiciled long enough to be capable of producing a truly national and original creation. Salisbury is as representative, as typical, and as national as the Parthenon. It is supremely English. It is so pre-eminently English, indeed, that it can still stand as the embodiment of its religion, of that form which alone is suited to the English religious taste and to its spiritual temper,—the form of the Established Church, a religion governed by law, administered by ceremonial, yet freed from despotism and therefore typically English. Salisbury is the ideal cathedral of such a religion. It was made for beautiful ceremonials which yet should have a congregational form,—for ceremonials which would have no need of the mysteries of Catholic symbolism. Its builders, though Catholics and Catholics of the thirteenth-century blindly-believing order, were nevertheless Englishmen before they were Catholics. In those soaring lines, in that vast yet orderly-disposed mass, in the rich yet serious tracery, and in the grandeur of the harmonious outlines, the English talent for moderation, its genius for order, its love and delight in wise reticence, and its insistent demands for unity and proportion are revealed and embodied. If England were now capable of producing so complete an architectural work, her genius would again run into this early Gothic mould,—into this precise mould which she made her own,—into the Early English, of which Salisbury remains as the most perfect example.

Another of the causes which combined to complete the perfection of this cathedral was the fact of its having been built within the short period of thirty-eight years. The plan of the original designers was thus scrupulously adhered to, not altered and changed and then the structure itself finally torn down to suit still later innovators, as has been the fate of almost every other cathedral in England. This admirable celerity of execution proves the freedom and the skill attained by its builders. It again reminds us of the Greek workmen who could design and complete the buildings on the Acropolis in thirty or more short years.

The history of the building of the cathedral comes down to us begirt with the usual decorative embellishments of legend and superstitious romance. That the old Sarum Cathedral, which had crowned the old hill fortification, being successively Brito-Roman, Saxon, and Norman, had for centuries exercised its jurisdiction over half the southern diocese of England, history affirms. Also that in the time of Bishop le Poer, this ancient church was found suffering from a number of inconveniences, such as scarcity of water, exposure, and the insults of the soldiery quartered in the castle hard by, is likewise no fable. But the modern imagination finds itself lacking in flexibility when asked to believe that the site of the new cathedral, in the smiling fertile valleys of the plain, was determined by an arrow shot from the ramparts of old Sarum; and one's credulity rebels at an acceptance of the other alternative offered, that of believing that the site was revealed to the bishop in a dream by the Blessed Lady in person. The subsequent building of the church was carried along under the impetus of a religious fervor in keeping with this latter statement. A great body of the nobles, returning with the king from Wales during the laying of the foundations, went to Salisbury, "and each laid his stone, binding himself to some special contribution for a period of seven years." Little wonder that the cathedral grew apace. It grew so fast that, begun in 1217, it was completed in 1258, the cloisters and chapter-house being added in the latter part of the same century. The history of the spire is less assured. It seems a question whether or not it formed a part of the original plan; but, erected in 1330–1375, it now stands as the fitting completion to crown the noble structure. Two supremely interesting features in the external design are noticeable at a first glance,— the boldness of breaking the general outline by two transepts instead of one, and the beauty and simplicity of the apsidal portion. The western front, compared with these two strikingly original features, loses in impressiveness, although in design it possesses a unity in composition rarely seen in English fronts. The perfection of finish so noticeable in the exterior of Salisbury is due to the marvellous care taken to insure accuracy in the masonry. As soon as one part was finished, it was exactly copied in the next; so that the completed whole presents an exactness and precision hardly paralleled, perhaps, in any other great building. This high degree of finish is in some measure accountable for the fault of severity in outline and the lack of shadow so often commented upon in this cathedral; but the supreme elegance and the rare unity attained more than outweigh such defects.

The same perfection of finish that characterizes the exterior is found in the interior. The halls of a palace could not be more consummately radiant in their perfection. The eye wanders in dazed delight over the glistening floor, over the glittering marbles, and the polished Purbeck shafts. The green of the latter material is only appreciable when polished; so that although the ten great bays with their clustered columns are all of Purbeck, only the shafts gleam with color. The eye sweeps in unencumbered freedom from length to length of the gloriously vaulted nave. The finely wrought embroidery of the brass choir-screen separates the apsidal portion of the cathedral from the nave; thus the cinque-cento glass in the Lady Chapel is clearly visible from the extreme western end.

At the Reformation, although Salisbury was spared the usual barbarities inflicted by the Commonwealth soldiery on the great cathedrals, it did not escape the fate of abandonment and desolation. Its true profanation was left for more experienced hands. In 1791 the architect Wyatt, with his original views as to how the eighteenth century could improve on the thirteenth, swept away screens, porches, chapels, tombs; he " flung stained-glass by cart-loads into the open ditch; destroyed ancient paintings, and levelled with the ground the campanile, which stood on the north side of the church," — all of which astonishing iconoclastic changes were deemed by the authorities of his time as "tasteful, effective, and judicious." Fortunately the unique and beautiful triforium, with its thickly clustered columns and its airy open arcade, as well as the splendor of the magnificent vaulting in the roof, escaped; in the upper stories of the cathedral, at least, the original work of the builders remains unspoiled. Among other changes Wyatt ordained that the knights and warriors, the courtiers and their stiff-stomachered spouses, should be ranged in two long rows beneath the arches of the great aisles. It is a monstrous arrangement, and yet it produces a certain grandeur of effect. These mailed warriors, these courtiers in ruffles and lace, these Elizabethan-ruffed countesses, — the former grasping their swords as if seeing in every gazer a Crusader's enemy; others, more at peace with the world and not quite so sure of heaven, lying with hands stiffened in supplication; while the ladies, of course, are cast in the very image of piety, — this goodly company looked not unlike some ghostly band, kept here to guard the sacred precincts. In the monuments every period of mortuary art is represented, from the era of the rudest sculpture to the refined and all too elegant creations of Flaxman, — "another lost mind," as Ruskin graphically describes this sculptor. There is the same massing of picturesque historic fates here as at Winchester; bishops and princes, courtiers and nobles, beauties and frail ones, having passed the dark portal, their effigies remain to commemorate their virtues and their deeds. Among the beauties lies the Countess of Pembroke, —

> "The subject of all verse,
> Sidney's sister, Pembroke's mother," —

whose epitaph has been written by a hand which will long outlast the limner or the engraver on more perishable marble or brass.

To be deeply stirred by these bygone histories, or even to vibrate to any very profound impression, when under the influences of the singularly cheerful atmosphere which pervades this cathedral, would be, I think, difficult. It may be owing to the particularly light and open character of the architectural effects, resulting from Wyatt's changes, to the absence of deep shadow in the mouldings, to a certain sense of thinness and meagreness produced by the severity of the decorations, and also, perhaps, to the fact that there is almost no old stained-glass remaining to insure enriching, sobering tones; but certain it is that Salisbury, in spite of its perfections, fails in impressiveness. It is not that the splendid edifice is lacking in grandeur or in dignity; but the resplendent light which penetrates into every portion of the vast building, and the extraordinarily airy, soaring character of the architectural lines, impart to this cathedral an unwontedly joyous aspect, one as far removed as possible from solemnity.

Cathedrals have a very distinct and unique climate of their own. The atmosphere of Salisbury differs as widely from the dusky twilight which underhangs St. Peter's vast dome as noonday differs from the hour of the setting sun.

The blithe and active verger, who had been busy locking companies of tourists into the choir and out of the cloisters since our arrival, seemed imbued with a spirit and temper which were doubtless the result of his cheerful surroundings. He had the alert vigor of an American stock-broker. His brisk business-like air and the hospitality of his smile were suggestive of a transatlantic personality, even reaching to the lengths of a really instantaneous appreciation of a joke.

Some tattered flags were suspended over a chantry in the choir. As the little verger appeared to have forgotten their existence, Boston asked their history.

"Oh," he replied, with a quick, soft little laugh, "I was n't goin' to mention 'um, sir;" then after a pause, filled up with another laugh, "since they was to commemorate our victories in the War of 1812."

"We don't mind your little victories," said Boston, quietly; "but — we don't see any flags of 1776." Whereat the red-faced Britons composing our party smiled, but rather feebly, while the bustling little verger laughed outright.

The two chief features in our tour of inspection were the chapter-house and the cloisters. The former is a little model of elegance. Of a later date than the cathedral, it reproduces the era when French geometric tracery was most in vogue in England. Next in interest to the charms of refinement furnished by the light gracefulness of lines whose intersections are like harmonies in a musical accord, are the sculptures filling the voussoirs and the spandrels of the arcades. These latter, even in their restored condition, brilliant as they are in modern paint, their decay having been helped out by the guessing of the modern chisel, still remain as among the most interesting of the specimens of early Gothic art. The sculptures under the windows within the chapter-house were the effort, also, of the chisel to substitute figures for the inspired pages of the Bible. Here the Creation, from the group of a very pre-Raphaelite Adam and Eve under a grotesque tree in the act of eating forbidden things, to the dramatic scene in which Moses is represented as striking the rock, is reproduced with remarkable truth and earnestness. The nationality of the sculptors is revealed in the fact that the vines in Noah's vineyard are trained on trellises in the Italian fashion.

All appearance of foreign influence is lost in turning into the cloisters. Here again the inspiration of the true English genius reasserts itself. The style of these rich elaborate arcades, with their thickly clustered columns and the large trefoiled decorations in the unglazed windows, marks a later development of the Early English than that seen in the cathedral; but the same grave severity of character is retained. Nothing more beautiful could be imagined than one's walks around those quadrangular cloisters. The contrast of the long gray arcades and the graceful ornate windows with

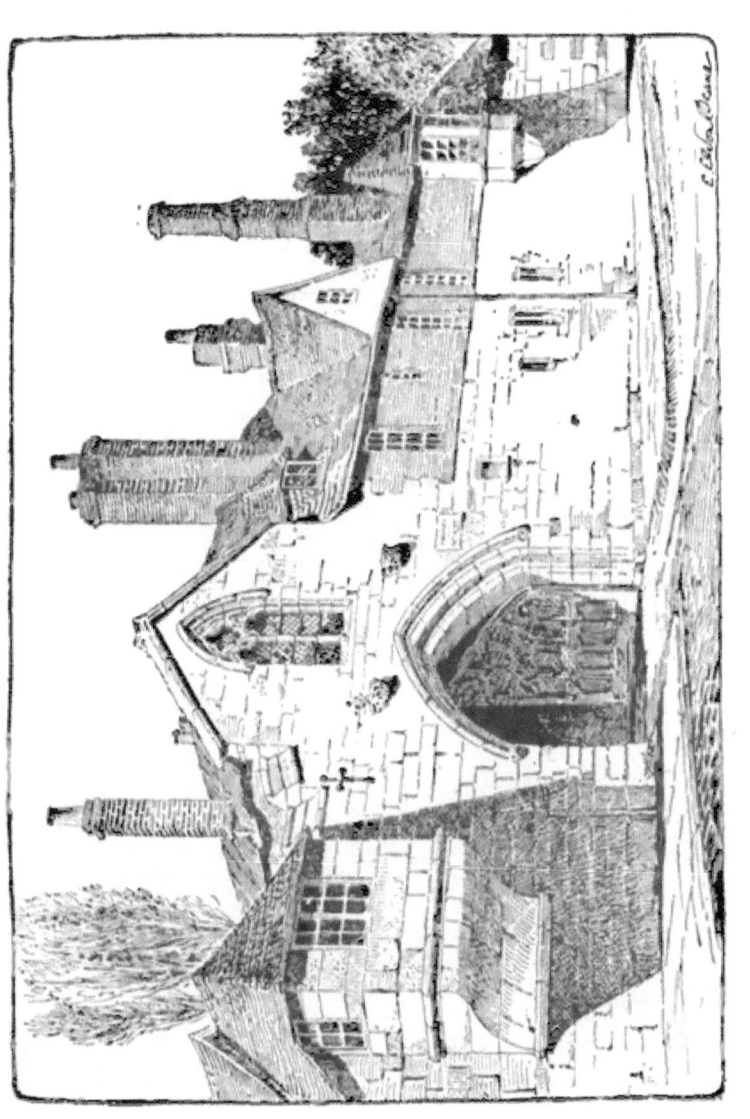

GATEWAY TO CATHEDRAL CLOSE, SALISBURY.

the smooth green cloister-garth, the patches of blue sky framed in the trefoil openings, and the dark shade cast on the greensward by two fine cedars, the sole inhabitants of this marble airy palace, form one of the most beautiful combinations conceivable of the delicacy of art and the refinement of nature.

The Englishman is never more an artist than when to noble architectural effects he adds the delicate yet perfecting note of a rural surrounding. Even the Italian may learn from him in this. The Italian, having been born of a prodigal mother, leaves too much to chance in his arrangement of natural effects; but the Briton has a master touch in the grouping of trees and in the laying out of a sward. He knows that as art lives by contrasts, so a great and beautiful edifice gains by the same subtle law. Who but an Englishman would have had the daring not only to group those low ecclesiastical buildings in the close so near to the magnificent cathedral, with its dwarfing spire and mountainous roof, but also to place about the green those charmingly lovely Elizabethan and Queen Anne houses, whose red gables and brown and gray roofs delight the eye with their broken irregular perspectives; whose ivied walls, trellised windows, and tiny blooming window-panes, with their suggestion of sweet domestic uses and of home-life, blend in perfect accord with the noble temple yonder, built for a great people's prayers?

The Englishman, whose home is his shrine, brings it to his church's altar, that it may rest within its bosom and blessing; and thus the cathedral, in the midst of these blooming homes, stands like some antique temple on whose steps garlands have been strewn.

CHAPTER XI.

STONEHENGE. — WARMINSTER. — LONGLEAT. — FROME.

THE afternoon of our departure from Salisbury was one of radiant loveliness. It was a perfect English day, one of those that seem to make fine weather in England different from any other. There is a peculiar quality in the best English weather, something at once rare and fine, from which all the vulgar pomp of over-luxuriance of sunshine and excess of heat and warmth appear to have been miraculously eliminated. If England, as a country, is the most perfectly finished agriculturally, from the point of view of climate it is assuredly the most highly civilized. It knows neither the extremes of heat nor cold; it is temperate, restrained, and when in fine humor, never loses its repose or its reserve. It is the climate of all others to produce a race of great men, — men who shall be as wise as they are courageous and as tender as they are strong; for men, like nature, come to their finest flower under temperate skies.

The weather had no reserves for us that afternoon. The fine golden light fell like a shower upon the land. Never had English turf seemed greener, or the hedge-rows more fragrant, or the trees more nobly tall and full, or the meadows richer in tone and color. The cottage windows were ablaze with carnations. The vines were laden with their burden of roses. In the fields the very cattle felt the influences of the fine soft air, of the pure ethereal sky, and of the odors and perfume which the earth sent up as its incense of praise and worship. Under this sky of blue, in this bath of warm air, the oxen moved lazily, luxuriously, treading their deep furrows with an absent, dreamy look, their dull natures insensibly stirred by the loveliness and the fairness of the hour. Men stopped their work to lean on their hoes and rakes. They shouted across a field or two, for in such weather man has the instinct of companionship; there is a compelling sentiment in such skies as these. Doubtless, if a girl or a woman had appeared, we should have witnessed a bit of rustic love-making; but only the field-hands and farmers were abroad in the wide grain-fields.

The drive out from Salisbury had been through a series of green fields, parks, and meadows. In an incredibly short time we had gained the open country. These rich, fertile valley-lands made progress swift and easy. Our drive was to include a climb into the hill-country, up into the famous Salisbury Plain that we might see Stonehenge; thence we should proceed to Warminster, in all comprising a distance of eighteen or twenty miles. As there were complications in the matter of roads, we had armed ourselves with two county maps and a guide-book, and had taken besides the additional precaution to receive minute and particular directions from the innkeeper of the "White Hart." We started forth equipped, in confident certainty; but behold, not five miles from Salisbury, we were at a stand-still. We were facing an opening of four roads. The county maps, with characteristic impartiality, gave us the choice of all four, as all lead up into the hill country, but did not enlighten us as to which one went directly to Stonehenge. The guide-book treated the subject with the fine scorn of a book whose pages were dedicated to a history of Druidical ruins. The innkeeper had been wiser than either, and had not even mentioned them. So we sat still and discussed the perplexity, knowing by the interrogatory movement of Ballad's ears that he was quite as much in doubt as we.

Suddenly a foot-passenger appeared walking towards us on the right-hand road,— a gentleman carrying a fine bunch of roses in his hand. As he drew near, to our question as to which was our road he responded with charming courtesy, coming close to the carriage wheel as he answered,—

"Your road is to the left along the river; but farther on you must turn to the right, and still farther to the left again. If you will allow me I will mark it out."

He laid the roses on the travelling-rugs, drew a pencil and a bit of paper from his pocket, and proceeded to sketch, with remarkable swiftness and skill, a rough draught of the direction of the road. A moment later, barely waiting to receive our thanks, he had lifted his hat and proceeded on his way.

"And there is a tradition extant that Englishmen are rude!" I exclaimed, as Boston plied the whip on Ballad's dark coat.

"Englishmen are only rude when they travel. It is their way of carrying war into an enemy's country."

"If they leave their politeness at home, they assuredly forget none of the practices of the art!" I answered, with the soft tones of our helper's London voice and the readiness of his kindly impulse still strong upon me.

His sketch served us better than the maps or the guide-book. In an hour we were toiling up the first long hill of the Salisbury Plain.

We had passed, in an hour's space, into a world as changed as if an enchanter's wand had whirled us from a fairy-land of verdure to the abode of some aerial sprite dwelling in a desert. Salisbury Plain is an endless succession of hills, sans verdure, sans trees, sans water, sans anything that grows save grass, and a short stumpy inferior quality of that. Far as the eye can reach it rests on a ripple of these low, barren, naked hills. To make the descent of one is to begin the ascent of the next. This unending succession of undulatory lines ends by producing the impression of an arrested sea. It seems as if earth at some time in her changeful history must have been possessed of the fluctuant instability of the ocean's turbulent element. Nothing but the sea, when possessed by the demon of unrest, could be imagined as the fitting comparison to a bit of earth so full of strange contortions, of restless undulations, and of unstable outline.

The land is as barren and as uninhabited as the sea. There was no sign of hamlet or hut in all the wide expanse. The only proofs of man's existence we saw were those of his labor. A few hay-mounds here and there reared their pyramidal tops against the sky. A curse seems to have been laid on this strange fantastic tract of country,— the curse of desolation. Man, like nature, appears to have abandoned these bald hills to their fate. Desolation and sterility of foliage are so infrequent in verdant England as to make this striking note of contrast the more impressive. On our own wide continent earth has a hundred different faces, as she has many climates and temperatures; but the wonder grows that here, in this compact little island, there should be room for so many varied aspects and such sharp transitions. It appears, however, as if it were meant that England should be an epitome of earth, as man is himself Nature in miniature; and thus the Salisbury Plain is to be taken as a kind of sample specimen of the barren and the desolate.

History and tradition come to accentuate the emphasis of romance and weird unreality which nature has outlined. These hills have been as enriched by the vicissitudes of human experience as they are barren of any reliable records which shall reveal them.

The only rival of the hay-ricks are the barrows, — ancient burying-mounds, so ancient, indeed, that their history is lost in conjecture. The multiplicity of their number appears to prove at least that only an army could have yielded dead enough to people so vast a burying-ground. Here many a strong Roman and fair-haired Saxon found their long home. The plain, for centuries before the Conquest, was the natural battle-ground of the rude disputants for Britain's sovereignty. Celt and Roman alike had early seen the military value of these heights. Camps and rude fortifications held the more advantageous positions long before, with vast labor and at huge outlay and cost, the great fortress of old Sarum was built. If ever a battle-ground was in keeping with the horrors of war, this gaunt skeleton of earth's beauty must have seemed, to even the least imaginative Saxon, a fitting arena for the clash of arms and for the dark work of killing and dying. Earth itself looks as if it had been stripped and then left for dead.

Suddenly, as we rose on the top of one of the hills, a mass of strange ruins stood out against the sky. Over the brow of the next hill they were facing us. Rude in outline, and of giant height, the huge gray stones, black against the pale sky, were as bare and naked as the land on which they rested. Here were no flowing draperies of ivy or the velvet of green moss to soften the rough outlines and to make a bit of poetry out of decay. The "hanging stones" of Stonehenge stand as pitilessly exposed to the winds of the bleak desert on which they rest as did the bleaching bones of the rude warriors who found their graves here. Like bones that have been whitened in the sun, washed to polished smoothness by the storm and rain, these cyclopean stones bear evidences of the slow but inevitable yielding to the elements. That king of architects, the Tempest, has carved this barbaric heap into shapes to suit his own fancy; he appears to have tossed the huge fragments about in riotous

STONEHENGE. *Page 254.*

glee, till their present fantastic attitudes and positions have become the despair of the archæologist.

On a nearer inspection, when we alighted and walked around the strange monument, we saw that such intention as could be read in the position of the stones clearly showed some attempt at the formation of a circle or a horse-shoe. But whether we believe with Inigo Jones that Stonehenge was once a Roman temple, or with the learned Dr. Charlton that it is a Danish ruin, or with other archæologists that the Druids here erected one of their puzzling shrines, the ultimate result remains the same. Conjecture finds no solid ground on which to build the certainty of fact. For once, at least, the tourist need not bow his head in ignorance and humility; his guesses are as good as those of his superiors in that line. Whatever mystic rites in pagan temple of gods or heroes Stonehenge may have been built to celebrate, whether the temple of a religion which is dead or of a god as forgotten as the believers, Stonehenge and the Salisbury Plain appeal to the beholder as does the Nile with its mysterious company of the Sphinxes, as solemn reminders of that great workman, the voiceless Past. Both belong to a time and to an era of whose life and history we have lost the key. That deep organ chord, modern sympathy, would doubtless, if furnished with the clew to these remote, shadowy lives and alien beliefs, bridge the gulf and vibrate still to those distant echoes; but earth, rather than man, appears to have retained the dread secret of their fate, and to have been cursed, in virtue of this knowledge, with eternal sterility. Nature, whenever she has a secret to guard, is stricken mute; time having found, doubtless, that she is possessed of the common failing of her sex.

An hour after leaving Stonehenge, it became a question whether or not we also might not end by finding on the Salisbury Plain a fate similar to other warriors who have wrestled with its difficulties and dangers. Ballad, quite suddenly and without warning, became very queer in his hind legs. He began his vagaries by slipping, on all fours, down one of the longer hills. This practice not being to his liking, he gave every evidence of its being his secret wish to roll down. Only an embarrassment of harness and Boston's obstinate grip on the bit prevented his accomplishing this unexpected freak.

"It's the hills, Boston, and no wonder; there has been nothing but miles of them since leaving Salisbury," I cried, as we both alighted.

An examination proved that it was worse than rebelliousness. It was not the hills; it was a question of ankles. Both hind ankles bent completely beneath his weight.

And we were fifteen miles from Warminster, our destination! Fifteen miles, and not a hut or even a hovel to be seen!

We looked at each other as the full meaning of the disaster burst upon us. We then sat down by the roadside, and held a consultation, as Romans and Britons had done before us. Either the horse was dead lame, or he was dead tired. To settle the question, it would be best to experiment while he was still comparatively alive. The result of our efforts proved that he could walk perfectly well on a level without giving any symptoms of fatigue; also that he could ascend a hill without more than his habitual protest against being hurried. But at the first beginning of an incline came the terrifying droop of the hind quarters, a look in his eyes as if the world were going from beneath him, and that dread bending of the hindermost ankles. The ankles on examination seemed to be neither bruised, nor inflamed, nor sore to the touch; but when going down-hill, a pair of india-rubber adjustments would have served him quite as well.

However, we must push on or prepare to spend the night on this desolate road. Push on we did, literally. Boston pushed the carriage up the steeper hills, making an improved brake of himself going down, as I tugged vigorously at the bit.

This mode of procedure brought us, at the end of an hour, to a rude little hamlet lying in a valley. The hamlet consisted of a dozen or more huts and thatched houses and a small tavern. The landlord of the latter was at our bridle before we had fairly reached the first house. The village grouped itself in various attitudes of curiosity and interest. Every man present felt of Ballad's ankles, while every woman freely gave her opinion; but none could tell us more than we ourselves had discovered.

"He's not a-gone lame, sur, and he ain't been stung, nather. It's a bit of weakness, sur, — he ain't used to the hills," was the innkeeper's reassuring verdict. "He'll go along safe now if you case him a bit."

"All the same, I'd rather stop here over night," I whispered to Boston.

"In this wretched tavern? Why, it's impossible," he answered, in what I feared was an almost audible tone.

"Oh, I don't in the least mind. Can you give us a room?" I asked of the innkeeper.

The man's face fell.

"We 'er full, ma'am, thank ye, ma'am," pulling his forelock; "we haven't a bed left."

At his answer a woman's face emerged from a side door, flourishing two arms up to the elbows in flour paste.

"Perhaps the Pierces' would take 'em, John," she cried out; then she as suddenly withdrew.

"They're quite respectable folk half a mile up the road, and takes travellers in now and again," explained the innkeeper.

"But can't you take us in yourself?" I almost pleaded; for the twilight was falling fast, and Ballad in his present condition, and the prospect of fifteen miles more of this desolate country to pass through, did not appeal to my imagination.

"I'm sorry enough, ma'am, but we can't;" and his face fell again.

The crowd, instead of thinning, had been growing larger. Some farm hands, evidently fresh from the fields, and bearing equally strong evidence of having come fresh from something less harmless, pressed emphatically about the carriage. One or two were unmistakably drunk. One whom Bacchus had rendered bolder than the rest pushed his way towards me, and began to sing a coarse song in my honor. The innkeeper gave him a blow that sent him and the song in the dirt. The women snickered, and the men laughed.

Evidently this was no place for us, whether Ballad had ankles or not; so we whipped the latter's unoffending back, and with a curt good-evening were off.

The country was again as desolate and hilly as before. The moon, on which we had relied as our lantern after the night should set in, with the usual obstinacy of her nature when counted on for a particular exhibition of her powers for shining, had sulkily retired behind a cloud. Again neither house nor building was visible. Never was there such stillness. The sound of Ballad's heavy footfalls and our own voices made the loneliness and our remoteness seem the more oppressive. The dumb companionship of sheep and cows or the twitter of a bird's note would have been of infinite comfort, to reassure us that some link of life was near to connect us with the living, breathing, active world; but nothing save the echoes of our voices came back to us, as if even they had failed to find a home.

Reach Warminster we did, when the night and we were nearly spent. At last came the cheering light of the distant town. Earth took on more civilized forms, and the world looked very much as usual, set in the mould of a small provincial town, as we drove through the Warminster streets to our inn.

An experienced hostler the next morning explained the mystery of Ballad's ankles. Again the trouble lay not in the ankle, but in something else. It was in the carriage that the true difficulty was found. The latter had no brake. It had been built for the level country about Chichester. But for these obstinate hills a brake was not only essential, but it must be made of extra grappling-power. The hostler advised our waiting until we should reach Bath, as there were no good carriage-builders in Warminster. The hills between this town and Bath, which we hoped to reach in our next day's drive, were, he assured us, comparatively trifling.

We gave Ballad a day and a half in which to forget his late experience. When he appeared early on the following morning, he started off with such merriment and light-heartedness as proved that only our own lack of forethought had been to blame for the recent unpleasantness.

Our road to Bath was to include a drive through Longleat, the famous and splendid seat of the Marquis of Bath, and was to pass through Frome, one of the most ancient towns in Southern England.

Longleat is an easy distance from Warminster; but the heat and dust on the highway made the hours seem trebly long. Once within the gates of the great estate, however, and we experienced anew that peculiar sensation which we had noticed as belonging to all such parks. Beneath the airy avenues of the great trees we were in another climate. These vast, perfectly finished, and carefully arranged estates have a climate as distinct from the highway or plebeian fields and meadows as a great cathedral has from a glaring little wayside chapel. Beneath these plumed trees the noonday appears

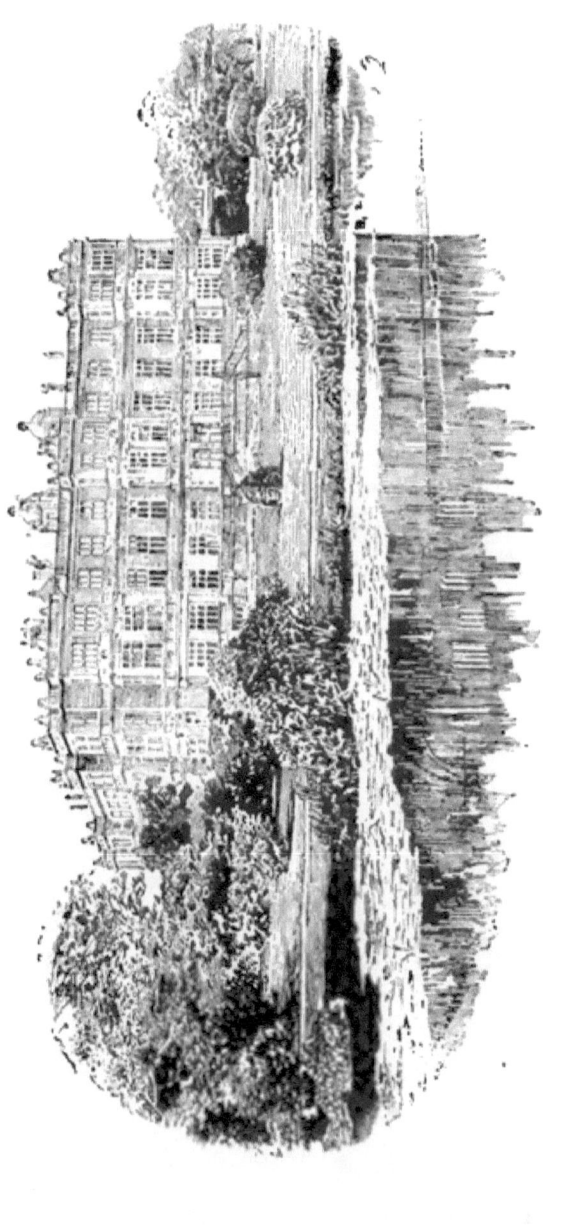

LONGLEAT HOUSE. *Page 262.*

never fully to penetrate; the glare of hot spaces of ground is unknown, so artfully are the laws of landscape-gardening administered; the stretches of turf and meadows are cooled by the well-placed groups of trees; they are broken by a fountain there, a gleaming pool beyond, by the rise and fall of hills with their trailing robes of shadows, or by the heart of gloom that dwells in the dense woods.

At Longleat the art of man is surpassed by the glories of nature. Somersetshire is perhaps the loveliest of the English counties. The romantic character of its scenery certainly places it among the most highly picturesque; and Longleat is set in the very heart of the county, where the blended loveliness of its hill and valley scenery, its superabounding richness and fertility, appeared to have focussed into highest beauty. From the celebrated Prospect Hill, the chief glory of Longleat Park, the eye sweeps over a glorious landscape; the country, dipping into the valleys beneath one, rises on banks of hills beyond to the very heavens; the noble trees on the hill have been spared and their foliage trimmed to form a natural frame to the enchanting outlook; thus the scene is broken into a series of pictures, a gallery whose masterpieces can be the better grasped and enjoyed.

With the inconstancy of true lovers of the beautiful, we decided that the charms of Longleat far exceed the glories of either Arundel or Goodwood. While it lacks the character of feudal splendor peculiar to Arundel, and the vast outlook to be had from the Goodwood heights, which command both the sea and the land, Longleat has a more highly finished air of magnificence than either. This effect is due not alone to the rich Somersetshire setting; the character of Longleat House is in itself singularly impressive. It is both a palace and a home. To the stateliness of the former it adds that air of domestic usage which the Englishman alone, of all the inhabitants of great mansions, has been able to impress on a huge pile of masonry. The house is nobly set on a vast carpet of turf, in the midst of glowing parterres. Its original builder, Sir John Thynne, the founder of the house of Bath, went to Padua for his architect, and the present building stands externally as John of Padua originally left it. It was built according to the style then in vogue in Italy, the Tuscan. But in spite of this most composite of the renaissance styles, the architect has made the great house more English than Italian. He borrowed his Doric columns and his Corinthian capitals from Greece, and the plan of his elevation from Italy; but the whole as a whole is pre-eminently English. It has a massive elegance and a soberness of dignity which have nothing in common with Italian architecture. The architect brought with him his love for immensity. The delight in the vast is inherent in the Italian, whose buildings and churches must be his refuge from the torrid skies and the burning suns of his tropical summer, and beneath whose roofs he seeks to find the breadth and largeness of his open-air spaces. Longleat House is a replica of the vast Italian palaces, whose walls seem to enclose acres of space. Its glorious dimensions make the historic visit of George III. and his queen with their suite numbering forty, over a hundred and twenty-five persons sleeping within the same house during the royal occupancy, no very wonderful feat of hospitality. In view of such a multiplicity of windows, doubtless each visitor found himself in undisputed right of both pillows.

Longleat, in the proud regalia of her history,

boasts not only the glory of entertaining royalty; her fame is further enriched with the shadow of romance, and darkened by the stain of crime. One of her earlier owners, Mr. Thomas Thynne, not having come into the world late enough to benefit by the wisdom of a recent philosopher, committed the indiscretion of marrying a widow. That she was beautiful goes without saying. That she was young — her previous lord, the Earl of Ogle, leaving her to learn all the wiles of widowhood at the tender age of twelve — relieves us of the necessity of pressing indignation to the point of abhorrence. In three years the lovely if youthful Lady Ogle had learned all the arts which belonged to her condition. She had succeeded in ensnaring the affections of the owner of Longleat, whom she married, reserving, however, all the joys of her favor for a rival, a noble Swedish count. Longleat never saw its new-made mistress. The bride, after the marriage ceremony, in spite of the magnificent preparations made at Longleat for her reception, suddenly developed a taste for a wedding journey. There could have been nothing very singular in so innocent a preference in a young beauty, who presumably wished to parade her happiness

and her new gowns before the world. But when
she went abroad with her trousseau, leaving the
groom behind to enjoy the bridal arches and the
Longleat festivities alone, her conduct, by her own
sex at least, was adjudged as savoring of eccen-
tricity. When, a short time after, the poor abandoned gentleman was shot and killed by four Polish
bullets instigated by Swedish hatred and Swedish
gold, the clew to the lady's erratic impulses appeared to have been found. But crime, it was discovered, was no better passport to the affections of
this singular, twice-widowed beauty than had been
her murdered husband's ardor. The Swedish Count
was dismissed, while she turned for solace to the
Duke of Somerset, drowning remorse, if so deep a
passion ever stirred the lady's becalmed soul, in the
intoxications of the political intrigues which made
Queen Anne's Court so admirable an arena for
restless spirits.

No shadow of crime or trace of tragedy rested
on the great house on that brilliant morning, as
we turned to take our last look at its splendor
and beauty. As if to dissipate even the memory of that dark occurrence, the sun had cleared
the skies of the wind-clouds, and was pouring

a flood of golden-dusted light over the huge gray pile.

There was fully an hour's driving before we were out of the Longleat Park, thickly peopled with its herds of deer and cattle scattered through its great lawns and woods; but an hour was none too long to linger over those seven miles of garden loveliness.

The remainder of the forenoon's drive to Frome was a continuation of the verdant valleys and the richly wooded uplands which we found made the charm and the picturesqueness of this beautiful Somersetshire County.

At Frome there was to be a long midday halt and rest. We had prepared ourselves for a vast outlay of admiration, since all early English history teems with recitals of Frome's importance and activity in early Celt and Norman days. We had counted on finding the Frome streets lined with picturesque houses and rich in an antique architectural setting. But the Frome of the dark ages must have disappeared with its ancient importance and dignity. Modern Frome we found chiefly a little town full of little shops, with only a series of hilly streets to give it even a moderately unique appearance. The centre of interest was no farther away than our inn. On our arrival we found an unwonted bustle and activity. There was a flying about of white-capped chambermaids and an agitation in the demeanor of the solitary waiter which announced at once that the extraordinary was about to take place. It was with difficulty that we succeeded in awaking even a response to our appeal for luncheon. Oh yes, they might be able to give us a luncheon if we could wait; in an hour maybe, or perhaps even later. Meanwhile we could sit in the smaller coffee-room. At high noon, with an English sun heated to summer heat, with a drooping horse before one and a hungry gnawing within, one is not disposed to be as actively belligerent against fate as when confronted with such trying circumstances under less helpless conditions. We meekly gave signs of accepting our destiny. Our humility, however, met with its reward. The landlady suddenly appeared in the large hall, resplendent in pink ribbons and a rustling black silk, and was immediately touched with the spectacle of our dejectedness.

"Mary, send up some cold 'am and beer and the muffins immediately; they won't be 'ere yet. — Hit's a party, ma'am," she continued, addressing me in an undertone of subdued excitement, "as his comin'; hit's the choir from the town, over heighty; and perhaps you'd like to see the tables, ma'am, while your luncheon's being spread." She led the way with smiling, triumphant complacency.

The tables were, in truth, a fine sight. There were four long dazzlingly white cloths spread on tables forming a quadrangle. Fine old shapes of antique glass and silver gleamed among the dressed hams, the tongues, the turkeys, the jellies and salads, each dish brave in its pretty toilet of curled papers.

"There's heighty covers laid, has you see," smiled the landlady, as she surveyed the spectacle with the eye of a general who had massed her forces and to whom the victory was already a foregone conclusion; "they're hall from one church, — the choir, and the wardens an' their wives, and the vicar himself and his lady, — and there they come now."

We stepped out on the balcony leading from our own modest coffee-room to look at the "heighty." The vicar and his lady were very easily picked out, and their identity established. The rest of the company were most unmistakably middle-class; farmers, smaller gentry, and provincial tradesmen composed the orderly mass that clambered out of the high drags and the long open wagons. The company embraced all ages, from the very youthful maidens who turned crimson with bashful self-consciousness as the equally crimson youths helped them to alight, to the venerable grandame and grandsire whose tottering steps were steadied by strong arms and filial care. Singularly enough, most of these people had a strangely familiar look. We were almost certain we had met most of their faces before, as, in truth, we had. The faces, or rather their prototypes, belonged to the owners of the quiet homesteads and the larger richer farms we had passed so often in our driving. Here were the stout motherly faces, a trifle redder and overheated now, and not so attractive in their over-trimmed bonnets as in the snowy caps, beneath which their calm eyes were lifted from the stocking-darning as Ballad's crisp footfall startled their ear. Here also were the old people, very smart in apparel, but quite as tottering and infirm as when they hobbled to the door-sill to see us pass. The younger girls and women were less recognizable in their prim Sunday attire, and assuredly not half so pretty as in their every-day costume of broad garden hat and apron.

Nothing could have been more orderly and soberly decorous than the behavior of the little congregation. Whether it was that the presence of the wardens and the vicar had a depressing effect, or whether this melancholy little band were merely suffering from the constitutional national malady,— that habitual dreary dulness which pervades all English holidays,— it is certain that if the success of the present occasion were to be gauged by its festival aspect, even its projector must have been haunted by the dark suspicion that it was resulting in failure. Since, however, the Englishman has not been brought up to associate the act of taking a holiday with the idea of pleasure, these loyal sons of the Church were doubtless munching tarts and genteelly disposing of ham without a suspicion that silence was not the most ideal compliment to their excellence. Even the many tankards of ale and beer which we saw going the rounds of the table appeared to have little appreciable effect on the flow of talk. Towards the last there did come from behind the swinging doors a subdued murmur of chit-chat, enlivened with a buzz of short low laughter. But to the end the awful presence of the vicar appeared to have its restraining effect; the talk was pitched to a church whisper.

I am disposed to believe that to our own soil have flown the wholesome heartiness, vivacious exuberance, and louder-tongued jollity in which older, gayer England was wont to indulge in those days when it seasoned its cake with that heartiness of enjoyment which won it its name of "merrie England." Our American way of taking pleasure may have a touch of plebeian plainness about it, considered from the standard of English reticence and self-restraint; but laughter — broad, strong, deep laughter — is one of the best national habits for a growing nation to cultivate. A people that laugh are a people who have little to fear from tyrants or despots, in whatever form they may come. An American joke keeps the political sky clear.

CHAPTER XII.

BATH.

FOR several miles before reaching Bath on our way out of Frome, Ballad had begun forcibly to resent the deceits practised on him by the suave hostler at Warminster. The hills, far from being trifling, might more truthfully have been described as formidable. What to Boston's and my own enraptured sight was a landscape rich in an altogether unexpected originality of character and formation, — steep conelike hills dipping into slits of valleys, hamlets and villages perched on the slanting inclines like nosegays on an Alpine-peaked hat, miniature waterfalls which looked as if turned on to order, a shining river running through the sinuous valley as if it were a liquid snake, quaint little chapels hanging in mid-air, and castles over whose battlemented walls we rode serenely, — a country, in a word, strangely fantastic for orderly, sober England, — was to

Ballad's weary and incompetent ankles only a land big with potentialities of suffering.

He had made a struggle, and a brave one, to put his best foot forward. He had had desperate spurts of energy going up the hills, ending in a complete collapse going down. The collapse had finally ended in rebellion. He refused even to attempt to propel his tired body an inch farther. Naturally, forcible measures were resorted to; but the strokes of the whip moved him as little as the most alluring entreaties. His feet remained rooted to the ground.

We were half-way down the long and truly magnificent descent of Coombe Down, one of the higher hills overhanging Bath. The city lay beneath us, — we could overlook its chimney-pots; but we had still before us at least two miles of steep down-hill work, and Ballad was beginning to show determined signs of his desire to lie down and die by the roadside. Die we were resolved he should not, at least not without the formalities of an attending physician and the privacy of a stable. Some means must be found to keep him on his legs.

"I never heard of a horse dying of weak ankles, did you?" I asked, a trifle nervously, as our poor beast again made a futile effort to take a little wayside repose.

Boston jerked the bit with such force that Ballad came very near performing a somersault in the air instead of accomplishing his own lazier intention.

"No, I never did; but it would be just our luck to have him invent a new way out of life. Get down, can you, alone? and can you take out a bag or two? The carriage must be lightened, and we must walk. You had better take the whip, and I'll lug the bags."

Such was our entrance into Bath! — Boston leading Ballad on one side, with the bags in the other hand, as I plied the poor creature with the whip.

It would have been funny even to us, as an incident in our experience, I think, weary and annoyed as we were; but what prevented our complete appreciation of the humorous side of the situation was the fact that the spectacle we presented evidently appealed to the humor of the passers-by. The people, indeed, as they passed, were at no pains to conceal their entire appreciation of the joke. Some inconsiderate draymen and farmers laughed outright. Children came to the gateways and snickered. The usual superfluity of street gamin shrieked and whistled in shrill glee. They attempted to form in line, as rearguard. Ballad had to be temporarily abandoned to his fate, as Boston plied the whip lightly about more responsive legs and ankles.

It is never the mocking jeers or the derisive laughter of the class below one which really hurts. What we term our own world alone has the power to inflict the deepest pain. What was really hard to bear were the suppressed smiles of the staid dowagers and the more open mirth of the large-hatted young ladies, who were out taking their late afternoon drive; for Bath at all seasons of the year, it appeared, is the abode of fashion. At the end of a half-hour I began to feel oppressively warm.

"Boston, would you mind holding the whip? I think he'll go now without being scourged all the time; the paving-stones seem to help him."

Once free, it was the most natural thing in the world to take to the sidewalk. Once there, it was the work of an instant to open a parasol. I had a comfortable sense now of having returned to the outward decencies of life. I even looked in at the shop windows, and took a flitting review of the Bath fashions. But in a weak moment I looked back.

Boston was still leading Ballad by the bit. Both were dusty, weary, and dejectedly travel-worn. The rubber cover was white with the pulverized macadam of the roadway. The bags were lopping over, and the umbrellas were sprawling about as if just recovering from an orgie. It was, in truth, a most disreputable-looking trap. In another instant I had returned to my post. One look at Boston's face, and remorse and contrition triumphed. I flew at the bags with that ardor which is born of repentance.

"At least I can carry these; it can't be very far now. Do you think he will last another half-hour?"

Boston was merciful. His quiver was full, but he did not make use of even his tiniest arrow. He could not, however, wholly conceal the smile which came when I resumed my place at Ballad's side, thus publicly acknowledging my renewal of relationship with them.

The remainder of the journey through the slippery, muddy Bath streets was accomplished under agonies of calculation. Was it best to urge Ballad on to the hotel, and would he hold together as a whole; or would it be wiser to have him and the carriage part company, and place both under shelter at the nearest hostelry, while we proceeded on our way? Some latent potentiality of will-force must have come to the rescue of our poor worn-out beast; for in spite of repeated slippings and fallings, in spite of renewed expression of his overmastering desire to lie down and be at rest, Ballad did nevertheless reach the imposing façade of the Grand Pump Room Hotel. It was one of those moments when the sense of deliverance is strong enough to assume, unconsciously, the form of a vague prayerful utterance.

In entering a city we had returned to all the stirring activities of city life. Bath was so real a city that it actually possessed horse-cars. Since leaving London we had been as free from their monotonous jingling as one can hope to be in a world now bent on rapid locomotion; but here again were these ugliest and most useful of conveyances, as crowded with citizens as is compatible with an Englishman's sense of justice.

We decided that Bath, in spite of its English-looking horse-cars, was the most foreign-looking city we had seen on English soil. It had a surprisingly continental air. It had the charm of the unforeseen, the attraction of the unexpected. Who would have thought of building a city in so small a valley, — a valley so narrow that its streets must needs run up the hills, like vines along a lattice? The least serious-minded inhabitant would have laughed such a plan to scorn. Yet here it is, — this charming, audacious lovely little city, — lying as contentedly in its valley as a rose in the hollow of a cup. The hills appear to step directly out of its streets. The streets, nothing daunted, climb diligently after them, till at a distance the landscape ends by describing those amazing perspectives so abundantly introduced by Albrecht Dürer into his drawings, where hill and city seem about to overwhelm the subjects in the foreground. Here are the same quaint juxtapositions, — the carefully tilled patches of ground, interspersed with stiff façades, and a spire now and then to break the uniformity. In Bath this combination of altitudes and depressions is finely alternated with the majestic aspect of the remoter hills.

The street life of the city has a compelling

magnetic attraction. One's walks become a succession of surprises and discoveries. No one street is like another. If one thoroughfare be on a comparative level, the next will seem to run straight up into the sky, or will take an abrupt French leave, disappearing round a corner to plunge into some subterranean depth. The question of just how much there is of interest for the tourist in Bath comes, in the end, to depend very much on whether or not he is a good walker. One may safely intrust one's self to the more luxurious methods of locomotion, for a reviewing of the fine panoramic effects of the outlying hills; but to learn all the secrets which this bewildering little city holds, one must have the strength and the ardor of the pedestrian.

We were waiting for the brake to be made, and also to see what effect a temporary rest might have upon Ballad. In the mean time our leisure was employed in making a number of interesting discoveries. Among other curiosities, we had stumbled on a nest of enticing little alley-ways in the older portion of the town. Dark, mysterious-looking passages, and queer, quaint worn steps led into still quainter streets; a whole serial, in fact, of old-time fragments and historic suggestiveness, we found, could be picked up in instalments along these out-of-the-way paths. Houses and streets seemed made to order for the most lurid tragedy-novelist's imaginative requirements. Mysterious disappearances could be effected along these murderous-looking streets with a turn of the hand, as it were, without even the usual formality of a trap-door. The houses, built on top of one another, looked as if hung out to dry on the hillsides; the secrets they held being doubtless in need of an airing. At twilight or in the dark of early night the most innocent shape, as it flitted through the evil-minded gloom, took on a tragic aspect; its very shadow seemed to pursue it with fiendish intent. Such spectral charms made the more modern parts of the city — the severer façades of the Royal Crescent — seem a fable. In these dingy byways the past lost its vague dimness, and seemed alive again, as if reborn under the touch of some conjurer's wand.

Under the glare of broad noonday still another phase of this older city's life revealed itself. As if to keep the streets and houses in countenance, a remnant of hardier, coarser England appeared to have survived the transformations of the last few centuries. To look on the strong brutalized faces of the men who fill these streets with gossiping groups at twilight, gathering in front of the open butchers' stalls, where the blood-flowing on warm days in no wise appears to disturb the sensibilities of the hardy stomachs; to listen to the men's deep rough laughter and their burly speech,—is to realize that England, like all old countries, hides in her forgotten pockets survivors still of that tough mediæval people, the roysterers of King Henry VIII.'s reign or the fighters of Elizabethan days, to whom contact with the more brutal sides of life presents no horrors. Nerves and sensibilities are a modern growth. We of the nineteenth century are the highly strung instruments, fitted to be played upon by steam-whistles, railways, mowing-machines, pistol-shots, and the racking noise of great cities. In our day ingenious man is the inventor of his own torture. In the Middle Ages the pleasing task of testing to what lengths human endurance could go was wisely left to the rack and to persecution-workers. Outside of dungeons and dark council-chambers, life was lived with keen animal ferocity of enjoyment. In looking on this remnant of that earlier system, in gazing on these giant frames and ox-like faces, with features and expression born of strong appetites and the latent strength that comes of surplus muscle, one is led to conjecture whether, after all, our modern diseases of exposed nerves and over-active sensibilities are not questionable gains. But the man who is great enough to turn back to form himself on these robust models, and who will contribute his experiments in primitive brutality to our inert age, is still to be born. The modern reformer is no better than the rest of us; he persists in believing in the future, — that poor over-mortgaged country, that issues to each one of us such unlimited letters of credit.

In sharp contrast with the physical hardihood to be seen in the Bath slums is the invalidism that from time immemorial has been the *raison d'être* of Bath. Fashionable Bath is nothing if not the "city of the sick man." All the life of the little city localizes itself about the springs and the baths. The invalid's throne is his Bath chair, and he is the most peripatetic of monarchs. In whatever part of the town one may chance to be, one meets two lines of invalids, — a slow solemn procession of believers going up in hope and faith to the Temple of Hygeia, the Grand Pump Room, and another line of pilgrims returning from the same. In the open square in the heart of the city, on which the Pump Room and the Abbey Church face, the little army of sufferers meet to saunter, lounge, and gossip. The Bath chairs are drawn up in line against the buildings facing on the square. With their hoods open, they look not unlike so many yawning graves. He who enters one, indeed, appears to have already opened tacit negotiations with the dread monster. But Englishmen would not be Britons if they failed in heroism even under the hood of one of these dismal hearses. The foxes of pain and anguish may be gnawing their vitals, but English pluck keeps bravery well up in front. To watch gouty and rheumatic England sipping relief from the steaming glasses in the Pump Room is a lesson in heroism. It is a regiment of soldiers performing a drill under orders. It is only the limp that betrays any evidence of suffering. The faces are as impassive and as immobile as so many masks.

On the faces of the wives and daughters of these heroic martyrs a fine observer might detect quite another expression. It is the look of those who also suffer and endure; but the mingling of pain and courage which compose it is of a very different character. It is one of enforced submission. Even a hero must draw his line of repression somewhere. An Englishman considerately draws it at his own family. The world must be met with a Spartan face, but the true Briton provides himself with a family pillow on which to do his private groaning. Thus gout is turned into a direct spiritualizing agency, and the submissive expression of angelic patience and sweetness which the rest of the world so admires in English wives is a product of home manufacture conducted on the strictest principles of economy.

In a circular recess of the Grand Pump Room is a statue of one of the two monarchs who have made Bath famous. This one is the statue of its last and uncrowned king, Richard Nash. In the King's Bath yonder is the effigy of its first ruler, King Bladud. This latter is doubtless a most accurate reproduction of the original, since beneath the statue runs an inscription to the effect that "he was the founder of these baths 863 years before Christ." The statue of one king is aureoled with legend and mystery; the effigy of the other with the halo which belongs to leadership, by whatever name it is known. The two kings between them mark the Alpha and the Omega of Bath grandeur. The periods are nearly two thousand years apart; yet, with the exception of a brief and temporary period of illumination, Bath may be said only truly to have lived at these two widely distant eras. Its one other period of fitful activity was during the Roman occupation.

It is impossible to resist at times the impulse to insist on the analogy existing between features and character, not alone in man, but in that more mysterious portion of the universe which we call Nature. The history of some countries seems written on their landscape. That cities should reflect the character and the lives of the men who inhabit them is scarcely to be wondered at, since, as muscle is carved by mind, so is the outward aspect of a city determined by the life that peoples its thoroughfares. Nature, at times, seems also to lend herself to this mute handwriting. To look, for instance, on these Somersetshire hills about Bath,—at their sudden depressions and their impulsive heights of exaltation,—at the sinuous, variable, wayward little river running through its valley, at the sharp contrast existing between the richly wooded uplands and the naked barrenness of some of the hill-tops, at the mingled secrecy and abandonment of the landscape, the confidence of the forests and the betrayal of the open meadows, — is to divine that the adventures in experience of such a landscape have been a history richly diversified by incident and romance. The prose of fact, for once, comes to sustain the frail poetry of intuition.

Bath owes much of its varied and extraordinary history to its exceptional situation. Geographically, it had been gloriously endowed at its birth. Besides its beauty it has possessed an indefinable charm for mankind. Some cities possess such a magnetic potency. Man appears to divine their existence wherever he may dwell. He can no more resist seeking them out, dwelling in them, and beautifying them, than he can escape the fated fascination of any other of the irresistible forces of the universe. Bath has been from the dawn of history such a little magnet. Men have sought her out, here in her deep hollow, begirt by her thermal springs; they have brought their gods and their families; they have built baths and temples; they have lived and loved and roamed among her hills and along her lovely valleys; and then they have as incontinently deserted her. Others came to awaken the dead and forsaken beauty, to clothe her anew in loveliness, only in their turn to leave her to ruin and decay. Thus did those dwellers come, during the Stone Age, whose remains and ruins in Claverton and Lansdown Beacon prove this whole district to have been densely populated at least a thousand years before Christ. Thus came King Bladud and his train; then the Romans; then, during the great ecclesiastical period, the monks and bishops. Again came desertion; and finally Beau Nash appeared to put the little kingdom of the springs on a sure footing of order and established sovereignty.

Geoffrey of Monmouth's monkish chronicle relates, in a bit of pleasing narration, the first known discovery of the healing properties of the Bath waters. A king's son, Bladud by name, being afflicted with leprosy, was forced to turn vagabond. His father, Brutus, was the son of that hero whose wanderings Virgil sang, and who, after the destruction of Troy, came westward and conquered Albion.

But afflicted Bladud, for all he was a great king's heir, could find no nobler occupation, cursed as he was, than swine-herding. His pigs were, however, gifted with those phenomenal qualities common to pigs tended by royalty in distress. They in their turn, catching their keeper's terrible malady, proceeded to repair with great promptness to the hot springs in the morass in which Bath now stands. After a few baths, taken without the formality of professional consultation, the pigs became cured of their disorder. Their royal keeper, having had the benefit of a philosophic course at the schools of Athens, had acquired sufficient logic to enable him to make the following conclusion: "If the springs have cured my pigs, why will they not cure me?" Whereupon he promptly plunged into the morass. He emerged as cured as his swine. In consequence of which happy miracle, Bladud was enabled to make his bow at court. With the virtue so freely attributed to legendary heroes, the chronicle proceeds to narrate that Bladud inaugurated his own reign by building in the morass a grand city, plentifully supplied with baths for both rich and poor.

Whether or not the "grand city" survived till Rome came to take possession, is not authenticated. Rome, however, was sufficiently opulent to supply her own luxuries. This invigorating mountain air once sniffed by a Roman nostril; this lovely landscape once lit upon by the all-discerning Roman eye,—and the Roman knew a good thing when he saw it if ever a man did,—assured to Bath, for a century or two at least, the protection of its dominion. The charming hills were covered, as if by a miracle, with costly villas; parks were laid out, and terraces constructed to delight the eye and the taste of the pedestrian; roadways were constructed over the hills to the sea, along which Britons and American tourists still travel; the city itself was beautified with houses and temples and baths splendid enough to tempt the invalid across seas and continents,—for the distance from Rome to these hot springs of Bath was, after all, somewhat of a journey for a gentleman in Trajan's time. But then, what will not a man do if his liver be out of order? The Roman, however, it must be remembered, above all other travellers anticipated the nineteenth century in the ease and comfort of his travelling arrangements. He carried, so to speak, all Rome with him. He had only to unpack his Saratoga to feel entirely at home. Here in Bath, for instance, he soon found himself in a miniature Rome. If he needed to pass an hour in worship, he had the beautiful Temple of Sul-Minerva round the corner. If he repaired to the baths, he found as complete and as varied a club life as at home. He would hear all the morning's gossip in the Frigidarium, and in the Eliothesium he could be quite as certain as at Rome of being properly oiled and perfumed. Later in the day, a very fair contingent of fashionable Rome could be met taking the air along these Bath hills. Altogether, a Roman might do a worse thing than to settle here.

At a stone's-throw from our hotel, closely wedged in among the tall modern houses of the present city, lies a mass of ruins. One looks down upon an apparently undistinguishable medley,— on broken fragments of columns, on grand bases separated from their shafts, upon bits of richly sculptured capitals and traceried cornices. These shattered fragments are all that remain to make this lost page of Roman history a vivid reality. Archæologists point in triumph to the unmistak-

OLD ROMAN BATHS, BATH.

Page 292.

able traces of all the parts of these once great and beautiful baths, — to the leaden pipes which still exist, showing the entire plan of its heating apparatus; to the green pools where the gold-fish still show their scaly golden armor, descendants of those finny tribes that the Romans placed here; to the votive tablets and coins which the grateful had hung on the walls as tributes of their cure. But neither the historian nor the archæologist can do more than does this green sluggish pool of water which washes the broad mouldy steps of the bath leading into it: this shadowy pool reflects two cities, — the one in ruins, gathered in pathetic fragments near its margin; the other erect and intact above it, towering in the majestic solidity of the present. Such is the history of nations.

When Rome fell, Roman Bath died. It came to life again under the reign of the mediæval kings called bishops and abbots. Monks took the place of pagan epicureans. An abbey and a monastery replaced the Temple of Sul-Minerva, on that plan of economy which inspired the early Christians to make paganism serve God after its centuries of devotion to the devil. When the church became the cathedral of the diocese, John of Villula built a Norman structure befitting its dignity. In his time Bath was the bishop's seat. With the removal of that throne to Wells in the latter part of the same century, the Abbey Church fell into ruin and decay. The present abbey was rebuilt in the fifteenth century by Bishop King. Something of the grandeur of the former edifice may be inferred from the fact that this present Perpendicular building, of very respectable size, occupies only the site of the Norman nave. From the banks of the river, the abbey's embellished turrets, its pierced parapets and the pinnacled transepts group effectively with the surrounding plume-like trees and the city's picturesque sky-line. But this abbey, in common with other less complete buildings, is best seen at a distance. Like certain friendships, its excellences are heightened when seen in perspective.

The next and last page of the history of Bath reads like a fairy tale. It is centred in the life of one man,—an ideal prince of adventurers, who, it is true, never ascended a throne, and yet ruled as autocratically as any despot; who discovered, early in life, that in order to command men it is only necessary to guide their pleasures; that royalty will make quite as obedient subjects as commoners if it discover a monarch strong enough to issue the fiat of Draconian laws. Never was there a sovereignty, founded on such fictitious usurpation of power, so powerful and prosperous as the fifty years' reign of Beau Nash's kingship in Bath. This solemn adjuster of trifles, this master of the ceremonies of polite life, this rigid arbiter of fashion, who took dandyism as seriously as statesmen take statescraft, did for Bath what neither Rome nor bishop, nor kingly visitors had been able to achieve. He found Bath a city of dung-hills; he left it the beautiful and finished city which we now behold. In 1631 physicians did not dare recommend their patients to take the waters internally; "for the streets are dung-hills, slaughter-houses, and pigsties; . . . the baths are bear-gardens, where both sexes bathe promiscuously, while the passers-by pelt them with dead dogs, cats, and pigs," writes a certain Dr. Jordan. Another writer adds: "The roads are so bad it is scarce possible to get to the city in the winter. Every house is covered with thatch, and at every door hangs a manger to feed the horses, asses, etc., which bring coal and provisions into the town; and nothing but obscenity, ribaldry, and licentiousness prevail." Even ten years later, when Queen Anne made her famous entry into Bath, the city was still notoriously squalid, and the pleasures of the town were of the coarsest order. But Richard Nash, Esq., was a better ruler than stupid Queen Anne. When he came the face of things was changed. First he reorganized the pleasures, and then he reconstructed the city. The town, as we now know it, was either almost entirely the work of his direct energies, or the improvements were due to the impetus which the radical changes he wrought inspired. The new and enlarged streets, the churches and chapels, the Guildhall, the Grand Pump Room, the Stall Street baths, the numerous benevolent institutions, were the direct offspring of one man's genius for the organization of the pleasures of life. He may have been, as Goldsmith calls him in his inimitable portraiture, "the little king of a little people;" but the puerilities of his aim are dignified into grandeur in view of such wide-reaching and substantial results. The lesson of Nash's life is that it furnishes such a commentary on the relative values of human endeavor. How rarely are the noblest purposes and most heroic self-sacrifice rewarded as were the selfish petty ambitions of this man! Such may come to be the true secret of successful sovereignty, — that a prince should descend to the human popular level of presiding over quadrilles and issuing his fiat for the height of shirt-collars and the color of waistcoats, — to lead the fashion, in a word, both in manners and in dress, and thus make existence for simpler men a less expensive outlay of mental capital.

The sky is full of signs that the world will grow in wisdom with the coming centuries; but the world, be it ever so wise, will always have this point in sympathy with sheep, — whenever a leader arises it will be quite certain to follow.

In the mean time the brake had been finished, and Ballad, impatient of cures, having devoured all the oats within reach, had begun a species of refined cannibalism on his own person. He was eating his head off, the hostler said.

CHAPTER XIII.

THE DRIVE TO WELLS.—AN ENCHANTED NIGHT.

THE brake worked like a charm. It worked so well that we began to feel as if we had personally invented it. We experienced something of that joy which comes to a successful patentee. Ballard trotted merrily down the steepest hills; or rather, the merry trotting began after he had discovered the brake. At first, as a horse of enlightened intelligence, he received the evidences of its working-power with fine incredulity. At the top of the first hill he promptly reined himself in. In any other horse this self-assertive action might have been termed balking; but Ballad was too sensitive to outside influences to be classed among true balkers. A few caressive supplications, and he was induced to make a venture downwards. Then behold his amazement!—half of the weight of the carriage lifted and the vehicle held back, grappled as if by a hand of iron! He was as free from the load behind him now as if he had been on an independent flying expedition. Only the miracle, alas! was so far behind, so altogether hopelessly in his rear, that there was no chance of his ever being able to investigate it with satisfactory thoroughness. He had no choice but to walk, or rather to run, by faith. In view of our latter-day scepticism, it was beautiful to see how admirably a blind acceptance of hidden laws may work.

To get away from Bath was almost as serious a matter, in the amount of hill-climbing to be done, as it had been to reach the low-lying city. Just how deep is the valley in which the city rests, and how steep and high are the surrounding hills, can only be justly estimated by those who drive or by the pedestrian. As usual, we had not gone far before we found ourselves belonging to the latter class of journeyers. The brake, Ballad had been quick to discover, did not help him any the more in going up the long hills. He therefore speedily gave us to understand that a closer companionship, one which brought us nearer to his heart and head, would be more to his taste.

On this occasion we had determined to try a little rebellion on our part. Only recently, just out of Longleat, we had stumbled on a way of making the slow up-hill half-hours delightful. In rummaging in one of the bags for a remote and secretive pocket-flask, on our way to Frome, we had stumbled on a pocket edition of Shakspeare instead.

"Give it to me. It is a gift from the gods. Now we have something for the up-hill work. I can read a play as we walk along,— something we both know fairly well; then we'll drop it at the top, when the trotting begins, and begin again at the next long hill. What a find!" I had exclaimed.

The plan had worked as only a charm can. No more tedious dull moments, when the scenes in the landscape dragged, or the sun was too ardent a lover, or the wind too miserly to blow, or the hour just one short of starvation. Here were balm, contentment, and inspiration for the dull *entr'actes*.

On how many hill-tops had we not left a brace of those immortal lovers, whose woes and whose tearful joys are a part of our own intenser experiences! Viola, gay Rosalind and her Orlando, Egypt's dark enchantress and doomèd Anthony, or Romeo and Juliet, breasting their stormy sea of love,— such was the wondrous company we had conjured up as fellow-travellers. Even when the book was laid aside, thrust in between the two carriage cushions, in readiness to be pulled out at the next ascent, it was still the echo of that melodious passion and the rhythm of that ecstatic verse that filled the trees and was wafted towards us on the light summer air. This reading of Shakspeare amid the scenes and the land that he loved so well, whose fair and finished charms seem to fill the airy atmosphere of his work as do the violet skies of Greece each line of Homer, made the great English bard and his glorious company of immortal heroes new and strangely realizable. As the eyes of the spectators at Athens could sweep past the stage out to the Piræus, to the sea that Sophocles made his heroes apostrophize, so here the great framework was still left,—that gay and smiling background on which has figured so many a tearful comedy, so many a tender tragedy. How many forests of Arden had we not passed! Over the velvet of Longleat or under the silvery Arundel foliage, surely it must have been over such turf that tripped Titania's fantastic court. Nor do all the *dramatis personæ* seem dead, living only in these glowing pages. Each rustic we met seemed to have in him the making of a boor or a clown. Dogberrys and Shallows we were quite certain we had seen again and again at the wayside inns and at tavern doors.

May not this, perhaps, be taken as the highest test of genius,—that it shall so transfix, on an imperishable canvas of truth, the types truest to its time and country that the portraiture shall remain forever an immortal picture of the land and the people? That genius which has not so painted the life about him as to make it forever true, so that so long as the people endure as a race or a nation the world shall know the people through the work and the work through the people, has not, I think, touched the apogee of human greatness in creative power.

Ballad, being merely a horse of talent, quite naturally could see nothing in genius except that it was very much in his way. (If Ballad had been a man and an author, he would have belonged to the modern American school of realists; he hated things he could not understand.) He soon developed very decided objections to Shakspeare. Whenever he saw that small green book come out of its hiding-place he knew his most formidable rival was about to take possession of us. He proceeded to put into practice a series of deep strategic manœuvres. He began by suddenly developing a fancy for running up the hills. He slackened his speed, it is true, as he neared the crest, but not long enough for the hated rival to be drawn forth.

On this particular occasion chance and the loose morality that governs the inanimate world came to his rescue. "Cymbeline," the play we had nearly finished before entering Bath, had gone astray.

"Have you looked in the Amusement Bag?" I asked of Boston, as he continued an unrewarded search through the various hand-pieces. The bags, early in the trip, we found were cryingly in need of being christened. There were five. Each one more or less resembled its fellow in size and complexion. They came, in the end, quite naturally to take the name of their contents. There was the Amusement Bag, full of the books, papers, maps, and one small and as yet untouched pack of playing-cards. There were also the Medicine Chest; the Upholstery Department, with the toilet and night-gear; the Restaurant, which ministered to temporary physical wants; and the Wine Cellar.

In no one of these over-full receptacles had "Cymbeline" hidden itself. Ballad, therefore, had his way with us. We cheerily took to the hills.

With every upward step the prospect broadened. To look over the land was to overlook a great sea of hills. In the valleys nestled the farms and the villages; on the hill-tops bristled a tall spire here and there, a quivering spear flashing in the sunlight. The crests of the hills were, however, for the most part unbroken surfaces of woodland or tilled meadows, so that the rhythm of their harmonious elevations was unspoiled.

The whole glorious prospect was splendidly lighted by an August sun, — a late afternoon sun.

Experience had taught us that it was greatly to our advantage to make engagements with twilight effects. To start somewhat late in the afternoon, that we might have the sunset, the long twilight hour, and later on clear moonlight, — if the lunar gentleman could be counted upon to appear, — this was the ideal driving-time. Wells was at just the right distance from Bath to make this arrangement feasible.

We had started only a little after three by the Grand Pump Room's stately clock, yet here on the hills, an hour and a half later, the shadows were already lengthening.

During the days of our town life, whilst we had been gaping at shop-windows, Nature, we found, had gone on steadily perfecting her summer tasks. At the end of five short days great changes had come upon the landscape. The grain-fields, which we had left still green and only timidly yellowing, were now quite brazenly golden. The wheat had even had time to turn coquette. She was so yellow a blond she could dare to wear poppies in her hair. The trees also looked fuller and more mature, as if to prove that even in five short days a good deal may be learned in the arts of symmetry and proportion. Their trunks looked uncommonly rich and brown, as the sun, dipping westward, sent broad, strong beams of light through the woods.

There had been a good stretch of fairly level road. Soon we came to a village. It was none too soon. The timepiece of our vigorous appetites had begun to set the hour of ravenous hunger. We stopped at the first little tavern, which happened also to be the only one in the straggling village. We decided to rest for an hour, that

Ballad's supper and our own might have a peaceful digestion.

The Restaurant had been plenteously filled before leaving Bath. We had no mind to trust ourselves to the problematical casualties of roadside-tavern fare. We proceeded at once to make an improvised dining-table of the box-seat of the carriage. A clean napkin gave our feast the appearance of a fashionable repast on race-day. Ham and chicken sandwiches with some crisp leaves of lettuce between, some of the famous Bath buns and the pastry puffs for which the city is noted, topped off with some foaming glasses of beer, — a delicate compliment to the tavern-keeper's vintage, although our own Wine Cellar boasted some Château Yquem of a classic date, — made a tempting and wholesome meal.

We did not long enjoy our feast alone. At the end of five minutes most of the village were present. When we arrived the village had been as dead as only an inland rural village can be. The opening of our lunch-basket was the signal for its brisk awakening. By the time we had spread the napkin the entire village — to a man and the latest suckling infant — was present.

Not being royalty, eating thus conspicuously in public might easily have proved embarrassing; but the evident enjoyment of the on-lookers took off all edge of discomfort. It was a lesson in the uses of levées and of their effect on the masses. No lover watching his mistress's rosy lips sipping golden Tokay could have evinced a more vivacious delight in dainty food than did our cordon of rustics. When we broke into the crumbling feathery pastry every countenance expressed pleased approval. As we drained the beer-mugs there was an audible smacking of lips. Naturally such delicate compliments to our supper deserved their reward. When we had packed the Restaurant we had not expected to feed a village; but never did a few Bath buns and tarts prove the disputed facts in a certain great miracle to be incontestably true.

Even the infants partook. A sweet, shy-eyed woman had come out of the tavern door. She held in her arms a young babe. Her appearance was the signal for several wandering babies, old enough to toddle, to gather about her skirts, that they might with more safety direct their greedy asking little glances upward. Two Bath buns made the happiest family ever seen out of a show. The mother's portion was shared by the infant.

"Are all these children yours?" I asked as she stood smiling in their midst.

She blushed a vivid crimson as she looked shyly askance at the row of curly heads about her knees. "Yes, mum, please, mum;" and she dropped a courtesy. "There's five of 'em, mum, I do believe," — as if counting them were an altogether novel experience. Then, emboldened, she came nearer, and took courage to look me full in the face. It was delightful to look down into her eyes, — the shy, soft, maternal eyes. "You see, mum, it's a long family, mum, and they came so fast I don't remember rightly. There's Willie, now, he's the oldest; he's off mostly to the vicarage, — he sings in the choir and does chores. But won't you be feeling tired, mum, an' come in and take a seat?"

"Thank you so very much, but we are going off presently."

"You have come a long ways, maybe, — from different parts," she still continued, as if she felt, now that the ice was broken, that talking to a stranger was after all not so terrifying an undertaking.

The other bystanders looked at her in undisguised admiration. Perhaps they had not suspected her hidden talent for dialogue.

"Oh yes," I answered her, to encourage so brave a venture; "we have come a long distance, — from London and from across the seas, — from New York."

"Yes; I said from different parts," she replied, not to be put down with any such overwhelming distances. They evidently conveyed no meaning to her mind. Her eye did not lighten; there was only an obstinate tightening of the facial muscles. Her geographical limits were bounded by the hills; but she was a woman, and was outwardly not to be put in the wrong. It was very evident, however, that we had improved our position as adventurous travellers with the male members of the group. They all gathered closer, and began to take an interest in Ballad and the trap.

At the outskirts of the village, as we drove off, there stood a lovely vicarage. It had the straight parapet and the mullioned Tudor casements, with the diamond-leaded glass of the period, to proclaim its three centuries of antiquity. The moss and the ivy had had so many years to weave their mantle of green over the door-lintels and the rain-stained façade that they had ended by clothing the entire establishment. A boy's voice through the shrubbery rang out clear and sweet. It was a snatch of some old glee, with quaint old-time changes in it.

"It is the choir-boy, Boston, doing a song as he tidies up the barn. How pure his voice is, and how true! It has the ring of a skylark. And how the song fits into the scene, does n't it? It is like a madrigal to that Lady of Light."

For the west was aflame. A great glory of light filled the western horizon, spreading in fainter tints up to the very zenith. The landscape lay beneath, calm, peaceful, serene, as only an English landscape lies under a tinted sky, its velvet cheek scarcely a shade deeper in tone. The sun meanwhile was rolling up his day-canvas. The scene was being set for moonlight effects. According to the most approved modern devices for stage-shifting one scene was melting imperceptibly into the next. The sun, being an older and very experienced hand, was making a series of pictures of each point of transition. We had had a blue earth and a blue sky, a paler daffodil firmament, and a darker, greener landscape; and now there was that rich light in the west, and in the east a pale yellow moon. For one brief moment the two chief actors in the scene faced each other. The sun gave his rival a long, luminous, splendid stare; then he dropped behind his breastwork of hills. Slowly the moon mounted to take serene possession of the night; slowly the color faded out of the west; slowly the earth took on her sombre evening garments; slowly the woods thickened into darkness, the bluish greens in the meadows turning into warm browns and blackened purples. Then, as the moon rose higher in the rich, dusky summer sky, the breasts of the hills whitened to silvery grayness, the plains became a lake of misty light, and earth and sky seemed floating in a wondrous illumined halo.

For several hours we lived in this silver world. We were still toiling up the Mendip Hills, and our road took us into the fairy upper fields of light. The moonlight streamed into the depths of the forests, making the far distances as bright as day. Above us the hills towered, their heights white with light; while the nearer hollows were as dark and deep as wells.

Then quite suddenly the descent began. The road now was as broad as a wide boulevard. It wound in beautiful, sinuous coils about the mountain-side. As we looked down into the valleys below, we saw a fantastically lighted, half-obscured landscape. The mountain-sides were swathed in mist, — a gauzy veil that coiled its light tissues about the jagged rocks. At a turn in the road, the yawning abysses were exchanged for brilliant, clearly cut bits of woodland scenery, as frankly revealing themselves as meadows at high noon. We were in the midst of all the stillness and the mystery peculiar to high altitudes. The noises of the night were hushed. In this enchanted region not even a fairy was astir.

Finally, like stars shining through a misty sky, the distant lights of Wells pierced the illumined gauze that covered the valleys. As we neared the town, there was no break in the enchanted spell of beauty. Still the moon shone clear in high heaven; still the trees were clothed in light as in a heavenly garment; still our broad roadway was a path of shining silver. It led us into the damp and misty valley, where the wandering night air was fragrant with perfume; it led us past the suburban garden and the whitened villas, and finally it ceased and became a little narrow cobble-paved street.

And this was Wells.

CHAPTER XIV.

WELLS, AN ENCHANTED CITY.

THE little city was under the spell. It lay folded, entranced, in the garment of warm white light. The houses did not seem quite real, as we passed them, wrapped in that soft mellow radiance. The stillness made the dream more vivid. The silent, white little city neither moved nor stirred as we drove through its sleeping streets.

Suddenly there came the flare of lamp and candle light to make broad streaks of dull yellow on the white paving-stones. It was the light from our inn.

A woman's figure, leaning against the door-jamb, started forward as we drove up. When Ballad was brought to a halt, she was at our side to greet us with a smile and a soft "Good-evening." She was our landlady. She was a young woman, but she was in widow's weeds; and her sombre draperies and dazzling white cap gave to her comeliness a look of distinction. It was only in keeping with the hour and the night, we said, that we should be received by a pretty, sentimental landlady, with a taste for moonlight revery. Her romantic turn, however, did not seem to have been allowed to interfere with a very decided genius for affairs. The inn was like wax; and our supper was quite a little banquet.

"Do you know that any woman who can keep one eye on her servants and the other on the moon is a being for whom I have a profound respect?" I announced to Boston, as we unfolded our snowy napkins.

"Would you mind my making it a trifle warmer than respect? I feel a positive affection for her just now. This is the best *bouillon* I have tasted on English soil," he replied.

In spite of its excellence we both felt we were eating the meal in more or less of a trance. For the windows were open, and the warm night air, like the soft flutter of a bird's wing, caressed our cheeks. We were so close to the street that the little garden belonging to the inn, across the way, sent a cloud of perfume into the chamber. We could see the tiny fountain splashing in the moonlight, — a thread of diamond dewdrops glistening in the white night. On the bench near it some people were seated; their voices stole up to us in pleasant, drowsy murmurs. But beyond it all, beyond the garden and the fountain and the trees, rose a wondrous sight. It was the cathedral, looming up to heaven, cut in solid silver against the sky.

"Come, let us go," I cried, pushing the table aside. "This is no time for eating or for swinish slumber. We'll make a night of it."

The figure leaning pensively against the inn door was still there as we passed out, looking unaffectedly up at the moon. This time it did not move; but it spoke in the soft, clear English voice, —

"It's a beautiful night, is it not? Wells is so pretty by moonlight! Shall you be going to the cathedral?" A white hand pointed the way. "And be sure to see the moat, beyond the gateway, yonder. It's most lovely to-night."

"She's as perfect as if she'd been made to order, — for us and the night," exclaimed Boston, in what for him was a tone of rapture.

The low eaves of the houses made a black shadow for us to walk in. Then came a great gateway, a long high wall, within which, stretching out to the borders of some lofty trees, was the grassy cathedral close. It lay at the feet of the cathedral like a whitened shroud. The trees, with their lace-like foliage, made the only shadows that fell upon the transfigured lawn. The great façade of the cathedral rose into the sky like some fair and disembodied spirit; it was as unreal as a phantom ghost. Its outlines seemed to float entranced in the mellow light. Then, as we came nearer, the vast and splendid surface resolved itself into shape and outline. The three low portals yawned like so many caverns. The columns bloomed like rounded limbs turned to the sun. The turrets soared aloft into the summer sky. But in spite of the bloom and the aerial lightness, there rested on the whole the spell of a statue-like sadness. A strange, quaint company covered that glowing surface. Earnest, saintly faces leaned out into the silver light. Under stone canopies, immobile as images of fate, stood the effigies of kings and martyrs. Apostles and tender women lifted upward adoring, pleading faces, blanched with celestial passion. Above, tier on tier of angels seemed to be ascending into glory. Truly, this was the ideal cathedral façade. It was an open Bible of Belief, imaged in stone.

Then the moon went under a light cloud; and there was only a black mass in the eastern sky.

There was light enough, however, for us to thread our way towards the other gateway. As we passed beneath its high arch, we came face to face with two people,—a man and a girl. As we made way for them to pass, I saw that their hands had been locked. She was so near that I could look into her eyes; they glowed like two fiery stars. Was it the shadow of the white burnoose she wore over her head that had blanched her cheek to the same whiteness of passion we had seen on those silent faces yonder? As they neared the cathedral, they stopped. The great mass was still in the gloom; but the light in the sky fell upon the living figures. They stood for a moment, quite still, looking up at the stony faces; then the man stooped and kissed her.

"I am glad he did. I couldn't bear to see them looking up at those rigid faces. It was like young love gazing at renunciation. Poor things! I hope it isn't a prophecy," I said; and we crept away beyond the arch a trifle guiltily. The darkness seemed to deepen, as we walked on; the air suddenly thickening, as if with the heat of some stifled human emotion. Then, as we came into the open market-place, a great brightness filled the night, lighting up a picture we were both glad and half ashamed to see; for our lovers had gained the opposite side of the great square, and on its white flagging a shadow etched itself in black, the shadow of the two clasped in each other's arms. Imaged thus, they lay motionless a moment; then, at the sound of our footfall, the figures started asunder, hurrying away beneath the friendly blackness of the window-caves.

For us, as we also hurried away, came a moment in fairy-land. The market-place, with its rows of silent-faced houses, was the last glimpse we had of the world, with its reminders of the realities of life. Was it, in truth, a real world at all, — this that we had entered after passing beyond yonder stately gateway? There was a path, it is true, that wound in and out among noble trees; but to what, if not to a realm of pure romance, belonged that fair and shimmering sheet of water which girdled the rounded bastions of that fantastically garmented wall? Beyond, in the misty distance, gleamed a vision of towers and turrets, the fairy palace of this fairy world. The walls were still stout and strong, but they were covered with trailing vines and studded with foliaged trees,— a breast of steel hung with garlands. The drawbridge even in the dead of night was down; a host of pixies might have crossed it; and, as if in answer to some unseen Lohengrin's trumpet-call, a flock of kingly swans floated, serene and calm, over the silvered bosom of the waters. Their cries, answered by the "Quack, quack!" of some ducks that formed their train, were the only sounds that took possession of the still, voiceless midnight. It was the myth of the Middle Ages come to life, apparelled in its matchless beauty and in the grandeur of its state.

The sweep of a hand across a guitar, just a liquid note or two from a human throat, and it would have been Italy instead of staid respectable England, that knew no better than to go to bed and sleep away such a matchless night, — it would have been the house of the Capulets instead of the palace of a bishop. How Juliet's round arm would have gleamed over the curve of yonder bastion, and what a mirror for the midnight of her eyes this glassy sheet, as Romeo climbed to her lips along that pliant ladder of vines! As it was, two North

American savages entered and took possession of the scene. Was it a presage of the future, a prophetic image of the dominance of our new race, — this reflection of our motionless figures in the waters of the moat? Were these the new heirs to the golden past, coming to take possession? Are we not, in truth, the rightful heirs to all this glory, this beauty of the past? For whom else if not for us lives this golden legend, — the legend of history, of romance, of mediævalism? Sentiment and imagination help us to cross the filmy bridge. Once in that delectable land a new and wondrous strength to do, to dare, to create new castles fairer than the world has ever seen, to sing songs such as human throats did never utter, should be our longed-for prayer of inspiration.

Something of this rhapsody I ventured to breathe to Boston. He listened with exemplary patience to the end; then for all answer he bade me look at the reflection of my face in the still waters. The features were so ridiculously puffed out, so exaggerated and distorted, that I turned away with a laugh. It was the malicious, contemptuous retort of the Past to the presumption of the Present. I accepted the lesson in all humility.

It was high noon before we were awake to see what the city was like by daylight. We expected that the illusion of the night before would be gone with the moonlight, but we were forced to admit that the town held its own uncommonly well. The little garden across the street was a brilliant glow of color under the broad sunlight. It was so gay and bright a spectacle, indeed, that we were quite willing to exchange it for the spectral camping-ground of the sentimental ghosts of the night before. The cathedral also had lost its shroud of mystery; it rose into the fair summer sky in stately majesty and splendor.

"All the same, in spite of its beauty, let us go about the town first, before making a tour of the cathedral. It's too fine a morning to spend beneath stone aisles," I said, as we strolled out.

"As you like, my dear," Boston complied; "only, to-morrow, you know, we must be off. The cathedral, Murray warns us, is a city by itself. We must choose between it and the town. We have lost half a day already."

"Lost half a day!" I burst forth. "Would you barter last night's midnight adventures for twenty ordinary days? Why, if time were measured by sensations, as it should be, such a night would count as a whole decade."

"By which method of calculation you would be about a thousand years old, with your talent for emotionalism," was Boston's chaffing retort. But in spite of the chaff, Boston, I could see, now that it was broad daylight, was more or less inclined to make light of the raptures of the previous evening. Man, even superior man, will never rise to the height of tolerating the indulgence of sentiment unless it leads to something, — to marriage, for instance, or to verse-making which can command a marketable price.

Our stroll through the city proved it to be a compact little town. It could be held in the hollow of one's hand, so to speak. The streets were lined by a fairish assortment of houses, old and new, those fronting on the market-place being the most pronouncedly picturesque. Here all the life and movement — a somewhat sluggish movement, at best — focussed itself. The noble gateways, the walls enclosing the cathedral close and the bishop's palace, — the stately towers of the one and the turrets of the other, — were a display of ecclesiastical splendor in marked contrast with the meagreness of the town. Wells is first and pre-eminently the bishop's seat and the site of his cathedral. The city is an accidental growth about their ramparts, like the growth of barnacles on a rock.

One little street, however, charmed us into making a tour of discovery along its narrow sidewalk. It had started bravely and fairly enough out from the market-place at right angles with our inn; then we found it taking strange and capricious turns and windings. The houses, half of them, appeared too old and decrepit to follow its whimsical vagaries. Many of them had strayed into back alleys, and others had sunk dejectedly by the way. One house, however, had taken on new strength and courage. Its old face was unblushingly made up with fresh paint; and its worn sign-board was offering, in a mosaic of blandishing pictures, a vista of enjoyment to the visitor who should venture within. It was a bric-à-brac shop.

We were ourselves suffering from a mild form of the mania. The fever had not been abated by the temptations which had assailed us at Salisbury, Winchester, and Bath. There was an air of conscious wealth and dignified reserve in the scanty but rare bits of tapestry, and the one or two old carven chests which filled these narrow windows, which there was no resisting. We must behold what lay beyond if it brought financial ruin.

An old man came forward to meet us as we entered. He wore a workingman's blouse and a long faded blue apron; their dull tone made an admirable background for his powerful face. The hair and flowing beard were as grizzled as a polar bear's, and the face was seamed with deep wrinkles, — the wrinkles of thought and care. But in his deep blue eye, as it met ours in a look of penetrating interrogation, there was an extraordinary light and power. It was the artist's nervous, quickened eye, impressionable and perceptive. If his looks were remarkable, his manner was entirely commonplace. We wished to see some Chippendale chairs? Yes, he had some, but he had forgotten just how much carving there was on them; would we take the trouble to look at them? They were in the other house. The house we were in, and of which we appeared to be making a more or less complete survey, would have furnished the delight and occupation of an entire day could we have consecrated it to such enjoyment. Trousseau-chests with rare Gothic carvings, Delft plate,

Sheraton sideboards, fourteenth-century mantelpieces towering to the ceiling, and admirable tapestries crowded each room through which we passed. They were as closely massed together as so much old rubbish. Then came an open courtyard, full of flower-pots and green with vines. The old house had been an inn for years past. He had bought it, our guide went on to explain, to hold all his " stuff" together. It had been scattered before in different shops. But even the inn was n't big enough; so he had bought the house adjoining. He proceeded to lead us to an upper loft. It was brilliantly lighted, and was filled with workmen. Old bits of tables, panels, and sideboards were standing about. Some of the men were busy polishing, mending, and repairing these; but most of them were bending over new wood, carving industriously. They were copying the old models before them. And we had traced to their source the secrets of Wardour Street! We knew now how the new work was made to look so miraculously old.

The master of the shop stopped to glance over the shoulder of a workman near the door. Out of the block in his hand emerged a half-draped figure. He was putting the finishing touches to the head.

"You must cut the throat down; it is too broad. Don't you see how slender the figure is? It ain't a Amazon or a Bacchante; it's a Psyche." The old man then took the knife, making one or two bold incisions. It was the stroke of a master. The throat now was as slender as a lily-stalk.

"The drapery over the knee ought to have some wrinkles in it; one or two folds would take away that rigid look," whispered Boston to me.

But the old man had heard him. He turned quickly with his wonderful eyes ablaze. "Ah! you know something about carving, then. You are an artist, sir?" he asked, with an entirely new manner,—a manner full of intensity and awakened interest.

"No, we are only art-lovers," replied Boston, smiling.

"Come, then, I'll show you something worth looking at. The chairs are in there; but there's plenty of time for them," with a wave of dismissal as if Chippendales were of a very trifling order of interest. "There are some carvings downstairs you will scarcely see beat anywhere, sir. They took the prize at the Exhibition, sir."

He led us hurriedly, almost tremblingly, down the rickety stairs. We repassed the dark alley-ways, the open sunlit court, the crowded stuffy rooms. Finally came a room, large, well lighted, with only two or three great pieces in them; but each was a *chef-d'œuvre*. One, a massive sideboard, was crowded with a wealth of figures in full relief.

"It's a scene from Chaucer's Canterbury Tales, sir. It's the starting out from the Inn. It's a fine subject, ain't it, sir?—and new, too. It won the prize."

There was no need of a prize to stamp the great work as a masterpiece. The figures were instinct with life. The entire scene was treated with wonderful naturalness and feeling; it was as animated as a living pageant.

Our praises brought a flush to the old man's cheek.

"You're very kind, my lady. I see you love art. Did I carve it all quite by myself? Oh, dear, yes! I haven't no workman could deal with such figures. You see, sir," — and in his earnestness (the shop-keeper had long since been lost in the artist) — in his earnestness the old man sat down beside us on a long carved settee and laid his work-worn hand on Boston's arm,— "you see, wood-carving has made great progress in our day, but there's only a few of us who really know the art. In the old days master and workman worked together, side by side. In our day it is boss and day-laborer. The boss must be overseer; he's too fine for dirty work. I'm boss, but I'm a workman too, and so I get along. I'm teaching my men myself, but it's slow work. They ain't educated, to begin with, and it's slow work teaching them mythology and how to handle their tools too. But it'll come,— it'll come, sir."

It was beautiful to see the fire that lit the old eyes and the flame that touched the wrinkled brow. The bent form, the eager trembling hands, the grand old head with its patriarchal beard and its ardent young eyes,— the immortally young eyes of the artist,— how admirably the figure fitted into the background of the rich strong carvings and the delicate grays and greens of the old tapestries! It was the art-spirit of the Middle Ages come to life, but to a life fettered, as is its period, with the shackles of a hoary antiquity.

We saw no Chippendale chairs that day; but we had stumbled on genius,— genius in carpet slippers and a blouse, but with a soul and a brow that had been kissed by the Muses.

"I see now just what kind of men those old mediæval workers must have been. They were dreadfully shaky in their grammar; but they knew the poets and the old gods and the Bible as we know Shakspeare. That old man has re-created an entire period for me. I know those old workers now."

"Yes, he was a study; and he was as shrewd as a Yankee. He had no Chippendales; he used them for purely strategic purposes. He meant us to buy his mantelpiece."

"Boston!"

But I desisted; I remembered in time that it was long past the luncheon hour, and that no man, under the dominion of hunger, can be expected to be just.

We were to devote the rest of the day to the cathedral; but just because it was an opposite neighbor, we indulged ourselves in making a little détour before entering it. Our feet involuntarily turned towards the moat and the bishop's palace. As it turned out, this proved the true and most perfect plan of approach. To cross the close and enter through the western front is the commonplace tourist's method. To assault the bishop's palace, and gain one's first glimpse of the twilight interior, as the bishop himself does, through the garden and the cloisters, is to see the great cathedral in its full strength of beauty.

As the drawbridge was still down, I crossed it. I saw that it was held in its defenceless position by ropes of vines and chains of moss. But the massive door beyond still looked formidable enough to resist a stout siege. I began to attack it vigorously.

"What are you doing?" cried Boston, who had stayed behind to look at the walls and the waters of the moat.

"I want to see what a drawbridge is like,—I never crossed one before,—and also to see—"

But we had been discovered. One of the panels of the great door opened, and in its narrow frame the figure of a particularly attractive young woman defined itself. She smiled, as if she had expected us. The smile and her prettiness produced their instantaneous effect upon Boston. The electricity of a pretty woman's glance is as yet the fastest known time made in the universe.

"We were told this was the way to the bishop's palace," said Boston, with his best bow, and with the unblushing mendacity men are capable of summoning on such occasions.

"You are quite right, sir. Visitors are admitted during the bishop's absence. Will you please step this way?"

The way led us along a velvety lawn and past sunny and exquisitely trim gardens. We followed with alacrity; or, to speak with entire truthfulness, only one of us strictly followed. My companion might be said to be enjoying a personally conducted tour of inspection. For so great became Boston's interest in our charming guide's intelligent explanations of the ruined hall, the moat, the terrace, and the wells, that insensibly, doubtless, he found himself walking by her side; and the paths were narrow (they always are when a man finds he must choose between two women). But, reader, I found it in my heart to forgive him. A man who could have remained indifferent under the soft spell of those brown eyes and that blooming complexion would remain unmoved before the spectacle of his wife in her best gown. One ought to be willing to pay the price for discriminating sensibility.

BISHOP'S PALACE, WELLS CATHEDRAL:
Page 332.

A bishop's palace I had always imagined would be different from the dwelling, however regal, of any other earthly potentate; and for once the intuition was sustained by reality. We had seen no such collection of buildings as this in England. Perhaps no one, indeed, except a bishop would have dared to appropriate so much of earth, on his way to heaven, for purely domestic and festival purposes. The conception which possessed the ingenious and affluent imagination of Bishop Jocelin certainly proved him a colossus in magnitude and magnificence of design. No other group of buildings so triumphantly attest the grandeur of mediæval ecclesiasticism. The cathedral, the chapter-house, the close, were in the original plan to be but a portion of the vast whole. The temporal side of a great bishop's state was to be represented by the adjacent palace, engarlanded by flower-beds, terraces, and lawns. The plan, one would have thought, might have satisfied the most exacting and luxurious of thirteenth-century bishops. But when the palace was completed, it was found to be on too modest a scale for the next spiritual incumbent; it was too small for occasions of state. Bishop Burnell thereupon in 1280, with the ease with which great lords in those days gratified a want or indulged a caprice, built him a great hall. The praise that it was the longest episcopal hall in England must have sounded sweet in his ears. Even the greatest of us have our little vanities.

The great banqueting-hall lies in ruins now. A portion of the walls is still standing; but the wide vacant windows, with their suggestion of festival state, are as so many yawning graves. There is a touch of malice the old sculptors little dreamed they were hinting in the grotesque heads beneath the drip-stones. They surround the old ruin like a band of jeering demons, grinning as if with satanic glee over its decay and abandonment.

In blooming radiant contrast with this image of death, stands the palace. It is a gem-like little building. Its ancient portion is in a perfect state of preservation, and the modern additions have been made with admirable taste. Its gables, turrets, lancet and Tudor-mullioned windows, make an enchanting *ensemble*. It is as chastely draped as a goddess, with its flowing garment of vines and ivy. A glimpse was allowed us of the interior, — of the gallery with its groined roof and richly carved doors, and of the vaulted lower story, formerly the old cellar and entrance, now restored and used as a dining-room.

We strolled later on towards the terrace. It overlooked the moat. The afternoon sun lay warm and dazzling on the sparkling waters, on the ivy along the walls, on the great and noble trees within the park. The beauty of it all was very different from that of the night before; but in full sunshine it was quite as much a region of pure enchantment. The views were as varied as they were surpassingly lovely. In the blue distance was Glastonbury Tor. Beyond the meadows, in the park, shone the jagged sides of Dulcot Hill. On the right, through the trees, the cathedral towers lifted themselves into the blue ether. On all sides the hills stretched away, surrounding the country and enclosing it, as the costly cathedral and the palace were enclosed by their own walls and ancient bastions; it was a double fortification.

On our way back through the gardens towards the cloisters, we noticed innumerable wells or springs, lying unenclosed and bubbling with life. These wells were at once the glory and the origin of the city itself, our guide explained. It was the discovery and the prevalence of these natural springs which decided the mediæval bishop to fix upon Wells as the seat of the diocese. The moat is still fed from St. Andrews, — " the bottomless well," the original great well of King Ine. It still rises close to the palace, and falls in a cascade into the moat. All the centuries have not run it dry. During the Middle Ages this well made the palace almost impregnable. Its continued abundance has preserved to modern eyes, in perfect preservation, an ideal picture of those earlier methods of warfare. In our own day the well has felt the modern movement. It has adapted its resources to modern utilitarianism; it turns several mills, besides serving to cleanse the city's streets.

After the glare on the terrace, the damp sweet coolness along the garden paths that rimmed the bubbling springs was full of refreshment. The delicate sound of the bubbling waters and the distant notes of the falling cascade made a delicious liquid harmony. No other music but that faint silvery tune would have fitted into the perfectly finished surroundings, or would have seemed in keeping with the domestic elegance of the gem-like palace, with the softened tragedy of the ruined hall, with the lovely scents and perfume of the white roses, the jessamine, the blooming vines, and above all, with the spiral loftiness of the cathedral towers. The melody of falling water is the most delicate of all sensuous sound, — it is music without the voluptuousness of rhythm.

We gave ourselves up to its witchery and to the scene. We might stay as long as we liked, and walk about, our charming guide considerately said.

"For the cathedral, sir, you see is quite handy," she added at leaving, as she lifted her dark eyes in farewell to Boston.

It was a novel view to take of so impressive a building, this of a cathedral being "handy;" but doubtless she only unconsciously reflected the bishop's own view of the edifice, — in time, very probably, his cathedral does come to assume the aspect of a personal belonging. Such was the attitude of the older holders of the See in the great Middle-Age days; and why should not such a feeling be hereditary, along with the office and the duties?

In whatever light the present bishop may view his noble temple, there can be no finer point from which to see it in its fullest beauty than from his own gardens. Subsequent experimental observations, taken at various other points, only served to confirm this first decision. First, through the trees you catch exquisite detached bits, — the traceries of the windows in the Lady Chapel and the southern transept framed into the freer breeze-blown branches; then the entire apsidal portion, together with a wonderful view of the whole southern side, transept, central and western towers, chapter-house, and Lady Chapel, rise in splendor above the tree-tops. From no other point is the cathedral at once so impressive as a whole and so supremely and astonishingly picturesque. With such a review of its great and stupendously lovely beauties, you are willing to accept Wells as Messrs. Fergusson and Freeman would have you, — you are willing to declare it the most perfect and complete of all the English cathedrals.

Then, if you happen to be less of a critic and master of technicalities than these learned gentlemen, if you will persist in using your own eyes, even if they be but those of an audacious amateur, as you proceed on a more detailed tour of investigation you will awake to the surprise of discovering that you touched the climax of the cathedral's grandeur

WELLS CATHEDRAL, FROM MOAT.

Page 338.

in that first view. As you endeavor to spell out its various portions, you cannot avoid encountering two prodigious disappointments at the very outset. The frankness of full daylight will reveal the fact that the western front is a failure, — a positive, undeniable, and obtrusive failure. This is the more vexatious since it possesses in a high degree a distinct note of impressiveness. This impressiveness is due to the effect which so rich a multitude of statues must inevitably present. Such an array of serried saints and martyrs is as overwhelming as an army. But sculpture should be to architecture what acting is to the drama. It should be thought embodied in action. It must subordinate itself to the feeling it is meant to express. In this Wells façade the structural values are displaced. The architectural design is but a screen to serve as a background for the placing of the figures in position. The result is a want of depth and earnestness in the superficial architectural lines, which not even the dignity, the grace, and the irresistible simplicity of the sculptures themselves can supplement or efface. Added to this, is the note of discord contributed by the two western towers. Their unfinished tops, for all their refined and noble finish of detail, gives them a truncated appearance. They are but the torsos of towers.

The next shock of surprise comes from the first view of the nave, or, to speak more exactly, of the nave and the inverted arches at the intersection of the transepts. The nave itself is as completely lovely as a perfectly finished statue. It is in the very best style of the Early English period. The wonder is the greater that it should have been disfigured by these curiously incongruous inverted tower arches. As an ingenious and clever architectural plan for strengthening the supports of the great central tower, one can conceive of the project being admissible on paper; but one is lost in horror at the thought of so monstrously ugly a conception being perpetuated in stone.

This fact once accepted, and the additional one that all perspective is rendered impossible, both by reason of the organ and the arches, and the remainder of the cathedral will be found almost unsurpassable in point of beauty. Nowhere in the kingdom, perhaps nowhere in the world, will be seen such a combination of all the highest elements of architectural beauty as one finds in this Wells choir, in its exquisite Lady Chapel, its retro-choir, and in its adjoining chapter-house. Where find such varied yet harmonious symmetry of design, such spirited yet chastened originality, such elegance in proportion combined with such a wealth of elaboration in detail? The choir, lofty, impressive, and gloriously lighted; the Lady Chapel, of such extreme beauty as makes it the model production of the very best age; the retro-choir, with its symmetrical arrangement of piers and clustered columns; the chapter-house, reached by a flight of steps as beautiful as is the magnificent building to which it leads, — surely such a collection of buildings under one roof is rare in any of the greatest building-ages. It is sufficiently rare in England to win one's consent to the verdict of those who know, to a full and complete assent with their praise of Wells.

These gentlemen, besides their praise, will tell you that Wells was completed within a comparatively short period, which partly accounts for its perfections. There was, of course, an early Saxon cathedral which had fallen into decay. On its ruins rose, in the thirteenth century, the now existing nave, transepts, the central tower as high as the roof, and the west front. The apsidal portions, the choir, Lady Chapel, and chapter-house, were the work of subsequent bishops during the latter part of the thirteenth and in the beginning of the fourteenth century. It was never a monastery nor a conventual church, but was always held as a cathedral proper. The cloisters, in proof of this, are only an ornamental walk about the cemetery, not designed to serve as a part of a monastic enclosure.

Of all the bishops whose lives and careers are most closely identified with this bishopric of Bath and Wells, none so appeals to modern sympathies as does the blameless, courageous Bishop Ken. He owed his bishopric to the latter of these qualities, and also to a corresponding generosity rare in the make-up of kings. He it was who at Winchester had the courage to refuse to receive that fascinating little wanton Nell Gwynne, who had accompanied her royal lover on a visit to that city. When the bishopric of Bath and Wells became vacant shortly after, Charles II. proved himself even greater than this stout Christian. He rose to the height of forgiving an injury. "Odd's fist!" he cried to his courtiers, "who shall have Bath and Wells but the little fellow who would not give poor Nellie a lodging?" And this "most holy and primitive of

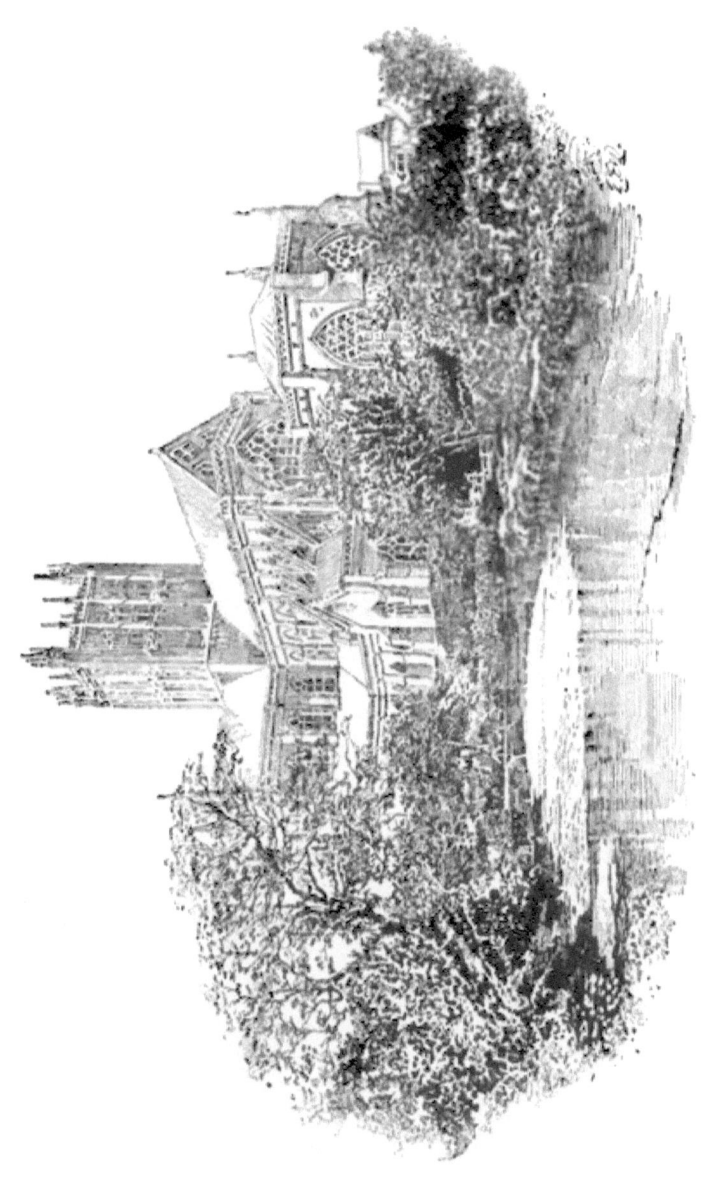

WELLS CATHEDRAL, FROM THE WELLS. *Page* 242.

bishops" could thenceforth take his strolls on yonder lovely terrace, and feast his poet's eyes on the loveliness of this goodly estate, until he was banished to Longleat; for he fell with his benefactor. But the author of those poetic hymns, "Morning, Evening, and Midnight," and the picture which history perpetuates of his singing to his lute at sunrise, as was his daily custom, can never be truly banished from the memory of men, not, at least, so long as gentleness, high courage, and lofty piety are loved and reverenced on earth.

CHAPTER XV

TO GLASTONBURY.

THE next morning, as we were strapping the last bag a few moments before leaving, an extraordinary bustle and noise came up the street and into the open windows. There was a great clattering of horses' hoofs, a clanking of heavy chains, and the rumble of stout wheels over the cobble-paved streets.

We looked out. It was to look down on a brilliant spectacle. An artillery company — guns, troopers, and officers whose sabres flashed in the morning sun — were clashing along the narrow thoroughfare. The town was in the streets; at least that portion of it which was not craning its feminine neck out of the windows was gathered in awed, admiring groups on the sidewalk. The groups scattered now and then, only to re-form, as the four or five young officers in charge of the company plunged their horses into the midst of the crowd to ring out the orders along the line. The troops, though evidently weary and whitened by the dust of prolonged travel, had that dashing, well-set-up air of the best military discipline characteristic of English soldiery. They were only travellers passing through a little provincial town *en route* for a northern city; but they entered the narrow street as if they were an army come to take possession of an enemy's country. Their entry was made in such form that it seemed only part of a well-arranged series of attack.

From the picturesque point of view, this peaceable invasion proved as good as a veritable assault. These scarlet coats lit up the dull gray streets into flashing brilliancy. The troopers' backs made a long line of flame across the low leaden-hued houses. The noise and the bustle in the streets made a bristling accompaniment to the clanking of the chains and the heavy thunder of the gun-carriages. The town, which had been asleep according to its custom of centuries, had suddenly waked up. Its slow pulse had been galvanized into a new life. A part, at least, of the active forces of the nineteenth century was sweeping along its sluggish stream, and the tidal wave was stirring the slow current. It was curious to note the contrast between the gaping townspeople and these alert-looking soldiers. The people looked on in woodenish wonder, with becalmed eyes, as they stood about in motionless attitudes. They might have been a fourteenth-century instead of a nineteenth-century provincial crowd, so alien and remote did they seem to the stir and the modern vigor these fine-looking artillerymen brought with them. It is only, we said to each other, as we leaned on our elbows, looking down upon the stirring little scene, — it is only by some such sudden and vivid contrasts as these, — by the introduction in sharp juxtapositions of these two periods, the period of the present projected into the midst of this fossilized past, that one can be made to realize fully the antique spirit that still inhabits these mediæval towns. Their real existence appears to have stopped three or four hundred years ago. They have lived on in calm, pulseless inactivity, virile only in the sense of being representative of some of the still surviving features of feudalism. Their real life is inrooted in the past. They are as unmodern and as unprogressive as if they had been bottled in the

Middle Ages, and had been preserved as specimens of the mediæval in the Museum of the Picturesque. Yet who would have it otherwise? These little towns are the nests which all the ages have been busy making for the immortal mating of those fugitive birds, Art and Poetry. Without them man would be as sterile, from the imaginative point of view, as a North American Indian. Their lifeless unmodern spirit helps to create and sustain the charming illusion of their remoteness, and the sense of their historic isolation. Their dulness seems only a part of their Quaker grayness. It is a calm which is in keeping with the twilight hush that broods under their cathedral aisles. Thus they charm into drowsy luxury of enjoyment the tourist's senses and faculties, as they continue to live on contentedly in the torpor of retrospection, by the fine subtle opiates of their matchless beauty.

These and other profound and philosophic reflections were brought to an abrupt close, — for the troops had been ordered to halt. The first four or five gun-carriages and two of the younger officers were to be quartered on our inn. In the twinkling of an eye the troopers were off their horses, the carriages had been quickly and dexterously wheeled into the courtyard, and a moment later the officers' swords were heard clanking along the wooden stairway.

The excitement which had pervaded the town now took possession of our little inn. It was thrown into convulsive throes of energy. The energy, however, appeared, by auricular evidence, to be concentrated in the male element of the establishment. The hostlers and waiters appeared to be in lively response to the sudden call of the emergency. But the women had evidently quite lost their heads. The maids stood about in conscious pairs, smiling vacuously at the troopers, twiddling their apron-strings. It was painful to learn, on Boston's going down to order Ballad to be brought round, that the appearance of the two young officers had even had the power to put the handsome landlady in a flutter. The rule that temporary paralysis invariably sets in among women at the sight of a few brass buttons and a uniform, was apparently to find no exception in this instance.

We were soon in need of other consolation than a talent for making light of a disagreeable situation. We waited a long half-hour, and still no

Ballad. As the sun was meanwhile mounting high, and noon was approaching, there was a better reason than mere irritation for our impatience.

"Confound the women! I wish they could do *anything*, even to answering a bell-rope, as well as a man," cried Boston, in his disgust and vexation.

"As the men of the establishment appear to have kept their heads, I'll go and see if I can't impress a hostler," I said. "There's nothing like carrying a war into an enemy's camp." And I determinedly opened the door.

It was to stumble on a bit of genteel comedy. In the door directly opposite was framed the figure of one of the young officers. He was in jaunty *déshabille*, and was holding in charmed dialogue one of the pretty chambermaids. Some point in his gay discourse appeared to render a pinching of the latter's rosy cheek necessarily explanatory. The girl was responding by a dazed little courtesy. My appearance was the signal for a hasty dropping of the curtain. The door was shut to with a bang; and the girl, in a cloud of blushes, disappeared round an angle of the hall-way.

It was our fate to witness still another encounter of this young gallant, which, however, did not have quite so brilliant a finish. Ballad had been at last brought to the door. There was the usual delay in the courtyard before the trap was entirely packed and loaded. Then, when the last hostler had strapped the last strap and had pocketed the last shilling, we issued forth to drive slowly and lingeringly out of the little town. We had turned, as was our wont, to take a farewell glimpse of the cathedral, at the first corner which was to hide the great structure behind a wall of house-fronts. As our eyes gradually descended from the glittering tower-tops, swimming in noon-light, into the glare of the streets, with a black shadow cut here and there by an eave or a window-ledge, three figures stood out in brilliant contrast against the whitened house-façades. Two of the figures were those of the two young officers. They were resplendent in scarlet coats and gold lace. The third was that of a young lady, tall and gracefully slender. She was walking along close beneath the wide window-ledges, to catch what shade their broad shelter might afford. She was carrying, as is the custom of English ladies in rural cities, a small wicker basket filled with odds and ends of shopping. A carriage followed slowly behind. As the three figures advanced, there was a little well-bred start of surprise on the part of the young officers; their hats were raised, and mutual greetings were interchanged; but beneath the young lady's richly feathered Gainsborough, a frigid distant smile met the eyes bent upon her. Two languid finger-tips were extended, a monosyllable or two were uttered, and she passed on.

"I'm glad they were snubbed,— and she was pretty too," I said to Boston, as we turned a corner.

"Why were you glad? They were perfectly civil, apparently, and they were rather fine-looking too, in their way," answered Boston, in the tone men use when they feel it necessary to defend one another.

"Oh, they were good-looking enough, but they had such a London swagger, and such a Londoner's talent for losing no time in sowing a wild oat or two. The modern man—"

"The modern man sows fewer than his grandfathers did."

"That's only a relative progress. Society will never be on a truly right basis until—"

"My dear, I'll grant anything. It's getting too hot for temperate argument or even for sane talk of any sort. Would you mind holding your parasol out of my eyes, please?"

The heat was, in truth, tropical. It was as hot as Naples or New York. Besides the heat to endure, there was a sirocco of dust. Why, of all days, had we chosen this one for a noon drive? Why had we not kept to our lately discovered plan of starting at sundown and arriving in the small hours, in the cool of the night, at our destination? We kept repeating this question — asked unwisely all too late, else there would be no errors in life to regret — most of the way along our torrid high-road to Glastonbury. The road, the views, the landscape, were spoiled for us. The sun beat his fierce light on a road as destitute of shade as a plain. The dust was as a wall between us and the outlying country. This drive from Wells to Glastonbury may be the most beautiful in England; for us it proved only an eight-mile journey of torture. The sole point of interest, as we neared the low-lying hills about Glastonbury was centred for us in the All-Weary Hill, where in the dim early centuries Joseph of Arimathea was supposed to have finally rested after his long brave pilgrimage. With that ardent disciple we felt now a new bond of sympathy. Our belief in the reality of his presence here was strengthened by the need of the proof that so reliable a fellow-traveller had survived the journey. Much after all, perhaps, of our fine incredulity regarding certain mythical statements might be changed into quickened belief were more of us, in these more comfortable days, subjected to the commoner hardships of life. We are out of touch with the old martyr's hardships and the toil of the early disciple's daily life; we no longer live in conditions which make the Apostle's simple faith or the propagandist's fervent undismayed audacity realizable. From the purely physical standpoint we are removed from them by far more than mere centuries of time. We are too well fed, too warm, too rested to believe very acutely in willing ascetics, in voluntary nakedness, or in gladly self-enforced labor and toil. Physically, our conditions are as changed as morally we stand far removed from the early primitive conditions under which great spiritual deeds were possible and almost easy. If Boston and I, for instance, had arrived here in Glastonbury by train, unwearied, unheated, unvexed by dust and the discomfort of enduring a broiling sun for nearly two hours, our interest in Joseph of Arimathea and the story of his resting on yonder hill would have fallen, without doubt, on dull, incredulous ears; but a little dust, heat, and fatigue made him and his journey seem entirely real. As a traveller, his experiences over-topped ours, it is true; but had he suddenly appeared among us, we should have sat down at the common board, — there must have been tavern-boards even in his time, — we should have interchanged experiences and clasped the hand of fellowship and rejoicing.

Had neither history nor guide-books been written to establish the authentic antiquity of Glastonbury, its age would have written itself. The town, as we drove into it, had the unmistakable mouldiness which centuries of life and bygone careers leave as a part of historic deposit. The church towers looked more like fortresses than belfries; and the narrow streets had the richness of gray coloring which old stones yield. The bits of moss, of lichens, the tufts of foliage here and there in the chinks of the old houses and in the cracks of the old walls, were like the gray, stumpy bits of beard old men grow, too thoroughly inrooted in unyielding soil to obey the razor or the scythe.

Chiefest and most beautiful of the old houses in this still ancient Glastonbury is the George Inn. The architectural authorities who tell you so much of its beauty do not tell you enough of its charm. The beauty lies in the unity and grace of its façade; but the charm is to be found in its having preserved so astonishingly the old methods of living. The walls are thicker, for instance, than many of the rooms are wide. The light which came through the picturesque mullioned windows was scanty and treacherous. The little sitting-room, which was coffee-room, inn-parlor, and commercial room in one, was as darkly lighted as a dungeon, and not much more commodious. It would have been impossible, in a word, on a hot noonday to have been more antiquely uncomfortable. Our ancestors presumably considered the compensations of safety as a happy exchange for larger comfort or freedom. But the nineteenth century, which has no use for walled towns or narrow streets or thick walls, prefers, on the whole, rather to play at mediævalism than to live it. This was our own first experience of a genuine fifteenth-century luncheon in a fifteenth-century inn. The comely serving-maid who brought in yesterday's shoulder of lamb, a huge cheese, and tankards of beer of the size and quantity accredited in fiction to the heroes of that strong age, made the fitting human completion to the rest of the picture, — to the little dark room, with its low ceilings, its fortress-like walls, and its rough deal furniture. There was nothing to mar the unity of the whole as a masterly bit of mediæval reproduction. As a final touch, there were the grunting of pigs and the cackling of hens in the courtyard, added to which was the pervasive odor of manure and hay from the stables, which, for convenience doubtless, had been built directly beneath the inn's sitting-room windows.

The innkeeper appeared to be enough of a connoisseur in architecture to prefer a prolonged contemplation of the unequalled beauties of the exterior of this famous little inn, to subjecting himself to any reminders of its internal deficiencies. On our arrival we had found him planted, with legs wide apart, at a comfortable angle for a protracted survey, beneath one of the lower windows. He was still there when, after luncheon, we had come to the point of asking our way to the abbey. He was again at his post when we returned some two hours later.

Our way, he told us, was not far. We were to cross the street, turn under yonder old archway, take a little alley to our right, follow between the two high walls till we reached a small green door which would open at the touch of a bell. All this sounded very mysterious and inviting; for ruins in these old countries have come to be as guarded and as ingeniously tucked away as bits of hidden treasure. To the stranger, part of their charms perhaps lies in these quaint and curiously unexpected methods of approach. The homeliness of this path along which we were proceeding, for instance, made our first sight of the great abbey's ruins doubly impressive. We passed through a courtyard filled with farm-wagons, rakes, and scythes. The long wall closed about rows of straggling, weary-looking old houses; and the little green door seemed not unlike those mysteriously commonplace doors in fairy-land which, once opened, usher one into paradise itself.

This particular paradise was a paradise of ruins. Glastonbury Abbey lies mostly on the ground.

Such portions of it as are still standing are the débris of a colossus. No one thing so strikes upon the eye at a first glance as does the immensity of it all, — the tremendous sweep of lawn, once entirely covered with the old conventual buildings; the grandeur of the still remaining walls, whose fitting roof seems heaven's vast vault; and the still standing glory of the great trees, whose tops overhang the nave aisles. It would be impossible, I think, for a magnificent building in ruins and Nature, grandly, nobly alive, to form a more deeply and profoundly impressive union than do these Glastonbury enclosures. Nature has supplemented what time and the desecration of man have attempted to destroy. These great lawns and giant trees have preserved at least something of that grandeur which must have been, even during its greatest day of glory, the noblest feature of this abbey.

That the abbey and its dependencies once covered sixty acres of ground seems entirely realizable, with this splendid sweep of velvet before one. The branches of the trees, as they play beneath the touch of the light winds, are Nature's gracious substitute for the lofty vaulting which once covered the long stretch from yonder distant nave to this crumbling, aerially roofed St. Joseph's Chapel. The latter, even in its decay, is still one of the most perfect examples of the transitional period. The Norman windows, with their rich embroidery of tooth-work and of embattled mouldings; the slender nave aisles, with their semicircular arches covered with roses, crescents, and stars in the spandrels; the noble doors, massive in their structural solidity,—make such a fusion of the best later Norman features and the Early English nascent forms as is unmatched for harmonious unity. As one deciphers the half-obliterated features of this once supremely lovely little building, one is lost in a rapture of wonderment as to what its perfect and completed whole must have been. What a miracle of luxuriance in ornament, what a harmony of flowing lines, and what an infinity of device in it all! Such portions of the great abbey as are still standing—the tall side walls, the few bits of sculpture still traceable in St. Mary's Chapel, the pier-arches, and the short, broken bits of vaulting here and there—everywhere repeat these notes of affluent richness in design, and the superabundance of ornamental wealth, which St. Joseph's Chapel first reveals. The abbey was built, in a word, before the sculptor's chisel or the architect's inventiveness had begun to tire. Both here rioted in the sense of an almost reckless fertility of invention. The Norman died here in a blaze of glory. The truer, more native Early English was cradled into birth by a parent whose own life was ending in the midst of a transfigured glory.

That the abbey was as rich in worldly possessions as it was glorious in architectural splendor, is a part of that history which made these great mediæval monasteries such a wondrous paradox. Within these sixty acres reigned for centuries a stupendous conventual hierarchy. These Benedictine monks had foresworn the world, only to repossess its luxuries under more assured conditions. When Henry VIII. came, they had become so drugged with the rich poisoned wines of enjoyment, that not only the monks but the abbot himself turned thief and common pilferer. The abbey treasures were deliberately stolen, hidden away, or sold by the pious ascetics who had voluntarily taken the vows of poverty and sanctity. Torre Hill, on which now bristles a sturdy tower, commemorates Henry's view of the situation. The abbot who refused to yield up his abbey into his king's hands, and then began a deliberate system of thieving to insure at least the possession of the abbey's treasures, paid for his short-sighted political sagacity and impiety with his life. With Whiting's execution, the monastery was confiscated to the use of the more powerful king. It was abandoned, and finally crumbled into ruin; but in its decay its utility may be said, perhaps, to have begun. The magnificent pile, as have so many of the great buildings at Rome, served as a quarry for desecrating builders. Half of Glastonbury town, as well as the long causeway across the Sedgemoor, has been constructed out of its fallen mass of ruins.

There are two incidents in the history of Glastonbury which stand out in luminous relief against the background of its later monkish luxury and its earlier days of ascetic piety. The one is the story of the life and career of Abbot Dunstan. The record of his brilliant achievements reads all the better in the pages of serious history, as a welcome relief to the interminable chronicle of the wars with the Danes, the chief political and military events of his day. But there is a tender episode in his career which has always seemed to me to throw a flood of light on the customs and manners of a period we are wont to liken to Cimmerian darkness. In his earlier days Dunstan, like Abelard, as well versed as he in the learning, philosophy, and poetry of his day, was followed by a train of pupils. The versatility of his gifts is proved by the statement that a lady summons him to her house to design a robe she is embroidering. He and her maidens bend together over their task; and a harp, which he has strung on the wall, "sounds without mortal touch in dulcet tones." The monk had anticipated the modern æsthete, you see, by just a thousand years; but he was a better lover than the emasculated specimens which hyperculture breeds in our day. As monk at Glastonbury, Dunstan became the spiritual guide of a woman of high rank, whose virtues were as great as her beauty was rare. In the simple, fervid English of those days the chronicler says, "and he ever clave to her, and loved her in wondrous fashion." It was only at her death that he became abbot.

The other incident in the history of Glastonbury is the one, above all others, which aureoles it with the halo of poetic associations.

The picture glows with the color of tradition. Two monks go forth into the morning to dig, in the now untraceable cemetery, the grave of one of the brothers. As the earth yields to their labor, their tools strike hard against a stone. Beneath the stone rests a stout oaken coffin. They wrench the coffin open, and behold, within lies the figure of a kingly, stalwart man, on whose breast rests the head of a yellow-haired woman. The figures are none other than those of the stainless king and his erring and beautiful Guinevere. A leaden cross beneath the stone bears the inscription, "Hic jacet sepultus inclytus Rex Arthurus in insula Avallonia." The story appears almost too obviously in consonance with the demands of historic justice to be taken for historic truth. Launcelot and the poets having done their uttermost to perpetuate Guinevere's perfidy during her husband's lifetime, the historians have felt it, perhaps, to be but the barest justice to place them, indisputably, side by side in death.

Legend and poetry seem far more fitting notes to issue forth from these "ruined choirs" than the reminders of the monks' fat living and their deep wassailing, which the massive square kitchen recalls. The building stands almost intact, beyond the main ruins. The cowled brethren of the fourteenth and fifteenth centuries, with such a capacious little fortress as their *cuisine,* were assuredly not starved. What a refinement of æsthetic and religious epicureanism is suggested by such a chapel as St. Joseph's, in which to worship of a morning, and the sitting down after Mass to such a dinner as these huge spits and yawning ovens must have furnished! One must be brought face to face with such a spectacle as Glastonbury presents even in its ruins, to have some of the great pictures of the past thrilled with a new life and meaning. To read of such a monastery as this and the history of its career, from its establishment sixty years after Christ to the dramatic finale on Torre Hill, can scarcely fail to interest the least imaginative reader; but to stand here within sight of these giant walls, before these vast perspectives and their crumbling glories, is to have the shadowy aisles filled with the pomp and splendor of those bygone ceremonials, with the long procession of the Benedictine Brothers, with the kingly abbot, who, as he swept in state from his monastery along the cloistered walk, could rest his eye on a fair and smiling country, which, far as he could see, was all his own. As the choir-boys'

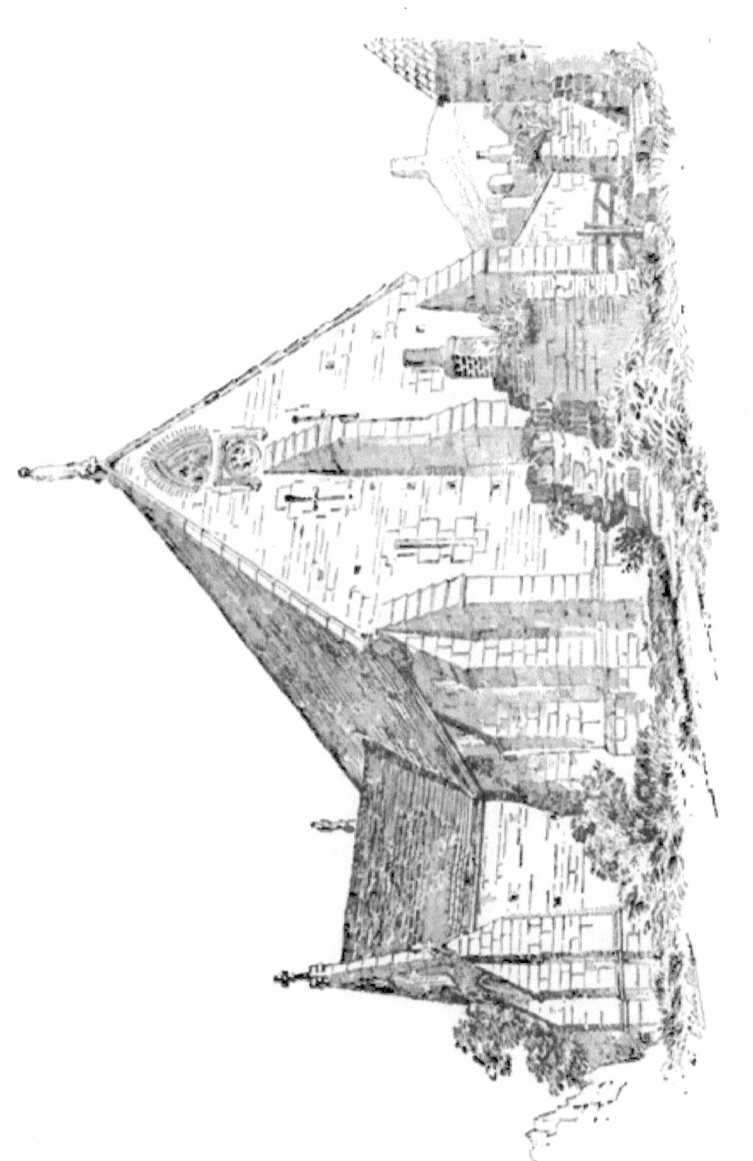

Tithe Barn, Glastonbury. *Page 364.*

chorals smote his ear, heaven and earth must indeed have seemed to clap their hands for joy over so royal a possession. Perhaps, if the sons of heaven had not attempted to appropriate so much of earth, the swift-footed Nemesis of the Reformation might have stayed its speed. It is a pity that these brethren could not have gone out in a greater blaze of spiritual glory. One would like to cover the abbey ruins with the veil of a sentimental tissue woven of wholesome admiration; but the monks were such a poor hybrid of man and beast that Henry VIII. for once at least poses as a righteous executioner.

CHAPTER XVI.

TO EXETER.

THE drive to Bridgewater was a dull one, in spite of our having secured the twilight as a torch and the stars as fellow-travellers. Bridgewater was as dull as its approaches, the town being in the heart of a long stretch of flat lands, the sole uninteresting feature we had seen on the face of this lovely Somersetshire. Bridgewater, however, might have been even less attractive than we found it, and it would still have been fraught to us with a serious import, for our reaching it at all was to mark an epoch in our journey.

It had been decided at Salisbury, between two tall and viciously feeble candles that refused to shed any save the most meagre light on the county-maps, the guide-books, and the discussion, that we should go from Bridgewater to Exeter by train. This decision had not been arrived at, as may well be imagined, without much and serious thought. The inception of the plan had grown out of a mistaken policy of which we had never been wholly able to rid ourselves,— the folly of asking advice. The hills about Bath and the betrayal of Ballad's weakness in the matter of ankles had engendered the vague fear in our minds that the Devonshire hills might prove to be even more prolific in disaster than Stonehenge and Coombe Down. On one or two incautious occasions we mentioned our fears to a friendly Somersetshire hostler; thereupon the entire county seemed to arise as one man to save us from what, it appears, would be certain peril.

"He's too light, sir; he ain't up to such rough work."

"The hills, sir, why, the hills is like the sides of a house; an' he's for easy-goin' travel, he is."

"You'd be left high and dry, tak' my word for it, sir; he'd drop on your hands after the first mile of stiff climbing."

When hostlers agree, how is the untutored, unhorsey mind to stand firm? We weakly yielded; and on one particularly bright, late August morning we all three took the morning express to

Exeter. The gain to Ballad of such an arrangement was obvious. Securely fastened in the freight-car, he was, perhaps, for the first time since the beginning of his travels, able to enjoy the scenery from an impersonal critical stand-point. Our own loss of two days' driving through the Devonshire lanes and hills was equally certain.

Through the narrow slits of the railway-carriage windows it was possible, however, to snatch swift if unsatisfactory glimpses of the country. For at least a third of our journey we were to be in Somersetshire; the landscape, therefore, still wore the smile of a friend. The morning, had it been made to order, could hardly have been better chosen for this our last view of this noble county. The sky had just the right quality of tone, and the atmosphere the perfect note of clearness, to bring into harmony the distant hill-lines and the softness of the nearer meadows. The country seemed to roll away as if in happy, conscious abandonment towards the brilliant edges of the morning horizon, carrying with it the wondrously tender green and gold and brown undulations. In the valleys the shadows were still nestling, as if loath to leave their midnight camping-grounds; on the hills was still lingering the faint blue mist, the breath of the not too broadly awakened day.

In spite, however, of such a banquet of beauty for a morning repast, the haunting sense of regret was not wholly stilled. A carriage rolling leisurely along a well-shaded lane, raising a light cloud of white dust, which the whiter smoke of the train voraciously devoured, seemed to emphasize with peculiar impressiveness the poignancy of our remorse. Why had we been wise? What, after all, were perpendicular hills compared to the joy and delight of our lost open-air days, with their leisurely calm, with Nature at arm's length, and Adventure perhaps, plumed hat and sword in hand, to meet us *en route?* The hills, now that we faced them, seemed commonplace enough, like most of the troubles in life which experience levels to the reach of our capacity. Already, what with our regret and remorse, the whole of our enchanting tour seemed to belong to a part of our past, — a glorious bit of experience relegated to the perspective of retrospect instead of being the living, acting present.

One event in our journey dispelled for a time these dismal thoughts. This event was our entrance into Devon. The country gave us no enlightening hint of the precise moment when we should cross the boundary-line between the two counties. But a short distance before reaching Taunton our sole fellow-traveller, a young Britisher of florid aspect, who had been diligently engaged in reading a strangely familiar-looking little brown book, "The Tourist's Guide to Devon," remarked, "We shall be in Devon in a few moments," immediately resuming the perusal of the little brown book. He belonged to the class of tourists who prefer to see scenery and a new country properly bound between the pages of a book, with well-arranged notes and statistical information; they are then quite sure of doing the thing thoroughly.

It was at Wellington, several miles farther on, that the first proofs of a distinctly different and alien beauty in the scenery proclaimed that Devon was equal to maintaining its reputation for certain high qualities. The land all at once took on strange depressions and abrupt alternations. Suddenly there burst on our sight a magnificent stretch of country. The spurs of the Black Hills projected into the landscape with the ruggedness of robust mountains. Farther on, the rude little villages, the primitive-looking huts, and the comparatively sparse population proved that the wilder characteristics for which Devon is so much praised are no fable. The romantic character of the land deepened in charm as we sped along; the streams were fuller and the dells more sylvan, while there was a bolder vigor of outline about the uplands and the remoter hills which made the feet long to press them.

No one — at least no American, I think — enters Devon without experiencing a peculiar thrill of interest. It may be partly because the imagination has been stirred immemorially by historians and novelists, by the traditions and descriptions of the romantic character of its scenery, or it may be due to its noble historic periods and its prolific breeding of heroes and heroic deeds; but certain it is that no other English county appeals to American sympathies with just the same quality of magnetic attraction as do the hills and the streams of Devonshire. Although it is English to its heart-core, in crossing its boundaries one has the sense of entering a different, though not a foreign, country. It seems to be apart from the rest of England. One has a vague sense that its Exmoor hills and its Dartmoor forests still abound in picturesque episodes, as they do in their legends of pixies and fairies. Devon is the fairyland of the imagination; it continues, by the sheer force of the magic that lies in its history and scenery, to be a part of the romance of our own lives. One of us, I remember, in his enthusiasm, went to the length of finding plausible reasons for these enchanting Devon characteristics, — for its individuality, its still-continued halo of romance, and its appeal to our transatlantic sympathies. The solution of them all was to be found in the fact that instead of Devon's being un-English, it was superlatively English: it was the ideal, the typical, the only truly national England; its landscape corresponded, as did no other in this green isle, to the traits of the national character, — for the Englishman is not as yet so highly and completely finished as are his sylvan Wilts or his rolling lawns of Sussex; whereas in this ruder landscape the contrasts abound which are prefigured in his own nature. And a hand was used with effective, sweeping gesture, I also remember, to include the smoothness of a near sunny patch of corn, the ruggedness of the distant hill-lines, the broad spaces of solitude, and the mingled brilliancy and delicacy in the atmosphere, in triumphant proof of this theory.

I also quite distinctly remember, although my note-book very considerately does not record the snub, that whoever was listener somewhat unfeelingly remarked, that the idea was suggestive and possibly worthy of consideration; but in view of the fact that we were rapidly nearing Exeter and the time had come to collect the hand-luggage, it would be wiser on the whole to dismiss it and to keep, instead, a sharp lookout for a porter.

The Rougemont Hotel was too near the railway station for the usual cursory glimpses one gains from a cab or an omnibus window, — glimpses which, like all first impressions, are valuable as a background, if only for purposes of future comparison or alteration. We had been assured, with much earnestness of asseveration, by each one of our guide-books in turn, that Exeter had preserved, in an extraordinary degree, its aspect of antiquity; that we should find it, indeed, an epitome of Devon's former greatness and glory.

In our five minutes' walk from the station to a superlatively modern hotel, the impression produced by this first shock of contact was that it might have been built yesterday. The force of this impression was certainly not diminished by the figure of the hotel porter in a London livery, who stood ready to grasp our hand-luggage, nor by the admirably appointed elevator, furnished with enough mirrors to satisfy even a Frenchman's vanity, nor by the large, airy, and elaborately upholstered apartment into which we were ushered. In themselves there is nothing, to even a sentimental pair of tourists, positively offensive in easy-chairs or in a spring-mattress. Boston, a little later, at luncheon, formulated both our disappointment and our subsequent appeasement, as he took his experimental sip of the ox-tail soup.

"After all, a good soup does tempt one to put up with civilization."

"Yes," I replied; "at its best and at close quarters civilization is, perhaps, an improvement on hoary antiquity."

We were soon to find, however, that Exeter was as rich in hoary antiquity as in the latest experiments in civilization for subduing man by making him comfortable.

An hour after luncheon, as we turned away from

the glaring brick façade of the Rougemont towards the city's thoroughfares, we had left in the twinkling of an eye three hundred years — nay, five — behind us, and were in the heart of the grandly beautiful ancient city. The antique picturesqueness of Exeter, it was obvious at the very outset of our tour of observation, was too abundantly rich in a sense of its own completeness to be either coy or secretive. Instead of one's having to seek for the jewels of the lovely old city among its dunghills, its glories are set in lustrous conspicuousness in the very centre of its crown. High Street, the city's main thoroughfare, is as crowded with its multitudinous collection of old houses, quaint churches, enticing low shops, and with the embroideries of its carvings, as an over-filled museum. The houses, in the variety and diversity of their architectural plan and arrangement and in the lovely blending of their sad soft colors, can best, perhaps, be likened to a collection of finely preserved old portraits, on whose garb and facial expression the seal of the long-ago centuries has set its mark of remoteness.

It is unquestionably, I should say, the most picturesque thoroughfare in England. This superlative degree of pre-eminence it maintains, perhaps, because of its possessing two entirely opposite traits, — it strikes you as being at once the oldest and also the youngest of streets. It has possessed the talent of preserving, amid all its ancient features, the art of looking perennially youthful. In our own day it is the busy, vigorous, commercial air of activity and prosperity, — the young blood coursing through its old veins, — which makes its life seem sympathetically modern. This characteristic strikes, I fancy, the key-note of Exeter's long-preserved vigor of life; she has always been in direct and active response to the stirring activities of her day. Like Rome itself, her cities have been built and destroyed, her people have been scattered and her tribes have perished, and yet she has lived on, renewing, phœnix-like, her youth and her vigor. The city, as a whole, possesses this dual aspect: it sits on its hills proudly, nobly, with an air of unshaken permanence and immovable stability, with something of the pride and the conscious dignity of the unconquered and unconquerable, — an attitude and bearing we are apt to believe belonged to the proud and passionate feudal towns, which they maintained as their heritage of heroism; yet the city's heart, the centre of its busy frame, pulsates with modern life, and is visibly thrilled with the modern movement. It is this union of antiquity and modernness which invests Exeter with the qualities and character usually found only in capitals. More than any other English city did Exeter impress us as an independent, autocratic city, one more used to wearing a crown than to bowing before another, — a kingly city, in other words, accustomed to meeting sovereigns on an equal footing.

The culminating point of the picturesqueness of High Street is the beautiful Guildhall, with its spacious Elizabethan colonnade, which projects, with its four grand columns, into the crowded street. The eye has endless sport and delight in deciphering the worn figures, in plunging into the fine shadows made by the overhanging galleries, and in resting on the noble mass as it proudly steps forth among the meagre nineteenth-century buildings, with their superficial smirk and pretentiousness. Among the many other rich and well-preserved treasures with which Exeter abounds, is an ideally perfect Elizabethan house in the cathedral close. Its two-storied projecting casements, entirely filled with the diminutive glass panes of the period, is said, by its proud possessors, to be the only house of similar design in perfect preservation in England. The house is now a photograph-shop; and its enlightened owner delights in showing an upper chamber, panelled to the ceilings with rare oak carvings, above which, in the frieze, are most of the famous arms of the English past and present peerage; for this upper chamber was once the famous Exeter club-room, and has resounded to the wit of Sidney, to the gayety of Raleigh, and to the grave eloquence of Drake. The smallness of the chamber, its rich yet severe finish, and its suggestion of cosiness and comfort were better than pages of history to picture the intimacy and the jollity of those bygone days, when the great and famous were not scattered about in large cities nor lost in giant club-houses, but met above an alehouse to plan their brave schemes of adventure and to laugh and sing as the cup went round.

Exeter is so rich in the consciousness of its dramatic and romantic career, that the fact of its being a cathedral city at all appears to be merely a matter of detail. It can, indeed, afford to regard as secondary in importance that which in other cathedral towns is the sole reason of their existence; yet Exeter Cathedral is such a priceless piece of splendor, such a truly royal ecclesiastical jewel, that it might well serve as the unique and solitary glory of a city's boastful pride.

A very obvious part of the charm of Exeter Cathedral lies in the fact that it has to be sought for. It is so well and dexterously concealed from view, as one passes along High Street, that one might be some days in town without so much as suspecting that one of the finest cathedrals in England was a near neighbor. It was almost by chance, I remember, that as we turned into a long quaint alley-way filled up with little low shops, we caught a glimpse of a green plot of grass and some trees in the distance. Our guiding instinct divined these to be the cathedral close. The crooked alley-way, with its jumble of lurking recesses, gay shops, and overshadowing projections, made the wide, airily open close, with its beautiful assemblage of old houses and the grand cathedral, set like some Eastern potentate in the midst of his silent court, doubly effective and impressive. There is a wonderfully appealing and persistent charm in such Old-World contrasts; the beautiful is rendered doubly attractive by the innocent deceits and the various devices which time and happy accident together have arranged as a part of the setting of the scene. One comes to the point, at the last, of finding an alluring coquetry in every crooked alley-way and dusky opening. In Exeter this species of what might be termed flirting with chance may be carried on to a most unlimited extent; for the city abounds in wanton little streets, in mysterious turnings and romantic alley-ways, that end by leading one into a maze of adventure. But the king of surprises holds his court in the cathedral close. No street was ever made up of such an innocent collection of projecting casements and unsuspicious-looking windows as the one that leads to the feet of the grand towers of the cathedral. Walking forward towards these towers which flank the cathedral like two colossal sentinels, gradually, and as if designed with the utmost skill and art so as to insure this slow first view, the path along the greensward leads one gently to the grand façade, and there you take your first full view of the glorious front. There are first impressions and first impressions, as there are cathedrals and cathedrals; there are impressions that are doomed to fall into the shadowy background of disillusion, as there are cathedrals which, like many another strong and beautiful experience, gather in volume of effect as the after-knowledge of their greatness deepens. But before some of the great and glorious triumphs of art, the first and the last view of their beauty remains the same; their all-conquering loveliness brings an overmastering ecstasy of delight. A certain strong and vivid current of emotion is sure, under the right conditions, to accompany such a moment. For art and music have this in common, that their most triumphant harmonies produce a like physical effect; the breath comes swifter, the eyes unconsciously moisten, and the throat is seized upon by that delightful emotional clutch which paralyzes speech and action. It was such an effect as this that Exeter produced on me. It was the first and only English cathedral I had seen that brought with it an overwhelming feeling of rapture. The delight and joy in its beauty marked the moment as an epoch in pleasurable experience. It was a moment to be classed with the San Sisto, with the Venus di Milo, and with Schubert's Unfinished Symphony moments.

To analyze the beauties of Exeter is only to add

another note to one's joy in them, their quality and rarity being of such an order as to warrant one's cooler admiration. The front is as unique in design as it is architecturally beautiful. There is that rarest of features in English cathedrals,— an elaborately sculptured screen, thoroughly honest in construction. In originality of conception this front is perhaps unrivalled, at least on English soil; there are three receding stories, so admirably proportioned as to produce a beautiful effect in perspective. The glory of the great west window is further enhanced by the graduated arcades which have the appearance of receding behind it. Above the west window rises a second and smaller triangular window in the gabled roof. Thus the triangular *motif* is sustained throughout, from the three low doorways in the screen up to the far-distant roof. This complete and harmonious front is nobly enriched by the splendid note of contrast in the two transeptal Norman towers, whose massive structural elegance and elaborateness of detail lend an extraordinary breadth and solidity to the edifice.

The grandeur which distinguishes the exterior is only a fitting preparation for the solemnity and

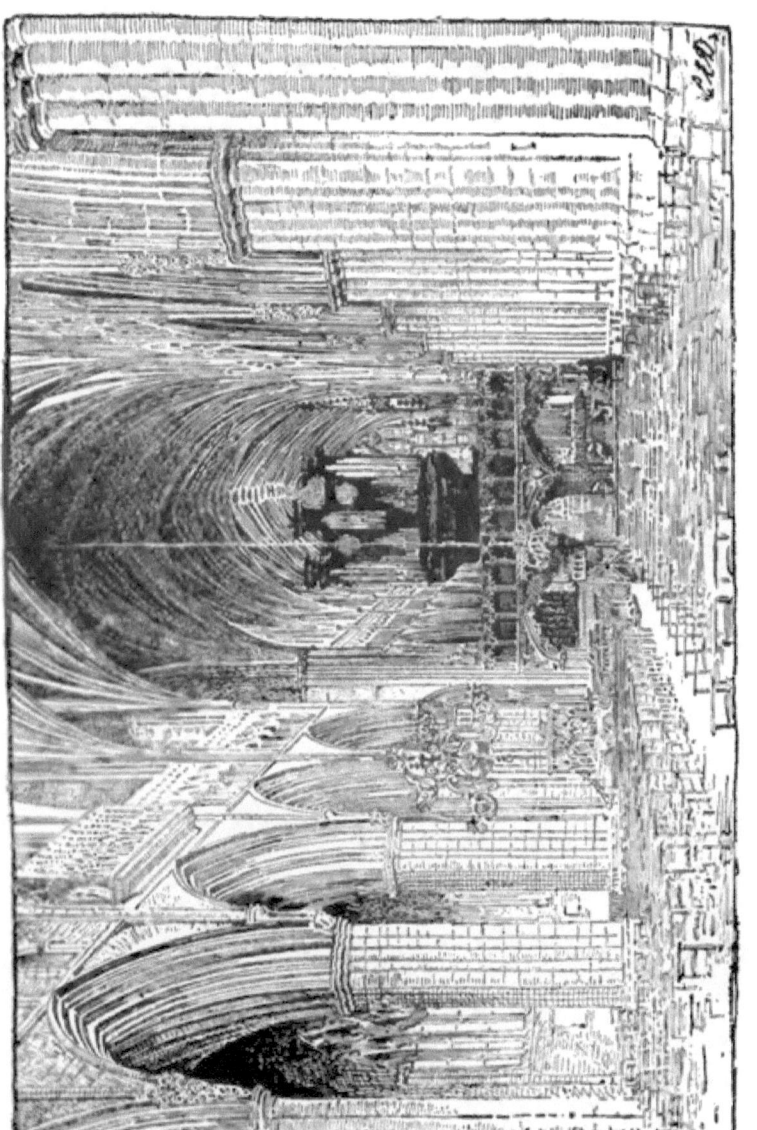

The Nave, Exeter Cathedral. *Page* 382

splendor of the interior. Passing beneath the thickly massed sculptures of the low portals, the effect of the vastness of the nave is striking in its immensity. Curiously enough, in this instance, this effect of immensity is not due to an unbroken stretch of nave-aisles or to a lengthy procession of pier-arches, but to the magnificent sweep of the unencumbered vaulting in the roof. An organ screen intercepts the line of vision at the entrance to the choir. This, however, is the sole obstruction which the eye encounters. Above, the great roof, with its unbroken three hundred feet of interlacing lines, rises like some mighty forest, its airy loftiness giving to the entire interior a certain open-air atmosphere of breadth and vastness.

For once, I fear, our sense of duty slumbered. Architecturally, we may be said to have been derelict in assiduous devotion to the inexhaustible beauties of this wonderful cathedral. The zest which had characterized our earlier attacks on the architectural peculiarities of Winchester or Wells had given way, before the enrapturing perfections of this interior, to the lethargy of a purely abstract and æsthetic enjoyment. We read from the pages of Murray, and we heard from the lips of the verger, that the geometric traceries in the windows were of the very rarest order of perfection, that the windows were themselves extraordinarily large and pure in design, that the roof was perhaps excelled by no other in its lightness and grace or in the beauty of its slender vaulting shafts and in their delicately carved bosses, that these bosses in their variety and carving were marvels of sculpture, also that the transformation of the interior from the Norman to the elaborate Geometric was a triumph of completeness and finish surpassing the less thorough reconstruction of Winchester and Gloucester; but we read and heard all this as in a dream.

What most deeply concerned us was the desire to secure an uninterrupted session of contemplative enjoyment. We had lost our hearts to the beauty of the cathedral, and cared little or nothing for a clever dissecting of its parts. We came again and again; and it was the glory of the cathedral as a whole — its expressive, noble character, its breadth and grandeur, the poetry of its dusky aisles, and the play of the rich shadows about its massive columns — that charmed and enchained us. It was one of the few English cathedrals, we said to each other, that possess the Old-World continental charm, the charm of perpetual entertainment, and whose beauty has just the right quality of richness and completeness to evoke an intense and personal sympathy; for in all the greatest triumphs of art there is something supremely human.

Our last visit was like a farewell to a friend. The occasion was the more sorrowful because we knew that it was not only our last of Exeter, but also that it was our last cathedral. The brief half-hour was imbued, therefore, with the sentiment and the solemnity of a final parting As if in response to our emotion, the organ poured forth a mournful tender groaning, the twilight shrouded the interior with a silvery pallor, and the faces on the tombs seemed to smile forth upon us a melancholy benediction of peace.

CHAPTER XVII.

FAREWELL TO BALLAD.

WE felt that if only in justice to Ballad, after his five days' imprisonment in the Exeter stables, we should all take a bit of an outing into the open country before the moment came when he was to take one road and we another. It was useless to deny that to two of us, at least, this inevitable separation was about to bring sadness in its train. To part with a friend is bad enough; but all human partings have at least this drop of honey in the bitter cup, — there is always mingled with the grief the cheering hope of a future meeting. But with even one's most intimate friends in the animal kingdom there can come no such soothing comfort. To bid farewell to a dog or to a beloved horse is the same as to bury him, — the world is so wide and men are so fickle. The opportunity is always open, of course, to prolong an intimacy with a four-footed companion by buying him. But friendship thus paid for usually, I find, ends as do all such mercenary relationships; when the period of cooling sets in sentiment evaporates, and the question of how much remains to be made out of a poor bargain is the ultimate result of all the fine frenzy. We had concluded, therefore, rather to part with Ballad than to run the risk of tiring of him. We preferred to leave him behind, that he, like the other features and incidents of our charming journey, might remain as an unalterable part of the delight still to come, — the joy we were yet to have in retrospect.

There were two or three days spent in exploring the country about Exeter; there were mornings in the lovely valley of the Exe, and a day and night given to Chagford, a wonderful little village set on a spur of the Dartmoor hills. These little trips gave us a series of delightful glimpses of Devon scenery, — of its rusticity and its wildness, of the charm of its woodlands and the grandeur of its noble hill-country. It was as if we had undertaken, with premeditation, a review of Devonshire's perfections. Nature and the season were in conspiracy to make these final days the harder. We were leaving a land of pure gold. The grain covered the fields like a yellow cloud. Here and there over the meadows were signs that already the harvest was garnered, amber mounds dotting the plains we passed on the last of our drives. The fields along the hill-sides were vocal with the sound of the mowers moving their scythes in rhythmic measure; and this music, which followed us into the thickly peopled Exeter streets, reminded us that if charming tours, like life itself, must come to an end, at least the harvest of pleasure is not over with the ending, but may be garnered and husbanded for future use and delight.

On one particularly sunny morning a sad little procession wended its way to the Exeter station,— two, that is, out of the five composing the company, were sad. The other three, it is to be feared, took a merely perfunctory interest in the proceedings; for, like mutes at a funeral, the chief reason for their being with us at all was their hope of making something out of the mourners. These unfeeling three were the hotel porter, who had come with us that he might point out the man who had placed Ballad in his box-stall in the train; the hostler who had attended to Ballad's physical wants while stopping at the Rougemont; and the usual odd man who never fails to make his appearance in England when anything unusual takes place, — the man who never does anything in particular, but who always contrives to get the fee for something that some one else has done. With so many escorts, much time was lost in coming to a decision on any point; and it was quite by chance that we found ourselves close to the freight-van in which Ballad was about to be whirled away from us to Chichester. A door was opened, a window unhinged, a considerate guard lifted me into the van, and behold, Ballad's sensitive, high-bred face was confronting me. At the first he received us with a start of affright, with quivering nostrils and high-arched ears; but at the sound of our voices the trembling ceased, his dark eyes lanced a glance of recognition, and to my caressive touch he responded by an answering whinny of glad greeting. It was hardly to be expected that the moment was as freighted with importance to him as it was to us. Even solitary confinement in a box-stall did not seem to have impressed him as the preliminary of our separation. Animals have a way of accepting the unusual, which in man would be termed philosophically stoical. I, for one, had no stoicism at my command.

I will not say that my emotion unmanned me, — I did not drop a tear; but I am quite willing to confess that I left the print of a very grateful and regretful kiss on Ballad's high white forehead.

I have sometimes wondered during the past winter, as I have sat seeing in the flames of the open fire the vision of those six weeks of pleasure, whether Ballad retains a vestige of the memory of our happy time together; whether his adventures as an experienced traveller have brought him wisdom, or whether, like so many another tourist, he carried no more home with him than he started out with. His gain must ever remain more or less a matter of speculation; but this I know, that in returning to the world the commonplace and the practical have been vastly less tedious because of our gay holiday. Life, it appears to me, may be made very endurable indeed if its pleasures are rightly managed; and surely, those pleasures are best that linger longest in the memory, that continue to vibrate, like cathedral chimes, long after they have ceased to be, and that are the more complete for being enjoyed with the best of companions.

THE END.

www.ingramcontent.com/pod-product-compliance
Lightning Source LLC
Chambersburg PA
CBHW020533300426
44111CB00008B/651